COMPARATIVE HEALTH POLICY IN THE ASIA-PACIFIC

STATE OF HEALTH SERIES

Edited by Chris Ham, Professor of Health Policy and Management at the University of Birmingham

Current and forthcoming titles

Noel Boaden: *Primary Care: Making Connections*
Angela Coulter and Chris Ham (eds): *The Global Challenge of Health Care Rationing*
Angela Coulter and Helen Magee (eds): *The European Patient of the Future*
Robin Gauld (ed.): *Comparative Health Policy in the Asia-Pacific*
Chris Ham (ed.): *Health Care Reform*
Chris Ham and Glenn Robert (eds): *Reasonable Rationing: International Experience of Priority Setting in Health Care*
Timothy Jost (ed.): *Health Care Coverage Determinations: An International Comparative Study*
Rudolf Klein, Patricia Day and Sharon Redmayne: *Managing Scarcity*
Nicholas Mays, Sally Wyke, Gill Malbon and Nick Goodwin (eds): *The Purchasing of Health Care by Primary Care Organizations*
Ruth McDonald: *Using Health Economics in Health Services*
Martin A. Powell: *Evaluating the National Health Service*
Ray Robinson and Andrea Steiner: *Managed Health Care: US Evidence and Lessons for the NHS*
Anne Rogers, Karen Hassell and Gerry Nicolaas: *Demanding Patients? Analysing the Use of Primary Care*
Marilynn M. Rosenthal: *The Incompetent Doctor: Behind Closed Doors*
Richard B. Saltman and Casten von Otter: *Planned Markets and Public Competition: Strategic Reform in Northern European Health Systems*
Richard B. Saltman and Casten von Otter: *Implementing Planned Markets in Health Care: Balancing Social and Economic Responsibility*
Richard B. Saltman, Josep Figueras and Constantino Sakellarides (eds): *Critical Challenges for Health Care Reform in Europe*
Claudia Scott: *Public and Private Roles in Health Care Systems*
Ellie Scrivens: *Accreditation: Protecting the Professional or the Consumer?*
Peter C. Smith (ed.). *Reforming Markets in Health Care: An Economic Perspective*
Peter C. Smith, Laura Ginnelly and Mark Sculpher (eds): *Health Policy and Economics: Opportunities and Challenges*
Kieran Walshe: *Regulating Health Care: A Prescription for Improvement*
Peter A. West: *Understanding the NHS Reforms: The Creation of Incentives?*
Charlotte Williamson: *Whose Standards? Consumer and Professional Standards in Health Care*
Bruce Wood: *Patient Power? The Politics of Patients' Associations in Britain and America*

COMPARATIVE HEALTH POLICY IN THE ASIA-PACIFIC

EDITED BY
Robin Gauld

Open University Press

Open University Press
McGraw-Hill Education
McGraw-Hill House
Shoppenhangers Road
Maidenhead
Berkshire
England
SL6 2QL

email: enquiries@openup.co.uk
world wide web: www.openup.co.uk

and Two Penn Plaza, New York, NY 10121-2289, USA

First published 2005

Copyright © The Editor and Contributors, 2005

All rights reserved. Except for the quotation of short passages for the purposes of criticism and review, no part of this publication may be reproduced, stored in a retrieval system, or transmitted, in any form, or by any means, electronic, mechanical, photocopying, recording or otherwise, without the prior permission of the publisher or a licence from the Copyright Licensing Agency Limited. Details of such licences (for reprographic reproduction) may be obtained from the Copyright Licensing Agency Ltd of 90 Tottenham Court Road, London, W1T 4LP.

A catalogue record of this book is available from the British Library

ISBN 0 335 21433 9 (pb) 0 335 21434 7 (hb)

Library of Congress Cataloguing-in-Publication Data
CIP data applied for

Typeset by RefineCatch Limited, Bungay, Suffolk
Printed in Great Britain by MPG Books Ltd, Bodmin, Cornwall

CONTENTS

Series editor's introduction vi
List of contributors viii
Acknowledgements xi
Abbreviations xiii

1 Introduction 1
  Robin Gauld
2 China 23
  Gerald Bloom
3 South Korea 48
  Soonman Kwon
4 Taiwan 69
  Tung-liang Chiang
5 Australia 91
  Stephen Duckett
6 Japan 122
  Naoki Ikegami
7 Singapore 146
  Michael Barr
8 Hong Kong 174
  Derek Gould
9 New Zealand 200
  Robin Gauld
10 Conclusion 225
  Robin Gauld

Name index 245
Subject index 249

SERIES EDITOR'S INTRODUCTION

Health services in many developed countries have come under critical scrutiny in recent years. In part this is because of increasing expenditure, much of it funded from public sources, and the pressure this has put on governments seeking to control public spending. Also important has been the perception that resources allocated to health services are not always deployed in an optimal fashion. Thus at a time when the scope for increasing expenditure is extremely limited, there is a need to search for ways of using existing budgets more efficiently. A further concern has been the desire to ensure access to health care of various groups on an equitable basis. In some countries this has been linked to a wish to enhance patient choice and to make service providers more responsive to patients as 'consumers'.

Underlying these specific concerns are a number of more fundamental developments which have a significant bearing on the performance of health services. Three are worth highlighting.

First, there are demographic changes, including the ageing population and the decline in the proportion of the population of working age. These changes will both increase the demand for health care and at the same time limit the ability of health services to respond to this demand.

Second, advances in medical science will also give rise to new demands within the health services. These advances cover a range of possibilities, including innovations in surgery, drug therapy, screening and diagnosis. The pace of innovation quickened as the end of the twentieth century approached, with significant implications for the funding and provision of services.

Third, public expectations of health services are rising as those who use services demand higher standards of care. In part, this is stimulated by developments within the health service, including the availability of new technology. More fundamentally, it stems from the emergence of a more educated and informed population, in which people are accustomed to being treated as consumers rather than patients.

Against this background, policy makers in a number of countries are reviewing the future of health services. Those countries which have traditionally relied on a market in health care are making greater use of regulation and planning. Equally, those countries which have traditionally relied on regulation and planning are moving towards a more competitive approach. In no country is there complete satisfaction with existing methods of financing and delivery, and everywhere there is a search for new policy instruments.

The aim of this series is to contribute to debate about the future of health services through an analysis of major issues in health policy. These issues have been chosen because they are both of current interest and of enduring importance. The series is intended to be accessible to students and informed lay readers as well as to specialists working in this field. The aim is to go beyond a textbook approach to health policy analysis and to encourage authors to move debate about their issues forward. In this sense, each book presents a summary of current research and thinking, and an exploration of future policy directions.

Professor Chris Ham
Professor of Health Policy and Management
University of Birmingham

LIST OF CONTRIBUTORS

Michael Barr is an Australian Research Council (ARC) Postdoctoral Research Fellow in the School of History, Philosophy, Religion and Classics at the University of Queensland, Brisbane. His current project is a study of nation building and elite formation in Singapore. A specialist in Singapore's political history, he is the author of *Lee Kuan Yew: The Beliefs Behind the Man* (2000) and *Cultural Politics and Asian Values: The Tepid War* (2002). He wishes to acknowledge the assistance of the ARC for funding his current position and his research visits to Singapore in 2003 and 2004.

Gerald Bloom is a Fellow of the Institute of Development Studies at the University of Sussex, UK. He is a medical doctor and economist, who has worked for many years on health policy issues in low- and middle-income countries. Over the past ten years he has been involved in several studies of the impact of economic reform on equity and efficiency of rural and urban health services in China. He has published widely on this topic and has participated in a number of policy meetings. He is active in the China Health Development Forum, which provides a link between researchers and policy makers.

Tung-liang Chiang is a Professor of Health Policy at the College of Public Health, National Taiwan University. He received a ScD in health policy and management from the Johns Hopkins University, Baltimore, USA, in 1984. Dr Chiang has played a key role in developing Taiwan's National Health Insurance, and has written extensively on health care financing and delivery in Taiwan. Currently, Dr Chiang is devoted to studying the relations between social transformation and health inequalities in Taiwan.

Stephen Duckett is Professor of Health Policy and Dean of the Faculty of Health Sciences at LaTrobe University, Melbourne, Australia. From 1994 to March 1996, he was Secretary of the Commonwealth Department of Human Services and Health. From 1983 to 1993, Professor Duckett held various operational and policy positions in the Victorian Department of Health and Community Services and its predecessors, including Director of Acute Health Services, in which position he was responsible for designing and implementing Victoria's case-mix funding policy. He is currently Chair of the Board of Directors of Bayside Health (the metropolitan health service responsible for the Alfred, Caulfield and Sandringham hospitals), Chair of the Board of Directors of the Brotherhood of St Laurence and Convenor of the Council of Deans of Health Sciences. Professor Duckett's research principally concentrates on the economics of hospital care, including the development and use of case-mix measures and methods of financing hospital care. His most recent publication is *The Australian Health Care System* (2nd edn, 2004).

Robin Gauld, PhD, is a Senior Lecturer in Health Policy in the Department of Preventive and Social Medicine, University of Otago, New Zealand, where he teaches on the postgraduate public health and health management programmes and is an Associate of the University of Otago's Asian Studies Research Centre. He previously taught at the City University of Hong Kong. Previous books include *Revolving Doors: New Zealand's Health Reforms* (2001), *The Hong Kong Health Sector: Development and Change* (co-authored with Derek Gould) (2002) and *Continuity amid Chaos: Health Care Management and Delivery in New Zealand* (editor) (2003).

Derek Gould holds BA (Hons) and Master of Public Administration degrees from the University of Hong Kong and a Certificate in Health Economics (High Distinction) from Monash University, Victoria, Australia. He was formerly Principal Assistant Secretary for Health and Welfare in the Hong Kong Government. Now retired from the civil service, he is partner in Kwok and Gould Consulting Ltd, a health care consultancy. An Honorary Assistant Professor at the University of Hong Kong's Department of Community Medicine, he also lectures on health care and public policy at various other universities. His research interests are policy analysis and health care financing/delivery systems. Among other publications, he is co-author (with Robin Gauld) of *The Hong Kong Health Sector: Development and Change* (2002).

Naoki Ikegami is Professor and Chair of the Department of Health Policy and Management at the Keio School of Medicine, Tokyo, from which he received his MD and PhD. He also has an MA degree in Health Services Studies with Distinction from Leeds University, UK. During 1990–91, he was a Visiting Professor at the University of Pennsylvania's Wharton School and Medical School, USA, and has continued to be a Senior Fellow at the Wharton. He is a board member of interRAI, Priorities in Health Care, and the Japanese Society on Hospital Administration. He has served as consultant to the WHO and World Bank, and has also sat on various national and state government committees. His research areas are health policy, long-term care and pharmacoeconomics. He is co-author with John C. Campbell of *The Art of Balance in Health Policy: Maintaining Japan's Low-Cost Egalitarian System* (1998).

Soonman Kwon is Associate Professor of Health Policy and Management at the School of Public Health, Seoul National University, South Korea. He received his PhD from the Wharton School of the University of Pennsylvania and was Assistant Professor of Public Policy at the University of Southern California from 1993 to 1996. Professor Kwon has held visiting positions at the Harvard School of Public Health (as a Takemi Fellow), London School of Economics and Political Science, the Universities of Duisburg, Trier and Bremen in Germany, and Hosei University in Japan. He has served on many health policy committees of the government in Korea. Dr Kwon's major areas of interest are in health care finance, industrial organization of health care, ageing and long-term care, and comparative health policy, on which he has published many articles. Professor Kwon's research has been funded by the Fulbright Foundation, Merck Foundation, Haynes Foundation, DAAD (German Academic Exchange Service), Friedrich-Ebert Foundation (Germany), British Chevening Scholarship and the International Labor Office.

ACKNOWLEDGEMENTS

Edited books do not come to fruition without contributed chapters. I extend the utmost of gratitude, therefore, to each of the contributors for their interest in this book project, for writing and delivering their various chapter drafts and for responding to my requests. Thanks also are due to Chris Ham and Open University Press for supporting the project. Finally, I am indebted to my wife, Ina, and children, Edward and Honor, for putting up with me while preoccupied with editorial tasks.

Robin Gauld
May 2004
Dunedin, New Zealand

ABBREVIATIONS

The following abbreviations appear in more than one chapter of this book. The definitions, where relevant, are sourced from European Observatory on Health Care Systems (2004) *The Observatory's Health Systems Glossary*. Copenhagen: World Health Organization Regional Office for Europe (http://www.euro.who.int/observatory/glossary/toppage).

DRG (diagnostic-related group): this refers to a mechanism whereby the provider or health care organization receives a fixed, pre-specified payment for each instance in which they treat an individual with a specified diagnosis

GDP (gross domestic product): the monetary value of all goods and services produced in a country or economy during a year

HIV/AIDS (human immunodeficiency virus/acquired immune deficiency syndrome)

OECD (Organization for Economic Cooperation and Development)

PPP (purchasing power parity): the rate of currency conversion that equalizes the purchasing power across the full range of goods and services contained in total expenditure and GDP of a country

SARS (severe acute respiratory syndrome)

WHO (World Health Organization)

1

INTRODUCTION
Robin Gauld

The Asia-Pacific is an extensive and important region, incorporating a diverse range of countries and island-states. This book looks at only a few of the jurisdictions in the region and, except for China, these are developed economies. In these jurisdictions and across the broader region are multiple variations of political systems, public service governance and organization, ethnic composition, financial markets, economic performance, and social infrastructure and development. Some countries, such as Australia and New Zealand, are advanced open democracies, with a strong historical emphasis on social services as a critical component of a civil and humane society. Some, such as South Korea, Taiwan and Singapore, have experienced phenomenal economic growth in recent decades and have shorter histories in actively developing social policy. Social services have emerged only as a mechanism to legitimize governing regimes and have been viewed as a means to enhance the 'productive' capacity of the state (Holliday 2000). Other states (for example, Timor Leste, the Solomon Islands, Papua New Guinea) have in recent times experienced considerable civil unrest and governance problems, and are focused on stability and development of basic infrastructure.

The region is marked by the fact that it hosts a significant proportion of the world's people. China alone, at 1.3 billion, is home to around one-fifth of the global population. Indonesia, with 220 million people, has the fourth largest population after China, India and the United States. With rapid urbanization, Asia has a growing number of 'mega-cities', with over 10 million people. The challenges urbanization presents – pollution, congestion, housing, water, sanitation and transport – are important to population health. Urbanization also often means increasing inequalities: between residents of rural areas and those in wealthier and faster-growing cities; and, within cities, between the rich and poor, as is evident in the stark contrasts between run-down shanty-town areas and modern apartment buildings and shopping complexes. Despite this, Asia continues to invoke images of rurality, tradition and quaint village life.

The Asia-Pacific is an increasingly interconnected area, as evidenced by the impact of the Asian financial crisis of the late 1990s, the growth in population migration and the swift transmission of, and responses to, the SARS (severe acute respiratory syndrome) virus in 2003. The gradual opening up of China's markets, a growing number of free-trade agreements between countries in the region, and concerns about terrorism and security are also propelling interrelations. Forums such as APEC (Asia-Pacific Economic Cooperation) and ASEAN (Association of South-East Asian Nations) have become key institutions through which member-countries in the region meet to discuss issues of trade, regional security and policy. Because of the growing importance of the region and its interrelationships, the importance of such forums for member-countries has, in many ways, superseded that of other international trade, finance and security bodies.

In recent years, there has been growing interest in social development in the region, particularly in Asia (Marshall and Butzback 2003). This has been driven by a variety of concerns. At a practical level, the Asian financial crisis undermined economies around the region, impacting on employment and poverty. In affected countries, this bolstered domestic and international pressure for increased attention to population welfare and social services. The more advanced of the Asian countries have faced pressures that naturally result from economic expansion: demand for the fruits of development to be invested in increasing and better-quality social services.

Academics have latterly increased their attention to social development in Asia, producing a variety of articles and books (Ramesh 2000; Tang 2000; Holliday and Wilding 2003). Notably, much of this material concentrates more broadly on a range of core social services such as education, social security, housing and health care. There is considerable interest in, and analysis of, whether there are specifically 'Asian' welfare models that differ from those in the Western world, and there are many publications that discuss elements of health care arrangements in specific countries (Arai and Ikegami 1998; Gauld 1998; Lim 1998; Liu 1998; Shin 1998; Campbell and

Ikegami 1999; Hall 1999; Gu 2001; Ramesh and Holliday 2001; Cumming and Mays 2002; Ramesh 2003). However, there remains a lack of dedicated analysis, brought together in one volume, of how health policy is made and how health care services are funded, organized and delivered in different parts of the region. This book seeks to fill the gap. It brings together, in one volume, a series of dedicated health policy-making and service provision case studies.

THE RISING IMPORTANCE OF HEALTH POLICY

Health policy has been defined as the 'courses of action proposed or taken by a government that impact on the financing and/or provision of health services' (Blank and Burau 2004: 16). It also includes the inactions of governments (deciding consciously not to act), and is influenced by a host of factors: public opinion, international issues, political ideology and changing social, economic and technological trends. Health policy is also closely connected to, and influenced by, other policy areas such as the economy, social policy and education. Health policy and service delivery arrangements are garnering increasing attention among researchers and policy makers in both national and international arenas. It is important to understand why this is.

First, in the wake of the global push for economic liberalism and free markets through the 1980s and much of the 1990s, there has been growing international concern about the impacts on the health of populations; there has also been recognition in many countries that 'market' models for health care delivery are not a panacea (Gauld 2000; Sen 2003; Nichols *et al.* 2004). Institutions such as the World Health Organization (WHO) and World Bank have issued reports advocating that healthy populations and access to health care are integral to economic and social advancement (WHO 2000; World Bank 2001). The United Nations' Millennium Development Goals explicitly cite a range of health outcome improvements as crucial to world development (United Nations Development Programme 2003). As Roberts *et al.* (2004) note, 'a consensus has emerged that health care is important both to improved health status and to general development goals' (p. 5).

Second, governments, including those case studied in this book, have substantial health care and health policy commitments. They are involved in providing large amounts of health funding, and are also often integrally involved in delivering health services. Moreover, health care is often one of the larger portions of the government budget. While many Asian governments have comparatively less financial commitment in health than their Western counterparts, instead concerning themselves with health sector regulation (where their commitments are considerable), they nonetheless bear a moral responsibility for ensuring their populations have health care access. By contrast, governments in many developed nations (for example, Britain, France, New Zealand and Sweden) are the principal health insurer, meaning that virtually all citizens have government-guaranteed access to health care.

Third, across the developed and many parts of the developing world, a range of factors is placing pressure on health systems and policy makers. None of the case study countries in this book is immune from these pressures, which include:

1. *Demographic change and ageing populations.* Certainly, in the developed Western world, there is considerable concern about declining fertility rates combined with increasing life expectancy (Anderson and Hussey 2000). In many developed countries, the number of live births per woman has dropped below the population replacement rate. This concern is shared in the Asian countries studied in this book. Hong Kong has the world's lowest fertility rate; Singapore, Taiwan and Korea each face declining fertility; and while China's population continues to grow, the demographic implications of its one-child policy are beginning to be realized. At the same time, people are living – and living in retirement – for longer. The basic implication for each of the jurisdictions under study is a decline in the size of the workforce and, therefore, tax base, to pay for an ever-expanding retired population with specific and often very costly health care needs.

2. *Increasing demand and limited funding.* Statistics show that health care demand is, almost without exception, increasing (OECD 2003). How to provide for this demand with limited funding and other resources has been a key concern for developed world governments and researchers since at least the early 1990s. Indeed, 'rationing' and 'prioritization' have risen to the top of many governments' policy agendas (Coulter and Ham 2000). As evidenced in chapters of this book, such concerns appear to have been delayed in at least some Asian countries, or have not yet figured due to funding mechanisms and health system structure. Yet, overall, there remains concern

about the pace of health expenditure growth and the increasing scope of health systems. A driver of increasing demand is, of course, technological advancement: the capacity to treat the previously untreatable, and the emergence of new drugs and therapies. Another driver is the expanding range of interventions sought by patients seeking to enhance lifestyle, physical performance and appearance.

3. *Patient satisfaction and service quality.* Of increasing concern across the developed world in recent years is the issue of health care quality. High-profile studies in a range of countries have revealed that medical error, ill-attention to process, and poor coordination and communication within hospitals and between health care providers are responsible for a significant proportion of hospital patient admissions and deaths (Wilson *et al.* 1995; Institute of Medicine 2000; Davis *et al.* 2002). Of course, this is of concern to the general public, politicians, health care managers and health professionals alike for reasons of basic patient safety and the financial costs of medical misadventure and substandard organization. Various demands and policy initiatives have resulted. These include new regulatory and monitoring regimes, new techniques of organization and information management, and new approaches to disclosing information about medical errors and adverse health outcomes. Linked to issues of quality, the gradual erosion of medical power and an increasing emphasis on involving the public in health care decision making, is patient satisfaction. This is inevitably driving health-care providers towards ensuring that patient experiences (as measured through exit surveys, complaints and other feedback channels) are positive, in turn creating pressure for improved administrative performance, facilities and health professional behaviour.

4. *The quest for new ways of organizing.* Recently, almost all countries have experienced or planned for health care reform. This is in response to the above-listed challenges and to a wave of health system reform that has swept around the globe since the 1980s (Ham 1997). For the most part, reforms have been aimed at injecting competition into health systems and boosting the role of the private sector. In many developed countries, expected results have not emerged. Latterly, the pendulum has shifted towards collaboration in health care delivery, a focus on primary care, citizen participation in decision making, and

'cross-sector' activity aimed at addressing broad determinants of population health (6 *et al.* 2002; Hunter 2003). This, too, has spawned reforms of health service governance and organization.
5. *The emergence of 'new' diseases and health risks.* The developed (and developing) world is experiencing an increasing incidence of non-communicable and lifestyle diseases, including heart disease, respiratory illnesses, cancers and diabetes. These are related to various factors, such as changing lifestyle and consumption patterns, and environmental conditions. For health planners and governments alike, this has meant an increasing emphasis on changing population behaviours to reduce the risk of such diseases. The appearance of communicable diseases such as HIV/AIDS and SARS has created a new set of challenges for national and international policy makers in areas such as surveillance, transmission patterns, treatment capacity, health promotion and border control. They have also posed international governance challenges and focused attention on public health (WHO 2003a).

THE COMPLEXITY OF HEALTH POLICY AND SERVICES

The chapters in this book make for a complex picture as each jurisdiction under study has its own history, culture, set of institutional arrangements, and solutions to common problems such as those outlined in the previous section. The picture is further complicated by the fact that health care differs in a range of ways from other goods and services.

There are basic differences between the nature of health care services and the delivery of other goods. Because of these differences, health care is frequently politicized and of inherent interest to governments. A crucial difference lies in the fact that health care is about maintaining life, preventing death and keeping people comfortable. Surrounding this are questions of justice and equity. There is difficulty defining the 'product' in health care, with multiple interventions and combinations occurring at various levels within the health care system and with the involvement of public, private and non-government sectors. There is also difficulty defining causal links between any one health or other public policy intervention (for example, employment, housing, welfare, education) on improving the health of the nation. This makes policy development, decisions about service configuration, and performance measurement particularly perplexing.

Those receiving health care rarely have sufficient information available to them with which to make informed decisions about who should deliver their care and how. In addition to a lack of providers in some fields to choose between, there are considerable imbalances between provider and patient about the 'product' being delivered. Moreover, patients are often in no physical or mental condition to make informed decisions. All the chapters in this book refer to powerful interests, such as the medical profession and pharmaceutical industry. The threat of them withdrawing services means such groups can tend to have unparalleled influence on decisions that shape health policy.

A final factor complicating any analysis of health policy, systems and services is the evolving and different ideas about what constitutes an appropriate structure and focus. Throughout the 1980s and early 1990s, thought among policy makers around the world was that competition and market creation would result in cost-effective and better-quality public services. This model has been applied through health policy reforms in many developed – as well as developing – countries, with varying results (Altenstetter and Bjorkman 1997; Ranade 1998). The insurance-based financing models in some Asian countries, particularly Singapore, have been studied as an alternative to state dominance (Ham 1996). Today, collaborative behaviour and a focus on primary care and the determinants of population health are seen as an appropriate basis for health care delivery, while the jury remains out regarding the best options for financing among the many alternatives and variations (Mossialos *et al.* 2002). That said, individual territories tend to emphasize different mixes of core values and goals in their health policy-making and service delivery systems.

THE STRUCTURE OF HEALTH SYSTEMS

The health systems discussed in this book differ from one another in a myriad of ways, potentially frustrating attempts at comparison. Among them are fundamentally different types of systems, with differing funding and service delivery mechanisms. There are social insurance systems (Australia, Japan, Korea, Taiwan and, to a degree, Singapore), government-dominated systems (New Zealand) and the Chinese system, with its mix of arrangements that defies classification. Even at an individual level, the systems are highly complex with unique histories, governance and funding arrangements, and mixes of public and private sector service provision. For example, in Japan, government dominates at the regulatory and funding end of the system, while the private sector prevails in service delivery; a similar picture can be found in Korea and Taiwan. In Australia and New Zealand, government is deeply involved in both funding and service delivery, although the private sector also has a significant part to play in provision.

In any health system there are two fundamentally different types of health care, often organized in different ways. *Personal health* involves services delivered by clinicians such as hospital specialists and general practitioners to individuals, while *public health* (often called *population* or *community health*) is aimed at trying to reduce the health risks of entire population groups. Because of its population focus, public health is an inherent government responsibility (Beaglehole and Bonita 1997). Despite its potential for disease prevention and health improvement, governments characteristically allocate only a small proportion of health funding to public health. The reasons for this are many: when disease is not present, there is little pressure for increased public health spending; many public health programmes are cheap to run compared with advanced hospital services; key determinants of health, such as the state of the economy and societal conditions, are beyond the ambit of the health sector; and alleviating social and economic structures that potentially affect the health of some groups may not fit with a government's wider public policy agenda. To further complicate matters, these forms of care will be delivered at different 'levels' of the health system: *primary*, *secondary* and *tertiary*.[1] Despite such complexity, there is general agreement in the literature that health systems feature some common structural elements that provide useful points for analysis (Mossialos and Dixon 2002). Health systems (and related policy) can be studied in terms of how they are regulated (or governed) and funded, and how services are purchased and then provided.

Regulation and related policy establishes the parameters within which health services are organized and delivered. In broad terms, regulation is a vehicle for control. It will be used for a wide range of purposes, including: to provide a focus and set the boundaries for funders and providers; to limit the scope of the system and services; control organizations, personnel and their interrelationships; and to lay out the rights of patients (Saltman *et al.* 2002). Thus, in any country, regulation is the material of much political debate. Regulation is expressed in the laws governing health care. These may be state-level laws, but will also include the rules that various provider agencies and professional groups establish to guide their practices and behaviours. Implementing and monitoring regulations is generally a task assigned to a central government department such as a ministry of health, athough any health system will host a range of regulatory bodies.

The *funding* function is essentially about financing health care. Funding can emanate from a variety of sources, including government (via taxation and other revenue sources), individuals paying for services at the point of use, insurance schemes (including compulsory social insurance and private insurance often subscribed to by employers and individuals), non-government organizations and foreign sources (Mossialos and Dixon 2002). Funding, of course, will flow in different directions through the health care system and, depending upon funding arrangements, may entail an entire institutional structure. This might include bureaus that regulate, monitor and collect information about funding, together with any number of funding (or insurer) bodies. Australia, Singapore, Japan, Korea and Taiwan, each with their own insurance-based funding model, have regulatory and funding agencies. The funding role is inherently linked to regulatory policy pertaining to the scope, type and quality of health services.

Purchasing is a role often performed by funding bodies but, particularly through the market reform era of the 1980s and 1990s, many countries have pursued a split between health funding and purchasing. Here, separate purchasing agencies have been created with responsibility, within objectives set by funders, for assessing the health care needs of designated populations and then buying an appropriate range of services at negotiated prices from available providers. Thus, a funder (say the government or its core agency, a ministry or department of health) hands a predetermined health service budget over to another party to purchase an agreed range of services on its behalf that will fulfil government health goals (Ovretveit 1995). There may be one or several 'competing' or regionally based purchasers. This model was particularly evident in New Zealand through the 1990s, when dedicated purchasing organizations were established, and the distinction between funding and purchasing remains in place today. The purchasing notion, however, does not fit comfortably with the consumer-driven insurance models, where patients simply draw funding as required and spend it with a provider of choice, that characterize health funding in many of the countries studied in this book.

Providing is the business of delivering health care to patients. Again, there will be numerous combinations and types of providers in any country, including hospitals, general practitioners and other allied health professionals across the primary, secondary and tertiary care levels of the system. In health care provision, in almost any country, virtually every type of organizational form is found: large bureaucracies (hospitals), networks (different providers that collaborate to deliver services) and small businesses (solo and group practices). In terms of ownership, these will be public, private and non-government. The scope of provision will vary. For instance, in some countries, various 'welfare' services (such as rehabilitation, long-term disability and aged care) or 'alternative' therapies (such as osteopathy or traditional Chinese medicine) might be included in the health sector.

As noted above, most governments today are grappling with increasing service demand and restricted capacity to deliver. In some health systems, providers may be caught in a difficult position of having to either deny or increase provision within available funding, while lobbying funders and purchasers for improved resources. In other systems, notably those where private sources fund services, there may be pressure at the regulatory end of the system to confine health spending while providers continue to deliver on demand. Another key issue for providers (and funders/purchasers) today is service integration: essentially, ensuring that the many providers, either within large institutions such as hospitals or operating at the different levels of the health system, communicate and coordinate with one another to ensure that patients receive timely care, a seamless transition through the health system, and that diagnoses and laboratory tests are performed only once (Satinsky 1998). Of course, integration requires organizational systems that promote coordination, including incentives for this and for the building of relationships between implicated parties.

HOW AND WHAT TO COMPARE?

Any study seeking to compare jurisdictions must grapple with the issue of how and based on what criteria comparisons might be made, as well as the expectations of a comparative study. This section provides an overview of comparative policy studies and the approach taken in this book.

Comparative policy delves into the outputs and policy choices of governments and the way in which services are delivered. Its value is in the perspectives gained from analysing the different options available to policy makers, the ways policy is developed and implemented, and the varied policy experiences of different jurisdictions. Thus, comparative policy is primarily of use at a broad conceptual level: understanding what works in one country and not in another; how different territories deal with common issues; what the role and influence of certain interest groups, such as the medical profession, is; and why different jurisdictions have different policies and service delivery structures.

Comparing the health policies and systems of different countries is potentially an enormous and imperfect task involving trade-offs. Comparisions can be drawn in differing ways and at various levels – national, regional, organizational or by individual policy. Some comparisons rely on quantitative data, for instance comparing the relative performance of a particular policy field across a range of countries (OECD 2003). Such studies are often concerned with micro-issues such as cost-effectiveness and service utilization, and refrain from consideration of contextual issues such as political influences, policy frameworks or management processes. Other comparisons employ qualitative methods, such as through building individualized country case studies of the history and experiences across various policy areas (Moran 1999).

Most health and social policy comparisons use a common framework. For example, Scott's study of health systems in seven OECD countries was concerned with economic concepts of efficiency, cost containment, equity and choice (Scott 2001). Various studies have analysed the impact, following its proliferation through the 1980s, of market-influenced health policy and service delivery (Altenstetter and Bjorkman 1997; Peterson 1998; Ranade 1998). Health service funding and delivery issues have also been the study of comparison, including approaches to rationing and prioritization (Coulter and Ham 2000), and the role of the hospital (McKee and Healy 2002). Then there are various country case studies, such as those discussing developments in Europe (Saltman *et al.* 1998), South-East Asia (Tang 2000; Phillips and Chan 2002; Holliday and Wilding 2003) – although these are broader social policy studies – and developed countries (Moran 1999; Tuohy 1999). Common to all of these studies is the need to draw comparisons at a relatively abstract level, looking at issues such as regulation, funding, purchasing, providing and outcomes, as well as the role of politics, interests and institutions. In other words, to describe in detail individual country characteristics and then outline cross-country commonalities and differences around specific issues, seek explanations for these and discuss key lessons.

This book has a similar approach. While each chapter discusses a unique set of circumstances and institutions, it is built around a common set of issues. These include:

- the history of health policy and service development, assuming that history is a strong influence over present health care arrangements;
- the health system and services, including their scope, service provision at various levels, the role of government, the public and private sectors, service access and coverage, and the role of traditional medicine;
- health care financing and expenditure;
- health status and public health challenges;
- rationing and demand management.

REGIONAL OVERVIEW AND KEY INDICATORS

With the exception of China, the territories included in this book were selected on the basis that they fall within the realms of developed market-based economies. China was included for its role as a key emerging player in the region and, indeed, the world, and for its rapid transition towards a market economy. The territories also make for a diverse range of comparisons – for instance, between different cultures, small and large economies, city-states and geographically dispersed populations, and differing degrees of political development. This section provides broader contextual information on the territories under study. As to be expected, there are similarities and differences between them.

China, Hong Kong, Taiwan and Singapore are predominantly Chinese societies, although around 25 per cent of Singaporeans have other ethnic origins. Korea and Japan have notably homogeneous populations. The Western nations of Australia and New Zealand are dominated by people of European origin, yet have significant indigenous populations and growing numbers of new immigrants from Asia and elsewhere. Formerly focused on trade and relations with their British colonial masters and the European area, they today are firmly committed to intensifying ties with Asia. Many of the case-study jurisdictions have at one time or another been colonies. Four – Korea, Taiwan, Singapore and Hong Kong – have been referred to as 'tiger economies' in reference to their phenomenal economic performances in recent decades (Holliday and Wilding 2003). While lately experiencing a period of poor economic performance, Japan has been a global economic powerhouse in the post-war period. It remains one of the world's wealthiest states. China, meanwhile, is presently undergoing an extended period of high growth and foreign investment. However, the benefits of this are largely confined to urban areas and designated economic zones, while the rural areas, where most of the population resides, remain in poverty.

The jurisdictions exhibit a range of political and, in turn, policy-making systems. Although in transition to a market economy, China remains a one-party, centrally planned authoritarian state ruled by the Communist Party. Singapore might be described as a limited democracy that facilitates government by the People's Action Party. Taiwan and Korea have both been pluralist democracies since only the late 1980s. Korea was previously under military control; Taiwan was ruled by the Kuomintang. Japan has a longer history as a pluralist democracy, but is noteworthy for its constantly changing political leadership. Hong Kong has an executive-led government dominated by appointed policy secretaries and civil servants. While some of its legislative councillors are elected, the legislature's main role is in policy scrutiny. Australia and New Zealand's parliamentary democracies have long histories and tend to be dominated at any one time by one political party. Australia's federal system means that politics and policy involve a complex interplay between central and state governments. New Zealand, with its single-chamber parliament, has been referred to as an 'elective dictatorship', meaning that, once elected, governments have considerable freedom and capacity to implement their preferred policies, and do so swiftly. Its successive health reforms, discussed in Chapter 9, are a prime example of this.

In terms of health policy and systems, the areas under study host a fascinating array of variations of the arrangements discussed above. Insurance plays a strong role in some of the Asian jurisdictions, notably Japan, Taiwan, Korea and Singapore, although Australia also funds some health care in this way. Hong Kong, New Zealand and Australia share relatively high levels of state funding and dominance in their health systems. In the other jurisdictions, the private sector and individuals have a much stronger presence in health care funding, and private ownership is common across the spectrum of service delivery. Traditional medicine plays a significant role in a number of the case-study jurisdictions.

Common to all of the jurisdictions have been pressures for reforms propelled by a range of individual factors in addition to those outlined above. In some cases, reforms have been aimed at financing arrangements or at provision. For example, there have been recent reforms to the social insurance systems in both Korea and Taiwan, while in Hong Kong reforms were aimed at the governance and management of public hospitals. In other cases, such as New Zealand, the focus has been on systemic change. In each case, reforms and reform attempts have been complicated by factors such as political bargaining, interest group tactics and social pressures, highlighting the considerable influence that political context has on health policy in any country.

Table 1.1 presents data from each of the case-study jurisdictions, illustrating contrasting demography, economic development (and by implication capacity to support health system development), health risks and health status. The 'trends' that might be inferred from the table have significant implications for health policy and services, as discussed below.

Stark differences are evident in the size of the eight jurisdictions, in terms of both population and geographic area. China's 1.3 billion people live in an area only 20 per cent larger than Australia, which has a population of 20 million. By contrast, the city-states of Hong Kong and Singapore are small but densely populated. There are also considerable differences in wealth as measured by gross domestic product (GDP) per capita. Except for China, the case-study countries all fall into the range of relatively developed, wealthy societies. Each of the eight study areas has a low fertility rate, measured by live births per woman. Hong Kong's fertility is among the world's lowest and is a recognized problem for the government. Since the 1980s, in recognition of declining fertility and the population implications of this, the Singaporean government has periodically launched campaigns and policy initiatives to promote marriage and child-bearing. In recent years, Australia and New Zealand have actively sought new immigrants to ensure population growth and economic development. The Japanese, Korean and Taiwanese governments are also concerned about declining fertility and population replacement.

Perhaps as would be expected, given its level of development, China's infant mortality rate is significantly higher than in the other case study areas. It equals that of countries such as the Philippines,

Table 1.1 A comparison of key indicators

Indicator	Australia	China	HK	Japan	Korea	New Zealand	Singapore	Taiwan
Population (millions)	20.2	1 302	7.8	127.2	48.1	4.0	4.6	22.5
% Population > 65 years	12.7	7.4	11.0	18.6	7.9	11.6	7.2	9.0
Median age (years)	36.0	31.5	37.5	42.0	33.2	33.1	34.5	33.2
Area (km^2)	7 686 850	9 596 960	1 092	377 835	98 480	268 680	693	35 980
GDP per capita (US$ PPP)	26 900	4 700	27 200	28 700	19 600	20 100	25 200	18 000
Live births per woman	1.75	1.80	0.96	1.38	1.17	1.92	1.24	1.34
Infant mortality per 1000 live births	5.3	25.3	2.3	3.3	7.3	5.8	3.6	6.8
Life expectancy (male/female)	77.0/82.4	69.6/72.7	78.6/84.5	77.6/84.4	72.8/80.0	76.0/80.9	76.8/80.6	73.0/78.8
% GDP on health	9.3	5.4	5.1	8.0	5.9	8.2	3.6	6.1
Total health expenditure per capita (US$ PPP)	2 513	224	NA	2 131	948	1 835	993	776
Public spending (%)	68.8	15.2	51.9	77.9	44.4	76.6	25.0	65.0
Practising physicians per 1000 population	2.5	1.6	1.4	1.9	1.4	2.2	1.4	1.4
Obesity as % of population (body mass index > 30)	21.0	NA	6.5	3.0	3.0	17.0	6.0	4.0
Daily smokers as % of population (male/female)	21.1/18.0	53.4/4.0	25.2/4.4	47.4/11.5	64.8/5.5	25.1/24.8	24.2/3.5	45.0/4.1

Sources: Central Intelligence Agency (2003), HKSAR Government (2003), OECD (2003), WHO (2003a,b), Singapore Ministry of Health (2004), Taiwan Department of Health (2004)
Abbreviation: PPP = purchasing power parity

Mexico and North Korea. Japan, Hong Kong and Singapore have infant mortality rates among the world's lowest. Life expectancy in China, which is comparable to that in Bosnia and Hertzegovina, Hungary and the Solomon Islands, is lower than in the other study jurisdictions. Japan, Singapore, Hong Kong and Australia have some of the world's longest life expectancies, with New Zealand, Korea and Taiwan not far behind (WHO 2003a). However, a clear trend among all eight nations is increasing life expectancy and growing proportions of the population moving into the 'over 65 years' retirement age range. Reflecting this, the median age is also climbing among all eight case-study areas, and is a concern for policy makers and health service providers. Along with many Western European countries, Japan has one of the world's 'older' populations. This is of concern to policy makers because, as noted by the OECD of its 30 member countries, 'population ageing will cause total health care spending to increase by an average of nearly 2% of GDP by 2050' (Docteur and Oxley 2003: 19).

Looking more specifically at health care, there are significant variations in the level of GDP expenditure. China, Hong Kong, Korea, Singapore and Taiwan have relatively low expenditure (below the OECD member country average in 2001 of 8.4 per cent) when considered against Australia, Japan and New Zealand. With the possible exception of China, there is a common concern about expenditure growth, as intimated above. In most of the jurisdictions, this is outpacing general GDP growth. For example, through 1990–2001, Australia's health spending grew on average by 3.8 per cent against overall GDP growth of 2.3 per cent. Japan's health spending grew at a similar rate, against 1.1 per cent economic growth. At 3 per cent per annum, New Zealand's health spending growth was double its economic growth, while Korea's health spending grew at 7.5 per cent, compared with an economic expansion rate of around 5.2 per cent (OECD 2003).

Interesting divergences are evident in the public share of total health expenditure, with China and Singapore at the lower end of the spectrum. Korea and Hong Kong have low levels of public expenditure (compared with the OECD country average of around 75 per cent) yet, as discussed in the case studies in this book, their mix of public policies, funding and service delivery arrangements is such that there is virtually universal health service access. The public share is higher in Australia, New Zealand, Japan and Taiwan.

There are also differences between the numbers of practising physicians in the case-study territories. Australia and New Zealand have higher numbers, while Hong Kong, Korea, Singapore and Taiwan have fewer practising physicians per 1000 population. The picture is a complex one, however. In China, as noted in Chapter 2, a 'practising physician' has not necessarily received formal training or qualifications in medicine. Furthermore, there is a strong presence in all the case-study jurisdictions, except for Australia and New Zealand, of traditional medicine and traditional healers. In Hong Kong, for instance, the number of traditional Chinese medicine practitioners is equal to that of modern medicine practitioners. It remains unclear, however, what impact the presence of traditional medicine has on the utilization and number of practitioners of modern medicine.

A wide range of environmental and lifestyle factors influence population health. Tobacco consumption is a key concern for health policy makers around the globe as a cause of disease and death. It is a particular concern in the Asian region where the prevalence of smoking is high. As Table 1.1 indicates, smoking rates are particularly high among males in China, Japan and Korea, while the overall figures are offset by lower rates among females; in Australia and New Zealand, there is a gender balance. Obesity, and its potential to lead to illnesses such as diabetes and heart disease, is emerging as a major issue for policy makers in Western and, more recently, Asian countries. Table 1.1 shows that high proportions of Australians and New Zealanders are overweight. According to the OECD, obesity has doubled in Australia (and tripled in Britain) over the past two decades (LaFortune 2003: 20). Of particular concern is rising childhood obesity. A recent study revealed that child obesity rates in New Zealand had tripled since 1989 (*Otago Daily Times*, 24 March 2004). There is growing recognition in Asian societies that obesity, particularly among the young, is an increasing problem, driven by affluence, Westernization and consumerism (*The Economist*, 9 May 2003).

BOOK CHAPTER OVERVIEW

The chapters that follow examine the complex detail of health policy, service organization and delivery in their respective terrains. They each emphasize key issues germane to the health system and society. Chapter 2 details the challenges of health care organization in a rapidly changing China, in transition from a centrally planned state to a market-based economy. China is a vast country, with numerous variations in health funding and organization. Due to its social and political history, there is weak recognition of the notion of regulation or of rule of law, meaning this is often lacking or poorly applied. Furthermore, a significant proportion of the population lacks health care access despite the state appearing to be heavily involved in the health market.

Similarities can be found between elements of the South Korean and Taiwanese cases, as discussed in Chapters 3 and 4. Social insurance schemes figure strongly in both. Both also have relatively short histories of state involvement in health care, and have more recently merged insurance societies into a single national health insurer. While government, via regulatory mechanisms, dominates the organization of funding in Korea and Taiwan, there is considerable private sector involvement in service provision and patients are free to choose between providers.

Insurance, albeit in different forms, also features in the funding structures of Australia, Japan and Singapore (Chapters 5, 6 and 7, respectively). Australia's national Medicare scheme is a form of social insurance, although individual state governments are also involved in directly funding and providing services. The existence of federal and state governments means responsibility and blame for health policy issues often shifts between the two. A notable feature in Australia and New Zealand is the concerted attempt to control pharmaceutical costs, with a set of institutional arrangements dedicated to this. Japan has a history of parallel social insurance schemes for different population groups: those employed by large companies, the self-employed and state employees. Japan's 'fee system' for reimbursing providers is a fascinating method of cost control, while its key professional body, the Japan Medical Association, continues to wield considerable power in the policy process. Japan's health system is notable for its permanence, while an ageing population and the cost of long-term aged care pose considerable policy challenges. Singapore's insurance system, with three separate schemes, differs philosophically in that it is specifically focused on individuals to create incentives to stay healthy. This is in keeping with Singapore's strong anti-welfare, public health tradition.

Hong Kong's health system, discussed in Chapter 8, is an interesting mix of public dominance in hospital services with a largely private primary care sector. Health policy change in Hong Kong is a laboured and incremental process. A departure from this tradition, in the early 1990s era of managerialism, saw the creation of a semi-autonomous Hospital Authority to run government-funded hospitals as corporate entities. Since then, there has been increasing pressure for health system change, at both the financing and provider level, driven largely by factors outlined earlier in this chapter. As with Japan, the medical profession is a key player in the policy process. More recently, Hong Kong moved to officially recognize traditional Chinese medicine, which has a strong presence in the territory, establishing a regulatory body for this purpose.

New Zealand, discussed in Chapter 9, is justifiably described as the world's 'most restructured' health system. Through the 1990s, it had four different structures for health care funding and delivery, reflecting the political preferences of different governments. Notably, however, underlying institutions have remained largely unaffected. The funding and delivery of health care continues to be government dominated. That said, the reform era stimulated a number of developments in primary care organization, indigenous health care, pharmaceutical management and service prioritization.

The concluding chapter considers in detail the similarities and differences between the eight case study health systems and policies.

NOTE

1 Primary, secondary and tertiary care are definitions commonly used in the study and description of health services and systems. Primary care includes general or family practice, public health, optometry and physiotherapy. Secondary care includes standard hospital services: general medicine, general surgery, paediatrics and obstetrics. Tertiary care includes advanced hospital specialties and post-hospital rehabilitative care. Following this, policy may be directed at any one or all of these health system levels. In some cases, policy may be intended to shift funding and services from one level to another, say from more expensive secondary to primary care. In other cases, the intent might be to get providers at different levels of the health system to work together more closely.

REFERENCES

6, P., Leat, D., Seltzer, K. and Stoker, G. (2002) *Towards Holistic Governance: The New Reform Agenda*. Houndmills: Palgrave.
Altenstetter, C. and Bjorkman, J.W. (eds) (1997) *Health Policy Reform, National Variations and Globalization*. Houndmills: Macmillan.
Anderson, G.F. and Hussey, P.S. (2000) Population aging: a comparison among industrialized countries, *Health Affairs*, 19(3): 191–203.

Arai, Y. and Ikegami, N. (1998) An overview of the Japanese health care systems, *Journal of Public Health Medicine*, 20(1): 29–33.

Beaglehole, R. and Bonita, R. (1997) *Public Health at the Crossroads: Achievements and Prospects*. Cambridge: Cambridge University Press.

Blank, R.H. and Burau, V. (2004) *Comparative Health Policy*. Houndmills: Palgrave Macmillan.

Campbell, J.C. and Ikegami, N. (1999) Health care reform in Japan: the virtues of muddling through, *Health Affairs*, 18(3): 56–75.

Central Intelligence Agency (2003) *The World Factbook 2003*. Washington, DC: CIA (available at: http://www.cia.gov/cia/publications/factbook/index.html).

Coulter, A. and Ham, C. (eds) (2000) *The Global Challenge of Health Care Rationing*. Buckingham: Open University Press.

Cumming, J. and Mays, N. (2002) How sustainable is New Zealand's latest health system restructuring?, *Journal of Health Services Research and Policy*, 7(suppl. 1): 46–55.

Davis, P., Lay-Yee, R., Briant, R. *et al.* (2002) Adverse events in New Zealand public hospitals: occurrence and impact, *New Zealand Medical Journal* (available at: http://www.nzma.org.nz/journal/115-1167/271/ accessed on 13 September 2004).

Docteur, E. and Oxley, H. (2003) Health care: a quest for better value, *Observer*, 238: 18–23.

Gauld, R. (1998) A survey of the Hong Kong health sector: past, present and future, *Social Science and Medicine*, 47(7): 927–39.

Gauld, R. (2000) Big bang and the policy prescription: health care meets the market in New Zealand, *Journal of Health Politics, Policy and Law*, 25(5): 815–44.

Gu, E. (2001) Market transition and the transformation of the health care system in urban China, *Policy Studies*, 22(3/4): 197–216.

Hall, J. (1999) Incremental change in the Australian health care system, *Health Affairs*, 18(3): 95–110.

Ham, C. (1996) Learning from the Tigers: stakeholder health care, *Lancet*, 347: 951–3.

Ham, C. (ed.) (1997) *Health Care Reform: Learning from International Experience*. Buckingham: Open University Press.

HKSAR Government (2003) *Hong Kong 2003*. Hong Kong: Information Services Department.

Holliday, I. (2000) Productivist welfare capitalism: social policy in East Asia, *Political Studies*, 48(4): 706–23.

Holliday, I. and Wilding, P. (eds) (2000) *Welfare Capitalism in East Asia: Social Policy in the Tiger Economies*. Houndmills: Palgrave Macmillan.

Hunter, D.J. (2003) *Public Health Policy*. Cambridge: Polity Press.

Institute of Medicine (2000) *To Err is Human: Building a Safer Health System*. Washington, DC: National Academy Press.

LaFortune, G. (2003) Weighty problem, *Observer*, 238 (July): 20–1.

Lim, M.-K. (1998) An overview of health systems in Singapore, *Journal of Public Health Medicine*, 20(1): 16–22.

Liu, C.-T. (1998) A general overview of the health care system in Taiwan, *Journal of Public Health Medicine*, 20(1): 5–10.

Marshall, K. and Butzback, O. (eds) (2003) *New Social Policy Agendas for Europe and Asia: Challenges, Experience, and Lessons*. Washington, DC: The World Bank.

McKee, M. and Healy, J. (eds) (2002) *Hospitals in a Changing Europe*. Buckingham: Open University Press.

Moran, M. (1999) *Governing the Health Care State: A Comparative Study of the United Kingdom, the United States and Germany*. Manchester: Manchester University Press.

Mossialos, E. and Dixon, A. (2002) Funding health care: an introduction, in E. Mossialos, A. Dixon, J. Figueras and J. Kutzin (eds) *Funding Health Care: Options for Europe*. Buckingham: Open University Press.

Mossialos, E., Dixon, A., Figueras, J. and Kutzin, J. (eds) (2002) *Funding Health Care: Options for Europe*. Buckingham: Open University Press.

Nichols, L.M., Ginsberg, P.B., Berenson, R.A., Christianson, J. and Hurley, R.E. (2004) Are market forces strong enough to deliver efficient health care systems? Confidence is waning, *Health Affairs*, 23(2): 8–21.

OECD (2003) *OECD Health Data 2003*. Paris: Organization for Economic Cooperation and Development.

Ovretveit, J. (1995) *Purchasing for Health: A Multidisciplinary Introduction to the Theory and Practice of Health Purchasing*. Buckingham: Open University Press.

Peterson, M.A. (ed.) (1998) *Healthy Markets? The New Competition in Medical Care*. Durham, NC: Duke University Press.

Phillips, D. and Chan, A. (eds) (2002) *Ageing and Long-Term Care: National Policies in the Asia-Pacific*. Singapore: Institute of Southeast Asian Studies.

Ramesh, M. (2000) *Welfare Capitalism in Southeast Asia: Social Security, Health and Education Policies*. Houndmills: Macmillan.

Ramesh, M. (2003) Health policy in the Asian NIEs, *Social Policy and Administration*, 37(4): 361–75.

Ramesh, M. and Holliday, I. (2001) The health care miracle in East and Southeast Asia: activist state provision in Hong Kong, Malaysia and Singapore, *Journal of Social Policy*, 30(4): 637–51.

Ranade, W. (ed.) (1998) *Markets and Health Care: A Comparative Analysis*. London: Longman.

Roberts, M., Hsiao, W., Berman, P. and Reich, R. (2004) *Getting Health Reform Right: A Guide to Improving Performance and Equity*. New York: Oxford University Press.

Saltman, R., Figueras, J. and Sakellarides, C. (eds) (1998) *Critical Challenges for Health Care Reform in Europe*. Buckingham: Open University Press.

Saltman, R., Busse, R. and Mossialos, E. (eds) (2002) *Regulating Entrepreneurial Behaviour in European Health Systems*. Buckingham: Open University Press.

Satinsky, M. (1998) *Foundations of Integrated Care: Facing the Challenges of Change*. Chicago, IL: American Hospital Publications.

Scott, C. (2001) *Public and Private Roles in Health Care Systems: Reform Experiences in Seven OECD Countries*. Buckingham: Open University Press.

Sen, K. (ed.) (2003) *Restructuring Health Services: Changing Contexts and Comparative Perspectives*. London: Zed Books.

Shin, Y. (1998) An overview of health care systems in Korea, *Journal of Public Health Medicine*, 20(1): 41–6.

Singapore Ministry of Health (2004) *Ministry of Health Website*, Singapore (available at: http://www.moh.gov.sg).

Taiwan Department of Health (2004) *Department of Health, Taiwan, R.O.C.*, Taipei (available at: http://www.doh.gov.tw/english/).

Tang, K.-L. (2000) *Social Welfare Development in East Asia*. Houndmills: Macmillan.

Tuohy, C.H. (1999) *Accidental Logics: The Dynamics of Change in the Health Care Arena in the United States, Britain and Canada*. New York: Oxford University Press.

United Nations Development Programme (2003) *Human Development Report 2003: Millennium Development Goals: A Compact Among Nations to End Human Poverty*. New York: Oxford University Press.

Wilson, R.M., Runciman, W.B., Gibberd, R.W. et al. (1995) The Quality in Australian Health Care Study, *Medical Journal of Australia*, 163: 458–71.

World Bank (2001) *World Development Report 2000/2001: Attacking Poverty*. Washington, DC: World Bank and Oxford University Press.

World Health Organization (2000) *The World Health Report 2000: Health Systems: Improving Performance*. Geneva: WHO.

World Health Organization (2003a) *The World Health Report 2003: Shaping the Future*. Geneva: WHO.

World Health Organization (2003b) *Tobacco Control: Country Profiles*. Geneva: WHO.

2

CHINA
Gerald Bloom

Population 2002[a]	1302 million
Capital city	Beijing
Live births per woman 2002[a]	1.8
Under 5 mortality per 1000 live births 2002 (male/female)[a]	31/41
Life expectancy at birth 2002 (male/female)[a]	69.6/72.7 years
Total health expenditure as a percentage of GDP 2002[b]	5.4%
Government health expenditure as a percentage of total health expenditure 2002[b]	15.2% (not including compulsory work-related health insurance in urban areas)
Total health expenditure per capita 2001 (US$ PPP)	224
Practising physicians per 1000 population 1995	1.62 (refers to people in physician posts and does not necessarily imply levels of training)
Health system	The health system is difficult to characterize; most health facilities are run by government and most health workers are public employees, but these facilities derive almost all their revenue from user charges (some reimbursed by insurance). Perhaps the most accurate designation would be a transitional health system.

| Political system | Party-state in which the roles of the Communist Party and the government are closely intertwined. |

Sources: [a]WHO (2003), [b]Chinese Health Economics Institute

INTRODUCTION

It is dangerous to make general statements about a country as vast as China with a population of over 1.2 billion. The reality in Shanghai, a modern city with a per capita GDP equivalent to an upper-middle-income country, is very different from that in Guizhou Province, where many people live in remote rural villages on considerably less than the equivalent of US$1 a day. Furthermore, China has undergone several radical social, economic and institutional changes during the second half of the twentieth century and it continues to change at a dizzying rate. One theme underlying these changes has been the need to reconcile the objectives of building a modern economy and of widening access to the benefits of economic development.

The foundations of China's health system were built during the 30 years following the founding of the People's Republic in 1949. The development strategy at that time was based on collective agricultural production and centrally planned state-owned enterprises. The government invested heavily in the construction of health facilities and training of health workers. Its health policy gave priority to prevention and to meeting basic health needs. By the mid-1970s, China had experienced remarkable health improvements due, in part, to its widely accessible health services.

Since the end of the 1970s, China has been in transition to what its political leaders call a 'socialist market economy'. This has involved changing almost every aspect of economic organization. The political leaders' priorities during much of this time have been to foster rapid economic growth and manage an orderly change in the economic system. They have paid little attention to the health sector, which has had to adapt to the new economic and institutional environment. Many problems have emerged and health has gradually risen up the political agenda. The government is now emphasizing measures to spread the benefits from economic growth. These measures include improving the performance of the health sector. This will involve fundamental changes to the institutional arrangements within which health services are provided. Strategies for reform are closely related to other aspects of transition management.

BRIEF HISTORY OF HEALTH POLICY AND THE HEALTH SYSTEM

Creation of the health system

One can trace China's health system back to the founding of the People's Republic in 1949 (Horn 1969; Tang et al. 1994). At that time, the population suffered from a high burden of disease and premature death. One estimate is that average life expectancy was 35 years (Xu 1985). The causes of death and ill-health were mostly related to poverty, war and social disruption. China had prestigious medical schools and good medical facilities for elite groups, but most people depended on the many traditional practitioners and the few Western doctors, most of whom saw patients on a private basis. The new regime made health a priority and included a right of access to health care in its constitution. Life expectancy rose to 69 years by 1981 and 71.1 by 2002 (WHO 2003).

Health policy reflected the prevalent development strategies: mass mobilization for basic investments in physical and human capital, collective agricultural production and centrally planned industrial production in the cities. Almost everyone had access to land or a job. At national health conferences convened in 1950 and 1951, the government identified the following priorities for health work: (1) medicine must serve the working people, (2) prevention must be given priority, (3) Chinese traditional and Western medicine should be integrated and (4) health work must be integrated with mass movements (Tang et al. 1994). The government mobilized people in a number of mass public health campaigns to kill flies, reduce the number of schistosomiasis-carrying snails, and so forth. It also invested heavily in health facilities and health workers (Tables 2.1 and 2.2).

China established public health programmes based on the example of the Soviet Union. It established anti-epidemic stations and maternal and child health centres at every administrative level down to the counties to coordinate preventive activities, which were funded by government. These programmes were organized in parallel to curative health services.

Table 2.1 The network of health facilities, 1949–1995

	1949	1965	1975	1985	1995
Number of hospitals at county level and above	2 600	5 746	8 399	12 227	16 010
Hospital beds at county level and above ('000s)	80	633.1	977.9	1 508.6	2 102.8
Number of health centres	NA	36 965	54 026	47 387	51 797
Number of village clinics	NA	NA	571 425	777 674	804 352

Sources: Summary of Health Statistics of China 1948–1988 and 1990–2001; Summary of Health Statistics of China 2001

Table 2.2 Hospital beds and doctors per 1000 population, 1949–1995

	1949	1965	1975	1985	1995
Hospital beds	0.15	1.06	1.74	2.14	2.39
Urban	0.63	3.78	4.61	4.54	3.50
Rural	0.05	0.51	1.23	1.53	1.59
Doctors*	0.67	1.05	0.95	1.36	1.62
Urban	0.70	2.22	2.66	3.35	2.39
Rural	0.70	0.80	0.65	0.85	1.07

* This refers to people in doctors' posts, many of whom may not have had university training.
Sources: Summary of Health Statistics of China 1948–1988 and 1990–2001

One characteristic of China's social organization has been the household registration system introduced in the 1950s, whereby families could not move their place of residence without permission. This system has underpinned a sharp divide between rural and urban residents (Cook 2001). Rural residents have been entitled to little more than access to the means of agricultural production and minimal financial support has been provided for the poorest people. Urban residents have been entitled to a wide range of benefits in what Solinger (1999) calls 'the urban public goods regime'. Large-scale migration and the 'urbanization' of peri-urban areas have led to a blurring of the sharp rural–urban divide and some provinces have begun to end the registration system. However, substantial rural–urban differences persist. The following paragraphs discuss urban and rural health services in the late 1970s, when the transition to a market economy began.

The cities created a network of health facilities that extended from specialist hospitals to community and workplace clinics. Some facilities belonged to the Ministry of Health and others to enterprises and other government departments. A facility's 'owner' paid salaries and the facility charged for drugs, consumables, and so forth. Almost the entire urban population worked for state-owned enterprises or government institutions, which provided a wide range of benefits, including health insurance.

The rural areas were organized into communes, the units of collective agricultural production. By the late 1970s, most of rural China had a highly structured health service. Approximately 85 per cent of villages had a health station staffed by barefoot doctors, local people who had received some basic training. Commune health centres, staffed by doctors who had been reassigned from urban posts, provided routine outpatient and inpatient services. Each county had a Western and a Chinese traditional medicine hospital. The county health bureaux planned and supervised county-wide health services. The government paid the salaries of health workers in county health facilities and in some township health centres. The communes paid all other health workers. Individuals paid the remainder of the costs themselves. Most communes had a cooperative medical scheme, which reimbursed a proportion of the cost of care. This arrangement, combined with the low costs associated with the egalitarian pay structure, ensured that most people had access to basic health services.

The government encouraged the development of both Western and Chinese traditional medicine. It supported training institutions and hospitals in both traditions. Today, one commonly finds both types of health worker in front-line institutions and village doctors provide both kinds of treatment.

Transition to a market economy

Since the late 1970s, China has been in transition to a market economy. This has involved radical changes to almost every aspect of economic and social organization. The communes have been dissolved and a new tier of government, the township, has been established. Most agricultural production is the responsibility of individual households. State-owned enterprises have been given considerable autonomy and are expected to pay their own way. Many have radically reduced their activities and some have closed. There has been a rapid growth in the number of enterprises with a variety of forms of ownership (by village or township administrations, small private enterprises, joint ventures with foreign companies, and so forth).

The Chinese approach to transition management differs from the blueprint approach of the former Soviet Union (Rawski 1999; Stiglitz 2002). China's political leaders give high priority to social stability, paying more attention to the management of change than to the future structure of the socialist market economy. They describe transition as 'crossing a stream whilst feeling for the stones', expressing the unknown nature of the final destination.

The priority given to social stability strongly influences the policy process (Lieberthal and Oksenberg 1988; Liu and Bloom 2002). The national government articulates broad development objectives and defines certain fixed rules such as the primacy of the Communist Party, the maintenance of national unity and the prohibition of certain criminal activities. The formulation of a new policy involves the gradual construction of a consensus. The initial policy statement often states general principles. Its evolution into specific and enforceable regulations takes time. Meanwhile, localities have leeway in translating policies into new practices (Shue 1988; Oi 1999). Stakeholders (enterprises, workers, farmers, and so forth) test boundaries and re-negotiate relationships within the policy framework. This approach permits local experiments before the government alters the legal framework (Kelliher 1992).

The evolutionary approach to reform has had benefits and costs. China has experienced great economic success, and the government has avoided catastrophic mistakes during a period of complex change. The number of people living in poverty has diminished greatly. This has provided a relatively stable environment, within which stakeholders could have gradually revised their understanding of the ordering of social relationships. It has also favoured the creation of sustainable institutional arrangements.

On the other hand, interest groups have had opportunities to retard change, and individuals and institutions have been able to profit from the opportunities provided by partially liberalized markets. Woo (1999) argues that the gradualist approach to change has resulted in substantial economic losses. It may have contributed to growing differences between localities with strong and weak local administrations (Wang and Bei 1991), and has encouraged the development of informal arrangements that favour powerful stakeholders. The following sub-section discusses how a lack of appropriate institutional arrangements has affected the health sector.

Adaptation of the health system to transition

Figure 2.1 describes the management structure of the government health system in 2004. All but the lowest levels of government have their own hospitals, maternal and child health centres, and centres for disease control and prevention. Most township (rural) and

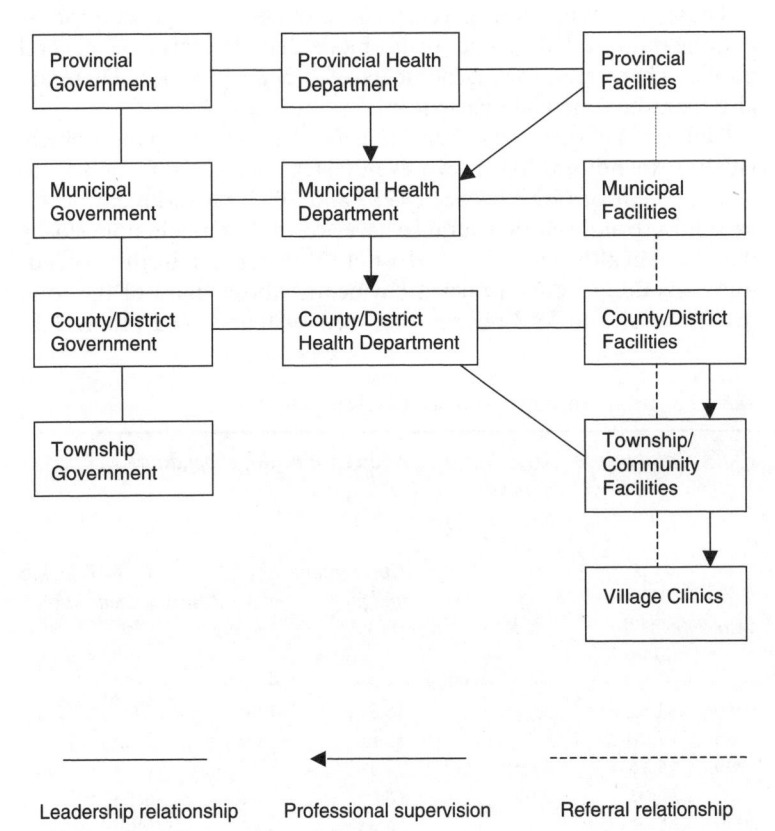

Figure 2.1 Management structure of the government health system. Based on a depiction of the management structure of the health system in Nantong City in Meng (2004).

district (urban) governments have financial responsibility for a health centre, which provides preventive and curative health services, but these facilities are directly supervised by the next level up (county or district). Most villages have one or more rural health workers working in small clinics. They may receive small payments from government but are not government employees. The family planning service maintains a similar chain of institutions at every government level. The system is characterized by extreme devolution of financial responsibility and the existence of parallel vertical administrative structures for curative and preventive services. Figure 2.1 shows notional referral relationships, but facilities compete with each other and lower-level ones rarely receive reports from higher-level ones.

There are many non-government providers. Large enterprises and the military have clinics or hospitals that also serve the general public. There are growing numbers of private facilities. There are also many commercial pharmacies.

China has experienced over 20 years of rapid economic growth. Health expenditure has grown even faster, increasing from 3.17 to 5.42 per cent of GDP between 1980 and 2002. Government health expenditure and health insurance have grown, but much more slowly than total health expenditure. Most of the increase in health expenditure was due to out-of-pocket payments, whose share of the total rose from 21.2 to 58.3 per cent between 1980 and 2002 (Table 2.3).

Table 2.3 Total expenditure on health, 1980–2002

Year	Total health expenditure (RMB billions)	Health expenditure as proportion of GDP (%)	Government budget (%)	Social expenditure (%)	Out-of-pocket expenditure (%)
1980	14.32	3.17	36.2	42.6	21.2
1985	27.90	3.11	38.6	33.0	28.5
1990	74.74	4.03	25.1	39.2	35.7
1995	215.51	3.69	18.0	35.6	46.4
2000	458.66	5.13	15.5	25.6	59.0
2002	568.46	5.42	15.2	26.5	58.3

Source: Chinese Health Economics Institute

This has been associated with a rise in the importance of market relationships in the health sector.

There are considerable differences in health expenditure between localities. In 2002, average health expenditure per capita was 932.9 yuan in urban areas and 268.6 yuan in rural areas (data supplied by the National Health Accounts team at the Chinese Health Economics Institute).

One important influence on the health sector has been the evolution from a centrally managed workforce to a labour market (Tomba 2001). The government's approach in the public sector has been to keep a national salary scale, while allowing facilities to pay bonuses. This has allowed differences in pay to emerge between categories of worker and between rich and poor localities. However, it has established a direct link between health worker income and revenue generation. Managers of health facilities have had little control over the hiring and firing of staff. Under pressure from local government officials, they have tended to increase their workforce regardless of activity; the average workload per health worker has decreased in many facilities.

Government health budgets have not kept up with the rise in the average earnings of health workers and, by 2000, government grants accounted for as little as 5 per cent of a health facility's expenditure. The government has tried to ensure access to services through price control. It has kept charges for consultations and bed-days low, but it has allowed health facilities to earn a 15 per cent mark-up from selling drugs and to charge more than the marginal cost of diagnostic tests. This has encouraged a costly form of medical care (Zhan et al. 1997; Dong et al. 1999; Tang and Meng 2004). The devolution of financial management has reduced the direct influence of higher levels of government. The major instrument of control is the annual review of the performance of local government officials by the Communist Party (Huang 1995), which provides very basic accountability upwards.

The government has radically devolved its administrative system (Ahmad 1997). Local governments collect tax and remit a share to higher levels, but they have full control over their own budgets. There are modest fiscal transfers (World Bank 2002). The limited public funds allocated for health are spent disproportionately in the cities and the more developed rural areas (World Bank 1997; Li Changming 2002). The health system has evolved differently in urban and rural areas.

Urban areas

The major challenges in the cities are associated with rapid rises in health care costs and growing social segmentation (Bloom 2004). The reasons for the rise in costs include the ageing of the cohort of people who joined government and labour insurance schemes during the 1950s and 1960s, the incentives to sell more drugs and prescribe more tests provided by regulated prices, the bias of insurance schemes in favour of hospital care and demand associated with rising incomes, growing inequalities and the influence of advertising.

Expenditure by work-related health insurance schemes has grown rapidly. Between 1978 and 1997, the number of people covered by government or labour insurance rose from 92 to 153 million and spending increased from 3.16 to 77.37 billion yuan (Tang and Meng 2004). The share of salary costs spent on health benefits rose from 5.8 to 9.1 per cent between 1978 and 1997. Meanwhile, the proportion of urban residents who were uninsured rose from 27 to 44 per cent between 1993 and 1998 (Gao *et al.* 2001). This was due to a combination of the reclassification of localities from rural to urban, the rise in the numbers of laid-off workers, the inability of loss-making enterprises to fund medical benefits and the large numbers of rural to urban migrants.

According to a survey by the Ministry of Civil Affairs in 2000, about 14 million urban residents were receiving financial support because they had incomes below the local poverty line (Hussain 2003). This accounted for around 3 per cent of the 458 million registered urban residents. Hussain (2003) points out that many more people have incomes close to the poverty level. The urban poor face serious financial barriers to medical care (Dong 2003). The government has recently announced that it will provide a basic health benefit for the poor, while local governments are experimenting with alternative benefit designs.

Rural areas

The institutional arrangements for rural health have changed a great deal (Bloom and Gu 1997). Governments of poor rural areas spend most of their budgets on salaries (World Bank 2002). They provide only minimal funding to local health services. In 2002, government health expenditure in rural areas was equivalent to 16.7 yuan per capita. County and township health facilities commonly receive less than 10 per cent of their budget from government; village clinics receive virtually no government support. The only exceptions are preventive services, which are better funded, but have to generate revenue to pay adequate salaries.

Health facilities compete for patients and supervision and referral has diminished. Government officials no longer influence day-to-day management, and they are more concerned with economic growth than health. Many local governments do not have the resources to monitor and regulate the health sector effectively. Health facilities have a lot of autonomy and there is an increasing number of private providers. The rural health services in many localities resemble a poorly regulated market.

Health facilities in wealthy areas provide an increasingly sophisticated mix of services, but at rising cost. Facilities in poor localities provide a smaller range of services than before, partly because they have lost their best personnel (Gong *et al.* 1997; Tang 1999). Preventive programmes have deteriorated in some localities. The cost of rural health services has risen quickly; the cost of an outpatient visit and an inpatient day increased two- to three-fold in county hospitals and township health centres between 1993 and 1998, compared with a 60 per cent increase in the overall consumer price index and a 41 per cent increase in the rural consumer price index (World Bank 2002).

According to government estimates, 32 million rural residents had incomes below the poverty line in 2000 (National Statistics Bureau 2001). Many more have incomes just above this very low level (much lower than the urban poverty line). The cost of medical care has become an important barrier to access and a significant factor contributing to household poverty. In 1998, health accounted for 5.7 and 2.8 per cent of total household consumption of urban and rural dwellers, respectively; it accounted for 8.5 and 6.2 per cent of the poorest quintile of urban and rural people, respectively (Gao *et al.* 2002). A minority of households spent a much higher proportion of their income on health. Liu *et al.* (2003) cite a survey which found that 18 per cent of rural households that used health services had spent more on health care than total household income for the year. They cite another survey of poor rural households of which 23 per cent said the most important cause of their difficulties was insufficient capacity to undertake agricultural labour and 22 per cent said it was disease or injury.

THE NEXT PHASE OF HEALTH SECTOR TRANSITION

The new policy environment

Recent policy discussions acknowledge that government needs to pay more attention to social welfare. One concern is the rising inequalities between localities, age cohorts and employment groups (Khan and Riskin 2001). Li Peilin (2002) argues that 'it is essential for future sustainable development in China to bring about a reasonable order of social stratification with the aid of the legal system' (p. 45). Another concern is the need to establish an effective social sector capable of meeting the population's needs. This involves the establishment of rules-based systems backed by a regulatory and legal framework and effective accountability arrangements. The report to the Sixteenth Party National Congress emphasizes the need for government action to spread the gains from economic growth and establish a rules-based regulatory framework (Communist Party of China 2002a). Tax revenues have been rising as a result of sustained economic growth, providing a major opportunity to allocate the additional revenue for new purposes.

The public has become increasingly concerned about the performance of the health sector. A recent survey found that the high cost of health care is the greatest worry of urban residents, even surpassing the risk of unemployment (Gong 2001). Rural people have demonstrated against high taxes and charges and the lack of public services of commensurate value (Bernstein and Lu 2000; Wedeman 2000). In the health sector, peasants have responded cautiously to requests that they contribute to health insurance schemes that mostly cover care in township health centres (Wang *et al.* 2001). Other sources of public concern have been scandals concerning counterfeit drugs and the slow response of the health sector to the SARS outbreak. There have been a number of newspaper reports of health workers accepting under-the-counter payments from patients or kickbacks from suppliers of drugs (Bloom *et al.* 2001). Policy makers have come to believe that major illness is an important cause of household poverty. All these factors have led China's leaders to pay more attention to health. In 1996, the government organized a national meeting to discuss responses to these problems. This was followed by a series of policy statements (State Council 1997a,b, 1998, 2000; Communist Party of China 2002b). The remainder of this chapter discusses issues these statements address.

Health challenges

The population is ageing and 7 per cent were over 65 years old in 2000 according to that year's census. This has been associated with a rise in the prevalence of non-communicable diseases (Lee *et al.* 2003). This rise has been exacerbated by high levels of tobacco use; the China National Tobacco Corporation accounts for 25 per cent of total world sales of tobacco. Changes in diet and high levels of environmental pollution have also contributed to the rise in non-communicable diseases.

The ageing of the population and rising prevalence of non-communicable diseases have contributed to the rapid rise in the proportion of household expenditure on medical care. The active family planning programme has resulted in very small family sizes, for whom the care of a dependent parent with a chronic disease is a heavy burden, particularly in cities where families have been limited to one child (Xiong 1999). Poor elderly people increasingly face a choice between forgoing care and financial destitution. This is particularly the case in poor rural areas, where household incomes are very low and only a tiny minority of people have health insurance. One of the greatest challenges the health sector faces is to develop appropriate ways of organizing and financing support and medical care for the aged and chronically ill.

China still has problems with infectious diseases such as hepatitis and tuberculosis. Their incidence is higher in the poorer parts of the country. However, very large population movements mean that all areas are affected. The impact of the 2003 SARS outbreak demonstrated to the highest levels of government the need to strengthen national capacity to prevent the spread of infectious diseases. There were 5327 reported cases and 348 deaths from SARS (Ministry of Health 2003) and the economic disruption was enormous. The government is investing heavily in a network of centres of disease control to improve disease reporting.

Another threat is posed by HIV/AIDS. Around one million people were infected in 2002, implying an adult prevalence of 0.1 per cent (Ministry of Health and UNAIDS 2003). The main transmission routes have been related to intravenous drug use and drug plasma sale. The second route has become much less significant since the government strengthened regulation of blood products. The disease has begun to spread to the general population. In parts of Yunnan and Xinjiang provinces, HIV prevalence among pregnant women has reached 1.3 and 1.2 per cent, respectively (Ministry of Health and UNAIDS 2003). Several factors make prevention difficult: a large illegal sex industry, rural–urban population movements, a high prevalence of reproductive tract infections in rural women, low levels of knowledge about HIV and insufficient regulation of health facilities. The government acknowledges the importance of preventing the spread of HIV, but is only just beginning to respond effectively.

Supply-side reforms

One of the major challenges government faces is the great variability in the quality of health services. During the Cultural Revolution, medical schools were closed and priority was given to training basic health workers. Doctors were relocated to rural facilities. Since the early 1980s, most of these doctors have left and a high proportion of health workers at village and township levels are not highly trained. A survey of rural health facilities found that 40 per cent of doctors had never been to college (Gong 2001). The government is introducing measures to license village doctors and certify the professional qualifications of other rural personnel.

The government is reforming the ownership, management and regulation of health service providers. One of the most serious concerns is the overuse of expensive and inappropriate drugs, largely in response to financial incentives. This is associated with side-effects, the risk of antibiotic resistance and high costs. Hospitals are now required to pay profits from selling drugs into a common fund to reduce the direct link between volume of sales and income. Charges for medical consultations have been raised. There is an increasing use of competitive tenders for drug procurement. However, government policy does not address other factors that contribute to the rise in drug expenditure, such as the predominance of fee-for-service payment mechanisms and the almost complete absence of regulation of the right to prescribe drugs.

The government is introducing reforms to reduce interference by government officials in facility management, select facility managers through a competitive process and give managers greater powers to hire and fire personnel. It is also rationalizing public sector employment, beginning at national level and extending gradually to lower levels. Implementation by health facilities has been slow, partly because of the government's desire to avoid major increases in unemployment. People who joined the labour force during the 1970s face a particular risk of unemployment, because many have had little training. There is strong political and moral pressure to protect them, which will ease as they reach retirement age. Meanwhile, training institutions are producing large numbers of health workers who will gradually dominate the health labour force. This will present a major opportunity for the introduction of new approaches for improving the quality of services.

The system whereby health facilities are largely responsible for their own investment has resulted in duplication of buildings, equipment and expertise. For example, 50 per cent of county and higher level hospitals had a computed tomography (CT) scanner in 1998 (Ministry of Health 1998). The State Development and Planning Commission now requires all municipalities to produce a regional health plan that largely focuses on facilities, equipment and staff. Many have done so, but have made very slow progress with implementation. This reflects government's limited influence, associated with low levels of public funding of health facilities. It also reflects how hard it is for government officials to change their role from central planners to regulators of the health system.

Given the small budgetary allocations to government facilities, it is difficult to unravel the meanings of public and private. On the one hand, government needs to reduce interference in facility management and remove regulatory controls that are no longer appropriate. On the other hand, it needs to play a more active role in monitoring and regulating facility performance. It is difficult to predict how ownership patterns of health facilities and government regulation will evolve. In a 1999 review of data from Guangdong, Shanxi and Sichuan provinces, Lim et al. (2002) found a small number of private hospitals in each province, between 1.3 and 2.1 private clinics per 10,000 people in sample counties and between 1.8 and 4.4 private clinics per 10,000 people in sample cities. A high proportion of village doctors were private. Local governments are just beginning to regulate private providers.

Health finance reform

One of the government's major challenges has been to establish an appropriate system of public finance (World Bank 2002). Local governments collect taxes and transfer a proportion of the revenue to higher levels of government according to an agreed formula. Some local governments are net recipients of fiscal transfers. The overall tax take has remained low as a share of GDP and inequalities in public expenditure have grown. The situations are quite different in urban and rural areas.

The financial problems of urban health services are associated with rapid urbanization and growing social segmentation. The government is addressing them with a combination of increased public funding of preventive and promotion programmes, a health safety net for the poor and health insurance reforms.

Government funding of preventive programmes and basic public health has lagged behind the growth in the urban population, while traditional programmes have not adapted to demographic and epidemiological change. For example, the workload of the Maternal and Child Health Service is low, but there are not enough community support services for the elderly. Government policy calls for greater funding of public health, but implementation is left to local authorities. In addition, the Ministry of Civil Affairs has been assigned responsibility for a health safety net for the poor and it is experimenting with a package of basic benefits for people living on less than their city's minimum living standard.

The government's principal strategy for financing medical care for the urban population is through work-related insurance. It has been searching for ways to cope with the rising cost of urban health care since the early 1980s (Tang and Meng 2004). It first tried to control demand through a variety of deductibles and co-payments. It began to experiment with health insurance reform in the 1990s. Two cities began to test new models of insurance and soon thereafter 57 cities were piloting health insurance.

In 1997, the government established a new Ministry for Labour and Social Security, to which it assigned responsibility for health insurance reform. The government subsequently published guidelines for city-wide insurance schemes (State Council 1998, 2000). These schemes vary, but have a common pattern (Dong 2003). All employees are expected to join the basic scheme, although many enterprises have still not joined. Employers contribute 6 per cent of salary and employees contribute 2 per cent. The revenue is divided between individual and social pooling accounts. The schemes vary in the levels of deductibles, co-insurance and ceilings. Individuals must draw a substantial amount from their individual account before they are eligible for funding from the social pool. The latter mostly reimburses inpatient care. There is limited provision for outpatient treatment of chronic illness. The schemes do not cover dependants, who must pay for their own health care. These schemes are new and there is limited evidence to date on how well they are managed. Enterprises can also enrol their employees in a top-up scheme to supplement the basic provision.

City governments have had great difficulty in establishing financially sound insurance schemes. One reason is the heavy reliance on referral hospitals for routine medical care. The government policy of encouraging the development of community health services is meant to address this problem. A second reason is the high levels of use of expensive diagnostic tests and drugs. A third reason is the demographic transition; a high proportion of payments is for the care of elderly people who worked for a long time for government or state-owned enterprises. The new insurance schemes are likely to experience rising costs as their beneficiaries age. There are several options for financing these demands. One is to ask young workers to make larger contributions, a second is to recruit many new beneficiaries into the scheme, a third is for government to subsidize some of the benefits, and a fourth is for government to transfer some state-owned assets to a special fund. Each option has important distributional consequences.

It is misleading to discuss the rural areas as if all localities are similar. Designation of a locality as 'rural' covers a spectrum of circumstances from very poor agricultural communities to rapidly industrializing peri-urban areas. The latter are mostly situated near big cities and have benefited from high levels of investment in labour-intensive production. One can envisage a gradual integration of health systems in the cities and the peri-urban areas. The following paragraphs focus on the rural areas that remain primarily agricultural, where around half of China's population lives.

During the late 1980s and the 1990s, the government allocated funds for investment in rural health infrastructure. As with many government programmes, the central government funded only a proportion of the costs and other levels of government were expected to contribute. A mid-term review found that the national government funded 2.7 per cent of total investment, provinces and counties funded 28.5 per cent, townships funded 20.9 per cent, facilities funded 40.9 per cent and other sources (such as local businesses) provided 7.1 per cent (Liu and Bloom 2002). Take-up of national government funding by poor counties was very low. Subsequently, the government added health facilities to the menu of possible investments by programmes aimed at reducing rural poverty.

The central government has acknowledged the financial constraints that rural health services face. It has proposed that every local government maintain health's share of total expenditure, with a target of 8 per cent of the total. However, many localities have not achieved this target. The underlying problem is the financial constraints that governments of poor rural areas face (World Bank 2002). The failure to increase fiscal transfers to poor localities largely reflects ongoing negotiations between rich and poor areas regarding their relative claims on public finance. It also reflects doubts by higher levels of government about the way that local governments use resources. This has led to an increasing interest in demand-side financing, which has taken the form of contracting for the provision of preventive services, the establishment of local health insurance schemes and a targeted health benefit for the poor, as discussed below.

The government has begun to experiment with contracting frontline health facilities to provide a specified amount of preventive services. These experiments have been small scale. However, if the government substantially increases its allocation for basic health services, this kind of contracting could spread. It might counteract the tendency for township hospitals to capture almost all of the resources for basic rural health services, leaving private village health workers with virtually no government funding.

There has been a lot of experimentation with local health insurance. Under the command economy, most communes had a cooperative medical scheme, to which the collective and individual households contributed. When people fell ill, they could claim reimbursement for a proportion of the cost of care. Most of these schemes collapsed after the communes were dissolved (Feng et al. 1997). During the 1990s, the Ministry of Health supported attempts to re-establish these schemes (Bloom and Tang 1999; Carrin et al. 1999). There were some successes, particularly in localities experiencing rapid economic growth, where governments provide a wide variety of social benefits (Cook 1999). There was less success in the poorer counties. A number of studies have explored the reasons for these difficulties. One factor was the very low level of government subsidy. Other factors included the low quality of local government facilities and a lack of trust in the management of health insurance funds and in the good behaviour of health service providers (Wang et al. 2001). The reform of rural health finance is inextricably linked to parallel developments aimed at improving local government management and accountability.

There has been a long-standing debate among policy makers about whether contributions to health insurance should be subject to the ceiling on local government levies and contributions of 5 per cent of average household income. The Ministry of Health argued that contributions to health insurance should be exempt because it provided great benefits. The Ministry of Agriculture disagreed, on the grounds that many rural health facilities used insurance schemes to increase salaries without providing more services (Du 2000). Government policy currently favours the spread of these schemes. Central government contributes a fixed amount per capita to schemes if lower levels of government and households each contribute matching funds. The funds are to be used to cover the cost of major illness. Should these schemes succeed, they could become a source of pressure on health facilities to provide better services at an affordable price. If their management and governance is weak, they could encourage increases in hospital costs and provide disproportionate benefits to the better off and those living near to hospitals. Where that happens, it will be difficult to convince people to continue to support them.

The government announced in late 2003 that it will establish a health safety net for the rural poor to be managed by the Ministry of Civil Affairs. Central government has allocated funds, and it expects lower levels of government to contribute. The present thinking is that beneficiaries will claim reimbursement for a proportion of their spending on medical care. There is debate about whether this is the best way to organize the scheme. People may decide not to seek care because they must pay for services before they can ask for financial support. Other issues include the selection of beneficiaries, the definition of major illness, the kinds of care to be subsidized and the measures needed to influence the performance of service providers. Government commitment to provide protection against the cost of major illness represents an important departure. One can expect lengthy debates about the design of this scheme.

The new government health policy includes a commitment to help very poor areas address health problems. Residents of villages in mountainous areas find it difficult to travel to health centres and depend heavily on village health workers. The policy states a general intention to increase funding of basic health services, particularly maternal and child health care, and prevention and treatment of epidemic diseases. However, details of the levels of funding, mechanisms for transferring the resources and strategies for monitoring performance have not yet been worked out.

There is a serious risk that health services will become more fragmented. The Ministries of Health, Labour and Social Security and Civil Affairs are responsible for different aspects of health finance. The State Planning and Development Commission is responsible for regional health planning and also for setting prices. No-one is responsible for overall coordination of health system development. The problem is complicated by the likelihood that the balance between the different financing mechanisms will vary, depending on a locality's level of development, the management capacity of local administration and governance arrangements.

Creation of appropriate institutional arrangements

China's experience illustrates the role of expectations and beliefs in health system performance (Bloom and Fang 2003). A major aim of transition has been to reduce administrative and political interference in the management of enterprises. Managers of health facilities have gained a great deal of autonomy. However, they have had to generate revenue to keep up with the rise in average levels of pay. It is widely believed that they sell more drugs and recommend more tests than necessary to increase their income. This belief reflects a relatively low level of trust in health service providers. There is also widespread distrust of local governments and how they spend revenue from taxation and other sources. One of the greatest challenges facing the health sector is to create institutional arrangements that foster trust.

The political leadership has acknowledged the importance of rules-based institutions. The government has identified a new role for itself as enforcer of regulations. To play that role, it needs to redefine its responsibilities, retrain officials and provide local personnel with incentives to enforce the law. This will take a long time to achieve. In the meantime, there is a growing interest in the role of the public as informed consumers and active community members.

There has been an explosion in the growth of the media. Almost everyone has a television. Televised drug advertisements have become an important source of information. Almost all drugs are widely available from the smallest clinics or specialized shops. There is also a wide variety of providers of health services. People rely on local reputations and word of mouth to choose providers. The government has begun to construct a regulatory framework, which includes registration of health workers, controls of drug quality, the setting of minimum standards for hospitals, and so forth. This should eventually reduce the transaction costs that people face in using the health sector. Meanwhile, there have been efforts to provide more information on how to use services well. Facilities are required to post information on prices of procedures and drugs. They may also be asked to post information on appropriate treatment for common diseases.

Several measures have been taken to make health providers more accountable to the public. Some facilities put pictures of their staff on the wall and provide complaints boxes and/or telephone complaint lines. Some take complaints into account in setting staff bonuses. Most villages have introduced competitive elections for local leaders. There is some evidence that this provides a deterrent to opportunistic behaviour by township government officials (O'Brien and Li 1995). Village leaders' complaints can also influence the performance of township leaders. There have been few documented examples of the influence of complaints on health sector performance. However, this may change with the increased attention paid to health by senior government leaders.

It is still early in the development of regulatory systems and accountability mechanisms in the health sector. It is difficult to predict the kinds of institutional arrangements that will emerge. However, it is safe to say that the outcome will be strongly influenced by the capacity of government to create rules-based systems and associated behavioural norms.

CONCLUSIONS

The challenge of SARS in 2003 provided policy makers with a graphic illustration of the weaknesses and strengths of China's health system (Liu 2003). The existence of parallel networks of health facilities meant that it was difficult to build up a full picture of the situation during the early days of the epidemic. The cost of treatment created a strong disincentive for people to seek diagnosis and care. On the other hand, once the political leadership recognized the seriousness of the problem, it mobilized government and Communist Party officials at every level to prevent a major epidemic. China established a network reaching most villages to ensure the identification and reporting of cases. The government is now giving very high priority to the consolidation of a national network, coordinated by the Centre for Disease Control, to ensure a rapid response to new disease outbreaks. However, at the time of writing, the extent to which government would act to address the systemic problems described above was not clear.

China's health system has reached a turning point. Policy makers at the highest level have recognized that government has to play a more active role. The creation of appropriate institutional arrangements has begun. It is impossible to predict the outcome of the present reform initiative. Nonetheless, it is likely that arrangements will emerge that combine characteristics of the market with a variety of social financing arrangements and new forms of government regulation and local accountability. No-one can predict the ultimate shape of Chinese society or of the health system that will serve it. The policy story will be a very long one.

ACKNOWLEDGEMENTS

The author acknowledges the assistance he was given in collecting relevant data by Zhao Kun and Zhao Yuxin of the Chinese Health Economics Institute. He also acknowledges financial support from the European Commission, Research DG International Cooperation (INC0) Programme project ECA4-CT2002–10030. Much of the work in drafting this chapter took place while the author was a Distinguished Visiting Fellow of the Institute for Advanced Studies at LaTrobe University. He benefited greatly from comments by Fang Jing and participants at a seminar at LaTrobe University.

REFERENCES

Ahmad, E. (1997) China, in T. Ter-Minassian (ed.) *Fiscal Federalism in Theory and Practice*. Washington, DC: International Monetary Fund.
Bernstein, T.P. and Lu, X. (2000) Taxation without representation: peasants, the central and local states in reform China, *The China Quarterly*, 163: 742–63.
Bloom, G. (2004) China in transition: challenges to city health services, in G. Bloom and S. Tang (eds) *Reforming Health Services for Equity and Efficiency in Urban China*. Aldershot: Ashgate.
Bloom, G. and Fang, J. (2003) *China's Rural Health System in a Changing Institutional Context*. Working Paper #194. Brighton: Institute of Development Studies.
Bloom, G. and Gu, X. (1997) Health sector reform: lessons from China, *Social Science and Medicine*, 45(3): 351–60.
Bloom, G. and Tang, S. (1999) Rural health prepayment schemes in China: towards a more active role for government, *Social Science and Medicine*, 48(7): 951–60.
Bloom, G., Han, L. and Li, X. (2001) How health workers earn a living in China, *Human Resources Development Journal*, 5(1–3): 25–38.
Carrin, G., Ron, A., Yang, H. *et al.* (1999) The reform of the rural cooperative

medical system in the People's Republic of China: interim experience in 14 pilot counties, *Social Science and Medicine*, 48(7): 961–72.
Communist Party of China (2002a) *Working Report of the CPC Central Commission for Discipline Inspection to the 16th Party National Congress*, November.
Communist Party of China (2002b) *Decisions of the Central Committee of the CPC and the State Council on Further Strengthening Rural Health Work*, October.
Cook, S. (1999) Creating wealth and welfare: entrepreneurship and the developmental state in rural China, *IDS Bulletin*, 30(4): 60–70.
Cook, S. (2001) *After the Iron Rice Bowl: Extending the Safety Net in China*. IDS Discussion Paper #377. Brighton: Institute of Development Studies.
Dong, H., Bogg, L., Wang, K., Rehnberg, C. and Diwan, V. (1999) A description of outpatient drug use in rural China: evidence of differences due to insurance coverage, *International Journal of Health Planning and Management*, 14: 41–56.
Dong, W. (2003) Healthcare financing reforms in transitional society: a Shanghai experience, *Journal of Health and Population Research*, 21(3): 223–34.
Du Ying (2000) Some opinions on rural health system reform, in *Proceedings of the Conference on Rural Health Reform and Development in China*, Beijing, November, pp. 43–50.
Feng, X., Bloom, G., Tang, S., Segall, M. and Gu, X. (1997) Cooperative medical schemes in contemporary rural China, *Social Science and Medicine*, 41(8): 1111–18.
Gao, J., Tang, S., Tolhurst, R. and Rao, K. (2001) Changing access to health services in urban China: what implications for equity?, *Health Policy and Planning*, 16(3): 302–12.
Gao, J., Qian, J., Tang, S., Eriksson, B. and Blas, E. (2002) Health equity in transition from planned to market economy in China, *Health Policy and Planning*, 17(suppl. 1): 20–9.
Gong, H. (2001) Present three most concerning issues to the general public. Beijing: Zhongguo Guoqing Guoli, #5 (cited by Dong 2003).
Gong, Y., Wilkes, A. and Bloom, G. (1997) Health human resource development in rural China, *Health Policy and Planning*, 12(4): 320–8.
Horn, J. (1969) *Away With All Pests: An English Surgeon in the People's Republic of China: 1954–1969*. New York: Monthly Review Press.
Huang, Y. (1995) Administrative monitoring in China, *The China Quarterly*, 143: 828–43.
Hussain, A. (2003) Urban poverty in China: measurements, patterns and policies, in *Focus Programme on Socio-Economic Security*. Geneva: ILO.
Kelliher, D. (1992) *Peasant Power in China*. New Haven, CT: Yale University Press.

Khan, A. and Riskin, C. (2001) *Inequality and Poverty in China in the Age of Globalization*. Oxford: Oxford University Press.

Lee, L., Lin, V., Wang, R. and Zhao, H. (2003) Public health in China: history and contemporary challenges, in R. Beaglehole (ed.) *Global Public Health: A New Era*. Oxford: Oxford University Press.

Li, C. (2002) Presentation to consultative meeting of the China Health Development Forum, April 2002, Beijing (available at: www.ids.ac.uk/ids/health/).

Li, P. (2002) Changes in social stratification in China since the reform, *Social Sciences in China*, 23(1): 42–7.

Lieberthal, K. and Oksenberg, M. (1988) *Policy Making in China: Leaders, Structures and Processes*. Princeton, NJ: Princeton University Press.

Lim, M.-K., Yang, H., Zhang, T. *et al.* (2002) *The Role and Scope of Private Medical Practice in China*. Unpublished report to the World Health Organization, Beijing.

Liu, C. (2003) The battle against SARS: a Chinese story, *Australian Health Review*, 26(3): 3–13.

Liu, Y. and Bloom, G. (2002) *Designing a Rural Health Reform Project: The Negotiation of Change in China*. Working Paper #150. Brighton: Institute of Development Studies.

Liu, Y., Rao, K. and Hsiao, W. (2003) Medical expenditure and rural impoverishment in China, *Journal of Health, Population and Nutrition*, 21(3): 216–22.

Meng, Q. (2004) The health systems in Nantong and Zibo initiatives, in G. Bloom and S. Tang (eds) *Reforming Health Services for Equity and Efficiency in Urban China*. Aldershot: Ashgate.

Ministry of Health (1998) *Health Resources and Utilisation since the 1980s*. Beijing: Statistical and Information Centre, Ministry of Health.

Ministry of Health (2003) *SARS Update* (available at: http:://168.160.224.167/sarsmap/).

Ministry of Health and UNAIDS (2003) *A Joint Assessment of HIV/AIDS Prevention, Treatment and Care in China*. Beijing: Ministry of Health and UNAIDS.

National Statistics Bureau (2001) *The Surveillance Report of Rural Poverty of China*. Beijing: China Statistics Press (cited in Gao *et al.* 2002).

O'Brien, K. and Li, L. (1995) The politics of logging complaints in rural China, *The China Quarterly*, 143: 756–83.

Oi, J. (1999) *Rural China Takes Off: Institutional Foundations of Economic Reform*. Berkeley, CA: University of California Press.

Rawski, T. (1999) Reforming China's economy: what have we learned?, *The China Journal*, 41: 139–58.

Shue, V. (1988) *The Reach of the State: Sketches of the Chinese Body Politic*. Stanford, CA: Stanford University Press.

Solinger, D. (1999) *Contesting Citizenship in Urban China: Peasant Migrants, the State and the Logic of the Market*. Berkeley, CA: University of California Press.

State Council (1997a) *Decision of the Central Committee of the Chinese Communist Party and the State Council on Health Reform and Development*, 15 January.
State Council (1997b) *Circular of the CPC Central Committee on Transmitting Some Suggestions on the Development and Improvement of Rural Cooperative Medical Care Submitted by the Ministry of Health and Other Agencies*, 28 May.
State Council (1998) *The Decision on Establishing Basic Health Insurance System for Urban Employees*, Document 44, Beijing.
State Council (2000) *Guidelines for Urban Health and Medicine System Reform*, Beijing.
Stiglitz, J. (2002) *Globalization and its Discontents*. London: Allen Lane.
Tang, S. (1999) Adaptation of township health centres in the poor areas of China to economic reform, unpublished PhD thesis, University of Sussex.
Tang, S. and Meng, Q. (2004) Introduction to the urban health system and a review of reform initiatives, in G. Bloom and S. Tang (eds) *Reforming Health Services for Equity and Efficiency in Urban China*. Aldershot: Ashgate.
Tang, S., Bloom, G., Feng, X. et al. (1994) *Financing Rural Health Services in China: Adapting to Economic Reform*. Research Report #26. Brighton: Institute of Development Studies.
Tomba, L. (2001) *Paradoxes of Labour Reform: Chinese Labour Theory and Practice from Socialism to the Market*. London: Routledge/Curzon.
Wang, H., Hu, Y., Li, Y. et al. (2001) *Report on CMS in Yushe County, Shanxi Province*. Hefiei: Heifei Kayak Society and Health Development Institute.
Wang, X. and Bei, N. (1991) *The Poverty of Plenty*. London: Macmillan.
Wedeman, A. (2000) Budgets, extra-budgets and small treasuries: illegal monies and local autonomy in China, *Journal of Contemporary China*, 9(25): 489–511.
Woo, W. (1999) The real reasons for China's growth, *The China Journal*, 41: 115–37.
World Bank (1997) *China 2020. Issues and Options for China: Financing Health Care*. Washington, DC: World Bank.
World Bank (2002) *China National Development and Sub-National Finance: A Review of Provincial Expenditures*. Report #22951-CHA. Washington, DC: World Bank.
World Health Organization (2003) *World Health Report 2003*. Geneva: WHO.
Xiong, Y. (1999) Social policy for the elderly in the context of ageing in China: issues and challenges of social work education, *International Journal of Welfare for the Aged*, 1: 107–22.
Xu, S. (1985) Health statistics of the People's Republic of China, in S. Halstead et al. (eds) *Good Health at Low Cost*. New York: Rockefeller Foundation.
Zhan, S., Tang, S., Guo, Y. and Bloom, G. (1997) Drug prescribing in rural health facilities in China: implications for service quality and cost, *Tropical Doctor*, 28: 42–8.

3

SOUTH KOREA
Soonman Kwon

Population 2004	48.1 million
Capital city	Seoul
Live births per woman 2002	1.17
Infant mortality rate per 1000 live births 2001	5.4
Life expectancy at birth 2001 (male/female)	72.8/80.0 years
Total health expenditure as a percentage of GDP 2003	5.9%
Government health expenditure as a percentage of total health expenditure 2000	44.4%
Total health expenditure per capita 2003 (US$ PPP)	948
Practising physicians per 1000 population 2001	1.4
Health system	National Health Insurance Corporation (social health insurer), private delivery system
Political system	Presidential system, single chamber (National Assembly)

Source: Ministry of Health and Welfare (2002); OECD (2003)

INTRODUCTION

The Republic of Korea (South Korea) is located in far-eastern Asia between China and Japan, and has an area of 99,460 km^2. With export-driven economic planning in the 1960s and 1970s, Korea achieved rapid economic development. It became a member of the OECD in 1996. A major element of government health policy in Korea is the national health insurance system with universal population coverage. The government played a major role in the implementation of this social health insurance scheme and its rapid extension to the entire population. However, a priority on the rapid extension of health insurance resulted in a policy of low contribution levels and limited benefit coverage. Delivery of health care in Korea depends predominantly on the private sector, and more than 90 per cent of hospitals are private. A fee-for-service payment system, which fails to provide physicians with incentives for cost-effective care, together with the for-profit nature of health care delivery has contributed to health cost inflation. Two major health care reforms were implemented in 2000 to improve the efficiency and equity of the health care system: health care financing reform to merge all insurance societies into one, and pharmaceutical reform to mandate the separation of drug prescribing from dispensing.

This chapter is organized as follows. First, it discusses the historical developments as well as the political and economic contexts associated with the health care financing system. Second, it conducts an overview of the main features of the national health insurance scheme. Third, it examines the characteristics of the organization of health care delivery and the payment system for health care providers. Fourth, it details health expenditure and outcomes. Fifth, it discusses two major health care reforms in Korea, namely health - care financing reform and pharmaceutical reform. The chapter concludes by outlining future challenges for Korean health policy.

HISTORICAL DEVELOPMENTS

Extension of national health insurance

Implementation of a national health insurance system with universal population coverage has been a major achievement in the history of Korean health policy. The main strategy of extending health insurance in Korea has been to make insurance mandatory for employees in the industrial and public sectors, and then to extend coverage to the self-employed. Health insurance for employees was previously based on workplaces, and for the self-employed it was based on regions. The Health Insurance Law was enacted in December 1963 by the military government immediately after its *coup d'état*. Because of the country's weak economic and social infrastructure, the law eliminated mandatory insurance coverage, and social insurance for health care was not actually implemented until there was a substantial revision to the Health Insurance Law in December 1976. This was prompted by the social development element of the government's fourth (five-year) economic development plan (1977–81).

In 1977, the first group to be covered by compulsory health insurance were employees of corporations with more than 500 workers; a medical aid programme for the poor (Medicaid) was also started in 1977. In 1979, health insurance was extended to government employees and teachers and to those working in corporations with more than 300 employees. Over time, it was incrementally extended to smaller firms. For the purpose of extending health insurance to the self-employed, the government implemented a pilot programme in three rural areas in 1981, and in one urban area and two additional rural areas in 1982. The health insurance programme achieved universal population coverage for the rural self-employed from 1988 and the urban self-employed from 1989. Therefore, from the initial introduction of social health insurance, it took only 12 years for the Republic of Korea to achieve universal population coverage.

Political and economic context

Beginning in the early 1960s, a series of five-year economic development plans, formulated by President Park Chunghee, improved the country's economic well-being. The government began to recognize the importance of a welfare system, and the fourth economic development plan of the mid-1970s placed emphasis on social development, aiming to distribute the fruits of economic development to workers. The substantial revision of the Health Insurance Law in 1976 was an important element of the social development plan. At that time, the government shifted the focus of its health policy from public health development and family planning programmes to programmes such as social security that benefited a broader range of population groups.

With a limited supply of health care institutions in the public sector, Korea decided to adopt a national health insurance approach rather than a national health service approach. A contribution-based insurance system made possible the introduction of health insurance with a minimum of government funding. The National Health Insurance (NHI) scheme was founded on multiple not-for-profit insurance societies that were based around enterprises and expected to be autonomous in operation. However, the public regarded social health insurance more as a welfare benefit, leading the government to design a health insurance system with very low contributions and, as a result, rather limited health benefits. The government's priority of rapidly extending insurance coverage throughout the population also contributed to limited benefit coverage with low contribution rates.

Both economic and political factors contributed to the rapid extension of health insurance to the self-employed, the last group to join the NHI scheme (Kwon 2002). First, the booming economy of the late 1980s substantially improved the ability of the self-employed to pay for social insurance. The economy of Korea enjoyed record high annual growth rates of about 12 per cent between 1986 and 1988, and large current account surpluses existed. The government had the fiscal capacity to provide a subsidy for the health insurance for the self-employed. Second, as a political factor, President Chun Doowhan and the presidential candidate of the ruling party, Roh Taewoo, were former military generals and wanted to obtain political support and legitimacy by proposing universal health insurance coverage. The impending 1987 presidential election prompted the ruling party to announce an expansion of social welfare programmes as a major item on their campaign agenda. In 1986, the government announced plans to include the self-employed in the NHI scheme, to introduce a national pension scheme and to implement a minimum wage system. The government was prompted to provide health insurance to the self-employed because of the increasing inequity between the amounts paid for medical care by the (insured) employed and the (uninsured) self-employed. This was because the social health insurance system reimbursed providers based on a regulated fee schedule, which motivated providers to charge higher (unregulated and market) fees to the uninsured.

Contrary to the rather smooth extension of health insurance to industrial workers, its extension to the self-employed faced tough resistance. Farmers refused to pay contributions and requested major reforms in the health insurance scheme such as a discount on or an exemption to the contribution.[1] Government responded to the farmers' protests by providing a health insurance subsidy for the self-employed. In extending health insurance to the self-employed, there arose hot discussions on the organizational arrangements of the universal health insurance system (Kwon 2003a). Debate centred on whether health insurance for the self-employed should adopt the then pluralistic approach of multiple insurance societies or should be a new single insurer by merging existing insurance societies of industrial workers. Through the nationwide contribution schedule and risk-pooling, the single insurer system had the potential benefit, at least in the short term, of a smooth extension of health insurance to the self-employed, avoiding its probable fiscal instability. The government decided to keep the existing approach of pluralistic insurance societies, mainly to minimize government's role in health-care financing in the long run. Another advantage was that it covered employees and the self-employed in separate insurance societies and avoided the problem associated with different degrees of income assessment between those two groups.

HEALTH-CARE FINANCING

Structure of the National Health Insurance scheme

Before the recent merger of all health insurance societies in 2000, there were three types of social health insurance schemes. These were for: (1) government employees and teachers and their dependants (10.4 per cent of the population and with a single insurance society); (2) industrial workers and their dependants (36.0 per cent of the population and with about 140 insurance societies); and (3) the self-employed (50.1 per cent of the population with about 230 insurance societies), the so-called regional health insurance. There was, and remains, a separate programme for the poor (Medicaid), which, as a part of the general welfare programme financed by the general revenue of the central and local governments, covered the rest of the population (approximately 3–4 per cent).[2]

The government set the statutory benefit package, and there was no difference in the statutory benefit coverage between social insurance societies. Before the recent merger, each insurance scheme consisted of non-profit insurance societies, which were quasi-public agencies and subject to strict regulation by the Ministry of Health and Welfare. Each insurance society covered a well-defined population group, and beneficiaries were assigned to insurance societies based on employment (industrial workers) and residential area (self-employed). Consequently, there was no competition among health insurance societies to attract the insured and no selective contracting with providers. Except for utilization review of sampled claims, health insurance societies were merely financial intermediaries that channelled funds to providers.

Contributions and benefits

For industrial workers and government and school employees, employees and employers shared the premium contribution equally. As of 1999, the average contribution was 5.6 per cent (of income) for government and school employees, and 3.75 per cent for industrial workers with a range of 3.0–4.2 per cent depending on the insurance society (subject to approval by the Ministry of Health and Welfare). Because reliable information about the incomes of the self-employed was only partially available, the health insurance societies for the self-employed and those for employees used different schedules to determine contribution levels. The contribution formula in health insurance for the self-employed consisted of two parts: income and property. The property-based part of the contribution depended on the property and automobile that a household owned. The income part of the contribution was based either on taxed income (for the relatively wealthy) or on estimated income. The calculation of estimated income took into account the age and sex of the insured, household property and the automobile tax of the household.

The government subsidized only the insurance societies for the self-employed, covering administrative costs and a part of the premium contributions of the lower income group. Over time, the government increased these subsidies. However, the relative share of government subsidy in the revenue of the regional (i.e. self-employed) health insurance had been decreasing ever since its introduction. In 1988, the proportion of government subsidy in the total revenue of the regional health insurance was 44.1 per cent. This fell to 25.6 per cent in 1999 (National Health Insurance Corporation 2000). A drop in the proportion of government subsidy to the regional health insurance led to a sharp increase in the contributions of the self-employed. Before the merger of health insurance societies into one, in July 2000, the revenue-sharing mechanism for risk pooling (the so-called fiscal stabilization fund) reallocated revenues across insurance societies, taking account of the catastrophic expenses and the proportion of the elderly. The health insurance societies for the self-employed were the major beneficiaries of the revenue-sharing mechanism, although it did not solve their problem of fiscal instability.

For insured medical services, the insured presently pays 20 per cent of the medical expenses in case of inpatient care. For outpatient care, there are differential co-payment rates depending on the types of health care institutions (clinics, hospitals, tertiary-care hospitals), ranging from 30 to 55 per cent. In addition to co-payments for insured medical services, the patient pays in full for uninsured services (e.g. ultrasonogram, magnetic resonance imaging, meals during inpatient care); this amount can be substantial due to the stringent benefit coverage. The social insurers' financial concerns have driven decisions regarding benefit coverage, rather than patients' needs for medical treatment and cost-effective medical interventions. On average, patients' total out-of-pocket payments account for as much as 34 per cent of inpatient care expenses and 64 per cent of outpatient care expenses (National Health Insurance Corporation 2002). The substantial amount of patients' out-of-pocket payments has called into question the fundamental purpose of health insurance – that of spreading the financial risks of the sick.

HEALTH-CARE DELIVERY

Organization of health care delivery

Korea has experienced a substantial improvement in access to health care, thanks to the consistent increase in the supply of health personnel and medical facilities. From 1976 to 2001, per capita numbers of physicians and traditional medical doctors have more than tripled (Table 3.1).[3] The per capita numbers of nurses and dentists have increased by five times. The per capita number of pharmacists has increased but at a slower rate than other types of health care personnel. Most graduates of medical schools get training as specialists and Korea is in short supply of genuine primary care physicians. From a societal perspective, it is very wasteful that most specialists practise as primary care practitioners rather than specialists in hospitals. The number of health care facilities has increased significantly over the last 20 years. Dental clinics and hospitals increased by five times and the number of physician clinics and oriental medical clinics tripled.

Table 3.1 Health resources

	1976	1981	1986	1989	1992	1995	1997	1999	2000	2001
Population per physician	2 009	1 631	1 304	1 067	904	789	735	672	649	630
Population per dentist	13 064	9 811	6 875	4 919	3 877	3 296	2 990	2 712	2 608	2 508
Population per nurse	1 468	994	684	482	NA	370	343	312	293	277
Population per tradititonal doctor	12 556	12 360	10 199	7 810	6 397	5 175	4 951	4 130	3 911	3 726
Population per pharmacist	1 730	1 530	1 315	1 187	1 106	1 042	1 004	952	929	913

Source: Ministry of Health and Welfare (2002)

The per capita number of beds has also increased substantially. The number of beds per 100,000 persons was up by more than four times in 20 years, from 104 to 422 (Ministry of Health and Welfare 2000).

One of the most distinct features of health care delivery in the Republic of Korea is its heavy reliance on for-profit hospitals that, in most cases, physicians both own and manage. As of 1998, almost 50 per cent of acute care hospitals were for-profit, 44 per cent were not-for-profit, and only 7 per cent were public (Korea Hospital Association 1999). More than half of the not-for-profit hospitals are private corporate hospitals with a *de facto* physician-owner. They are not-for-profit in legal terms, but behave as for-profit hospitals. This is because the tax law in Korea does not allow for-profit corporate entities in health care. Many hospitals originated from clinics with small inpatient facilities, and have been expanded by entrepreneurial physicians. Most private (both for-profit and not-for-profit) hospitals depend almost exclusively on patient care for their revenue without philanthropic donation or government subsidies. There is no difference for the health insurer in its dealings – for example, in fee schedules – with for-profit, not-for-profit or public hospitals. Public hospitals usually provide cheaper (uninsured) medical services and have a relatively greater share of Medicaid patients.

Hospitals have a closed system (no system of attending physicians) and employ their own clinical staff. The proportion of outpatient care in hospitals in Korea is much greater than in other countries. Most office (clinic)-based physicians are board-certified specialists, and those in the area of surgery even have small inpatient facilities. In 1999, a quarter of all beds were owned by physician clinics (Ministry of Health and Welfare 2000). Since these clinics and hospitals perform similar functions, and reimbursement to providers is by fee-for-service, referral means a reduction in income for the referring providers. These unique characteristics relating to health - care providers lead to fierce competition rather than coordination among physician clinics and hospitals. There is no formal gate-keeping, patient referrals or networks of health care provision are rare, and wasteful competition results in duplication of facilities and equipment.

Consumers have a strong preference for large (usually tertiary or university) general hospitals, which lead to waiting lines (excess demand) in the former types of hospitals, whereas physician clinics and small hospitals suffer from an excessive supply of beds. Neither demand-side financial incentives such as differential co-insurance rates, nor regulation such as the requirement for referral letters, seems to have solved the problem of large general hospitals being overcrowded with minor cases. Furthermore, because most hospitals are intended for acute care, the National Health Insurance system is in need of longer-term care facilities, especially considering the current increase in the elderly population. The flow of funds (among insured, insurer and providers) in the Korean health care system is depicted in Figure 3.1.

Government regulation of hospital licensing and quality is based on inputs rather than health outcomes. The Korean Hospital Association is responsible for accreditation of teaching hospitals. Because health care delivery in Korea is dominated by private providers, who resist quality control or monitoring by government or third parties, quality control has been a challenge. There are some private sector (commercial) initiatives measuring hospital service and consumer satisfaction. In the near future, government needs a policy to disseminate outcome-based quality of providers or link reimbursement to performance/outcomes of providers.

Payment systems for health care providers

Health care providers in Korea have been reimbursed by a regulated fee-for-service system since the beginning of the National Health Insurance scheme. Under the fee-for-service system, medical

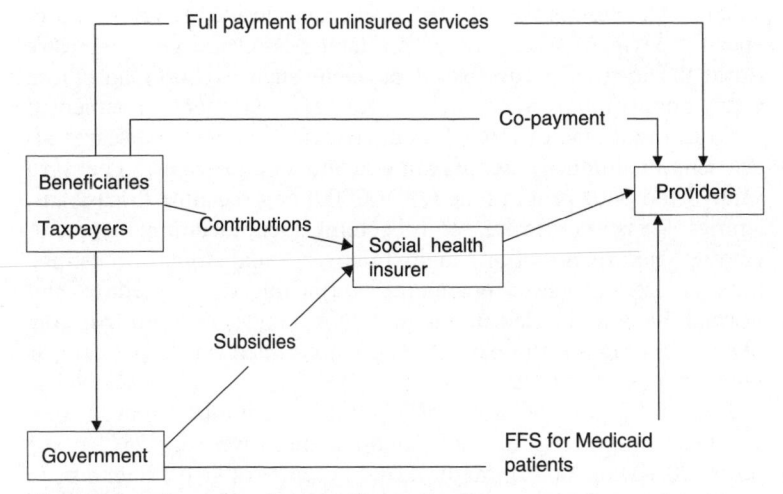

Figure 3.1 Flow of funds in the Korean health care system.

suppliers have incentives to increase the volume and intensity of services and to choose treatments with a greater margin. Differential margins from different medical services also induce physicians to provide more services with higher margins (i.e. overpriced services), resulting in distortion in the mix of medical care for patient treatment. The persistent distortion in the relative price of medical services has also affected the relative supply of medical specialties in Korea (Kwon 2003b). Some specialties, of which services are paid relatively generously, attract a greater number of applicants for residency training. Popular specialties include psychiatry, ophthalmology and dermatology, whereas radiology, thoracic surgery and anaesthesiology are less popular.

To avoid the effect of fee regulation, physicians substitute uninsured medical services, of which fees are not regulated, for insured ones. Even as the insurer has expanded benefit coverage, the proportion of patients' out-of-pocket payments of total medical expense has declined only slightly in Korea because of the increase in uninsured services. The rapid diffusion and utilization of high-cost medical technology, which is not usually covered by health insurance, are to some extent related to the provider incentive to induce patients to use more uninsured (and profitable) services. As of 1996, the number of computerized tomography (CT) scanners per 1 million persons was 17.48, making Korea a world leader along with Japan (55.4) and the USA (26.2) in the adoption of medical technology (National Health Insurance Corporation 2000).

To tackle these problems, the government decided to adopt a prospective payment system based on diagnosis-related group (DRG). Since the idea of a case-based payment such as DRG has faced tough opposition from providers in Korea, government implemented a pilot programme of DRG-based payment for selected disease categories to voluntarily participating health care providers. The third year of the pilot programme (1999–2000) covered nine disease categories (lens procedure, tonsillectomy/adenoidectomy, appendectomy, caesarean section, vaginal delivery, anal/stomal procedure, inguinal/femoral hernia procedure, uterine/adenexa procedure, and normal pneumonia/pleuritis) with 25 DRG codes depending on the severity and age of the patient. These accounted for 25 per cent of inpatient cases.

The evaluation of the DRG pilot programme showed that providers responded to the economic incentives of DRG-based payment (Kwon 2003b). Medical care expenses of given diagnoses in health care institutions declined by 8.3 per cent on average following their participation in the DRG pilot programme. The length of stay fell by 3.0 per cent on average. Heavy use of antibiotics and the resulting high resistance to antibiotics has been a major concern in Korea for some time. The DRG-based payment significantly reduced the use of antibiotics in inpatient care (by 29.6 per cent on average), while the use of antibiotics at discharge (dispensed when patients are discharged) decreased by 23.6 per cent. However, the use of antibiotics slightly increased after discharge, meaning that providers substituted non-inpatient (i.e. ambulatory) use of antibiotics for inpatient use to some extent. The DRG-based payment also reduced the average number of tests in inpatient care, from 5.06 to 3.85 (Ministry of Health and Welfare 2000a). However, providers substituted tests before hospitalization for those at hospital. There was also some evidence that the number of outpatient visits increased in the participating institutions.

Pilot programmes have shown that the DRG-based payment has not had a negative effect on quality as measured by complication and re-operation. The surgical procedures in the DRG pilot programme in Korea are not complicated ones and the rates of adverse outcomes are low in general. Once the DRG payment is extended to more complicated procedures, it might have a different impact on quality. To date, only a small proportion of participating health care institutions have tried to develop clinical guidelines or critical pathways. The DRG monitoring system by the government currently focuses more or less on the potential overcharge of patient co-payments, DRG 'creeping' (distorting DRG codes towards those with higher reimbursement) and distortion in 'outlier' (patients with extraordinarily high costs) classifications. Therefore, the DRG system in Korea is in need of a system monitoring outcome-based quality of care and appropriateness of discharge.

HEALTH EXPENDITURE AND OUTCOMES

Health expenditure

In 2003, Korea spent 6.0 per cent of GDP on health care. Although this expenditure is rather low compared with other OECD countries, it is partly due to Korea's rapid GDP growth. Since the growth of GDP in the future will not be as high as in the past, the proportion of GDP spent on health care is expected to increase. Despite the national health insurance programme, the role of social insurance in health care financing is still limited in Korea. Taxation and social insurance related to health care (national health insurance, Medicaid, workers' compensation) accounted for only 44 per cent of total personal health care expenditure (see Table 3.2). A high proportion of personal health care expenditure, 41 per cent, was borne by households through out-of-pocket payments.

Fiscal stability and cost containment is of major and imminent concern for the National Health Insurance system in Korea. National health insurance as a whole has experienced a deficit since 1997, but an accumulated surplus delayed fiscal crisis until 2001, by which time it was almost bankrupt. An ageing population, little incentive for physicians to provide cost-effective care under the fee-for-service system, and increasing demand for health care has contributed to the continuing trend of health care cost inflation. A recent hike in physician fees by more than 40 per cent following physician strikes against pharmaceutical reform was a critical blow to the deteriorating fiscal health of the National Health Insurance scheme. In the long term, changing financial incentives for providers to practise in a cost-effective way will be the most important factor for health care cost containment, and so payment system reform is urgently required.

Population statistics and health outcomes

Korea had a population of 48 million in 2004. The annual rate of population growth dropped from 3 per cent in 1961 to 1.57 per cent in 1980 (the natural growth rate was 8.0 per 1000 people in 1999), due to public policy and family planning programmes.[4] In 2000, the proportion of the elderly population (age 65 or older) was 7.1 per

Table 3.2 Public/private share of national health expenditure (%)

	1989	1991	1993	1995	1997	1999	2000
Government	8.7	8.3	9.9	11.1	11.5	10.7	10.1
Social insurance	23.3	25.1	23.5	25.4	29.5	32.4	34.3
Public total	32.0	33.3	33.4	36.5	41.0	43.1	44.4
Household	57.3	56.4	54.9	51.1	46.1	43.2	41.3
Private insurance	5.4	5.3	5.9	5.8	6.7	7.7	8.7
Others	5.3	5.0	5.9	6.6	6.2	6.1	5.7
Private total	68.0	66.7	66.6	63.5	59.0	56.9	55.6

Source: Ministry of Health and Welfare (2002)

cent, which is expected to increase rapidly to 13.2 per cent in 2020. Korea's dependency ratio was 40.4 per cent in 2000, but is projected to increase to 43.6 per cent in 2020. Life expectancy at birth was 80.0 years for women and 72.8 years for men. Life expectancy in 2010 has been forecasted as 77.0 years on average, 73.3 years for men and 80.7 years for women. The World Health Organization (2000) estimates disability-adjusted life expectancy to have been 65.0 years (62.3 years for men and 67.7 years for women) in 1999, which is lower than the OECD average of 70.2 years. Rapid ageing will increase health care expenditure and has serious implications for the social security system in Korea, particularly in the era when rapid economic growth is no longer expected.

The primary cause of restricted activity or disability is illness. According to a survey by the Ministry of Health and Welfare and Korea Institute for Health and Social Affairs (1999), major diseases with high prevalence per 1000 persons are dental cavities (184), skin diseases including allergies (170), arthritis (80), lower-back pain (64), gastritis and gastric ulcers (60) and hypertension (45). The prevalence rate varies depending on age and sex. Restricted activity due to illness leads to a loss of productivity, which was estimated to be 1.7 per cent of GDP in 1998 (Ministry of Health and KIHASA 1999). Lower-back pain and arthritis are the leading causes of loss of productivity, which are 0.30 per cent and 0.25 per cent of GDP, respectively. Loss of productivity due to accidents is estimated to be 0.24 per cent of GDP. Taking into account the cost of medical treatment, the cost associated with waiting and travelling and the cost of caregivers, the social cost of illness will be much greater than the cost of productivity loss alone.

Cardiovascular diseases, cancers and accidents are three major causes of death in Korea. Deaths from cardiovascular diseases and accidents have been decreasing steadily over the past 10 years, although those from cancer have been stable. Altogether, 58,000 persons died of cardiovascular diseases in 1999 (Ministry of Health and Welfare and KIHASA 1999). Mortality from cardiovascular diseases accounted for 23.3 per cent (20.7 per cent for men, 26.6 per cent for women) of all deaths, down from 29.9 per cent in 1990. Cancer was the second most prevalent cause of death in 1999, claiming 54,000 lives. Mortality from cancer accounted for 21.9 per cent (25.3 per cent for men, 17.8 per cent for women) of all deaths, up from 20.1 per cent in 1990. Accidents are the third major cause of deaths, accounting for 30,000 lives in 1999. Deaths from accidents accounted for 12.1 per cent (15.7 per cent for men, 7.7 per cent for women) of all deaths, down from 15.4 per cent in 1990. Although government has played a key role in social health insurance, policy for health promotion or public health is not extensive.[5] (Health has been regarded as the responsibility of individuals rather than government.) More active policy for health promotion along with research on determinants of health and its distribution across socioeconomic groups is called for.

RECENT HEALTH-CARE REFORMS

Merger of health insurance societies

In 2000, all (social) health insurance societies were merged into one single national health insurer.[6] Inequity in health care financing and the financial distress of many health insurance societies for the self-employed were major driving forces behind the reform (Kwon 2003a). Before the merger, social health insurance societies used different methods of setting contributions. The contribution from self-employed groups depended on income, property and household size, while income was the only basis for contribution among employee groups. The definition of earnings for contribution liability (contribution base) also differed in different insurance societies for industrial workers. For example, the contribution base in some insurance societies for employees included base salary only, while in others it was based on the total compensation. Differences across insurance societies in the method of setting contributions and the resulting horizontal inequity – people with the same earnings paid different social insurance contributions depending on which insurance society they were (mandatorily) enrolled in – in spite of quite similar benefits, caused concerns about the unfair burden of social health insurance.[7]

For members of the insurance societies for the self-employed in poor areas, the burden of the contribution as a proportion of their income was greater than for those in wealthy regions. Many regional health insurance societies in rural areas experienced serious financial distress. The aforementioned revenue-sharing mechanism among insurance societies did not rescue the rural health insurance societies from financial insolvency because this was more of a structural problem. In rural areas, the population is ever decreasing and in poor health, and the proportion of the elderly is increasing. Insurance societies in those areas faced expanding health expenditure, while their members' ability to pay was lower than in urban areas. Furthermore, gaps in fiscal status between urban and rural (or between rich and poor) insurance societies threatened social solidarity.

Before the merger, many health insurance societies were too small in terms of the number of enrollees to pool the financial risks of their members efficiently. Consequently, they were vulnerable to financial shocks from illnesses of their members. The absence of competition did not drive health insurance societies to merge voluntarily to improve their capacity of risk pooling. Many small insurance societies were not able to utilize the economy of scale in management either, and the proponents of the merger argued that it would reduce administrative costs. The proportion of the administrative cost in total expense was the lowest (4.8 per cent) in health insurance for government and school employees (single insurance society) and the highest (9.5 per cent) in health insurance for the self-employed (National Health Insurance Corporation 1999).

The unified system of health insurance has improved equity in health insurance contributions among the insured through a uniform nationwide contribution schedule. Income assessment of the self-employed will, in the future, be an essential element in improving equity in health care financing across the entire population.[8] Merging health insurance societies has had the benefit of risk pooling on a national scale, and the single insurer has also reduced the administrative costs of the National Health Insurance system by achieving economy of scale in management. However, the national structure presents some policy challenges. For instance, the single payer has greater bargaining power as a monopoly purchaser (monopsony) relative to health care providers. The financial solvency and the efficiency of the unified health insurance system could hinge on its capability and willingness to use this bargaining power over providers, in which case it needs to play the role of a prudent medical care purchaser. Moreover, there may well be an optimal size for any insurance society beyond which it will suffer from managerial inefficiency, including bureaucratic failure and a lack of responsiveness to consumer needs.

Separation of drug prescribing and dispensing

Before pharmaceutical reform in 2000, there was no separation of drug prescribing and dispensing, meaning physicians and pharmacists both prescribed and dispensed drugs. Pharmacists long played the role of primary health care providers when the supply of physicians was scarce. Drugs, and consultations that pharmacists provided, were readily accessible primary health care to consumers, which is evidenced by the number of pharmacies compared to that of physician clinics. The tradition of oriental medicine, where the roles of physicians and pharmacists are not differentiated, has also affected the practice of medicine in East Asia, and physicians both prescribe and dispense drugs in China, Hong Kong, Japan, Korea and Taiwan. Traditional medicine in Korea depends a lot on medication in patient treatment, contributing to people's perception that the fees they pay are compensation for drugs rather than for physician labour (consultation). People also take traditional medicines for prevention, which results in a strong preference for medicines.

Without the separation of drug prescribing and dispensing, physicians and pharmacists had financial interests not necessarily to act in the best interest of patients. What was missing was the mechanism of check and balance between the pharmacist and the physician in the prescription of drugs. This resulted in the possibility of misuse of drugs. In addition, patients did not have access to prescription information about the type and amount of medication they took because they did not receive a prescription slip. Therefore, by separating the prescribing and dispensing of drugs, reform aimed to reduce the overuse and misuse of drugs, improve the quality and safety drugs, and enhance the patients' right to know about their medication (Kwon 2003c).

Separation of drug prescribing and dispensing in Korea has much more important policy implications than the simple division of labour between physicians and pharmacists. Since the fees for medical services are strictly regulated, dispensing drugs has been more profitable for physicians than providing their own services. The government set prices for insured drugs on the basis of the data that pharmaceutical manufacturers and wholesalers reported. Physicians, however, purchased drugs at costs that were much lower than the price that the insurer reimbursed. Higher margins from drugs induced physicians to prescribe and dispense more drugs in order to increase profit. For internal medicine, almost 50 per cent of the revenue of physician clinics came from pharmaceuticals. For family medicine, dermatology, urology and paediatrics, the revenue from drugs accounted for more than 40 per cent of the total revenue (National Health Insurance Corporation 2000). In tertiary and general hospitals, the proportions of drug revenue were 43.7 per cent and 45.4 per cent, respectively, of total revenue. The mandatory separation of drug prescribing and dispensing meant that the substantial profit from pharmaceuticals was no longer available to physicians and hospitals.

Due to the financial incentive for physicians and pharmacists to dispense more drugs and consumers' easier accessibility to drugs, Koreans consumed more drugs than people in other developed countries. The proportion of pharmaceutical spending in health - care expenditure in Korea was 31 per cent, compared with an OECD country average of below 20 per cent (National Health Insurance Corporation 2000). Because government regulated the drug price, high pharmaceutical expenditure was related to the overuse of drugs. When pharmaceutical spending included physician fees for prescribing and dispensing, it amounted to as much as 40 per cent of health care expenditure in Korea. At the same time, consumption of more drugs resulted in an increase in the level of resistance to antibiotics.

Facing strong opposition from physicians and pharmacists, civic groups consisting mainly of progressive academics and individuals who used to be active in the democratic movements in the former military regime, played a pivotal role in formulating pharmaceutical reform. They made pharmaceutical reform a major social issue and pushed the presidents of the Korean Medical Association and Korean Pharmaceutical Association to agree on major reform issues. However, there were three nationwide physician strikes before the implementation of the reform, which succeeded in pushing the government to modify some critical elements. This included eliminating the principle of generic prescriptions and raising medical fees substantially to compensate for physician income loss. How to overcome the opposition of provider groups will be a critical challenge for future health care reforms in Korea.

CONCLUSIONS

It took only 12 years for the Republic of Korea to extend its social health insurance to the entire population since its first introduction to employees in large corporations in 1977. The government's priority on rapid extension of health insurance made unavoidable a policy of low contributions and limited benefit coverage. Consequently, current social insurance for health care accounts for less than 45 per cent of personal health care expenditure in Korea. Furthermore, for-profit health care institutions are the dominant form of health care providers, and there is far less involvement by the public sector in health care delivery than in the financing of health care. Therefore, major challenges facing health policy in Korea include the extension of benefit coverage and payment system reform for providers.

To achieve better risk spreading, the National Health Insurance scheme should increase the insurance contribution, expand benefit coverage and decrease the level of out-of-pocket payments in healthcare utilization. The total expected expenditure for the insured would not change much because the decreased payment at the point of service would offset the increased contribution. At the same time, consumer exposure to risk of economic loss when ill would decline. However, convincing consumers of the benefits of increasing health insurance contributions accompanied by expanded benefit coverage has not been an easy task. Therefore, should the raising of insurance contributions not be feasible, it may be necessary to redesign the benefit package (a) to allow for high-loss catastrophic illnesses with a low probability of occurrence and (b) to make increases in cost-sharing for minor cases. Rather than being solely designed with regard for its impact on health insurance expenditure, the benefit package should take greater account of the cost-effectiveness of medical interventions, the response of providers to benefit coverage design and the burden of costs to patients.

The fee-for-service payment scheme has to an extent contributed to health care cost inflation. It is, therefore, necessary to reform the payment system towards a DRG-based prospective payment or global budgeting to cap total health care expenditure. However, as with pharmaceutical reform, which engendered physician strikes, payment system reform efforts would likely encounter considerable resistance from the public and Korean health sector interest groups. From a societal perspective, the total benefit of payment system reform would be greater than its cost. The main costs of reform would be concentrated around health care providers, and they would be likely to pose strong opposition to it with their superior financial and information resources. On the other hand, the benefit of payment system reform is so diffused to consumers that they would probably have little incentive and capacity to provide support for it. As a result, providers are likely to continue to have a dominating influence on any proposals for health policy change. The Korean government needs to carefully carve out a strategic plan for payment system reform, including how to deal with provider opposition.

ACKNOWLEDGEMENT

Financial support from the Hosei University Institute on Ageing, Japan, is gratefully acknowledged.

NOTES

1 Farmers are not a strong interest group in Korea. Nonetheless, by appealing to the public that farmers are a disadvantaged group, they often succeed in pushing the government to adopt policy for their interest.
2 The number of beneficiaries of the Medicaid programme varies from year to year depending on the fiscal capability of government and on the number of the poor, which, in turn, hinge on the overall economy of the nation. See Kwon (2000) for a discussion of the major issues in the Medicaid programme in Korea.
3 Traditional medical doctors are trained in schools of traditional medicine, which have six years of academic curriculum, as do schools of (Western) medicine and of dentistry. Traditional medicine is popular in Korea, and the entrance to schools of traditional medicine is competitive. Acupuncture is covered by health insurance, while only a limited number of herbal medicines are covered.
4 Korea presently has a serious problem with low total fertility rates: it was 1.17 in 2002.
5 Tobacco tax is currently one of major sources of financing for health promotion programmes.
6 Before the merger, the structure of the Korean social health insurance system was similar to those of Japan and Germany (before Germany introduced competition among sickness funds).
7 There also existed a difference in health care utilization across different insurance groups – the highest in public and school employee groups and the lowest in self-employed groups (Kwon 2003d). The differences resulted from differences in age structures, such as a larger proportion of those over 70 among the dependants of government and school employees, and those aged 20–29 among industrial workers. Financial barriers and the regional maldistribution of health care personnel and medical facilities also had a negative effect on health care utilization by the self-employed in rural areas.
8 Income assessment of the self-employed is a critical challenge for the social insurance system in Korea, and reform of the tax administration is urgently required (Kwon 2001).

REFERENCES

Korea Hospital Association (1999) *Hospital List*. Seoul: KHA (in Korean).
Kwon, S. (2000) Health care financing and delivery for the poor in Korea, *International Review of Public Administration*, 5(2): 37–45.
Kwon, S. (2001) Economic crisis and social policy reform in Korea, *International Journal of Social Welfare*, 10(2): 97–106.
Kwon, S. (2002) *Achieving Health Insurance for All: Lessons from the Republic of Korea*. ESS (Extension of Social Security) Paper #1. Geneva: International Labor Office.
Kwon, S. (2003a) Health care financing reform and the new single payer system in Korea: social solidarity or efficiency?, *International Social Security Review*, 56(1): 75–94.
Kwon, S. (2003b) Payment system reform for health care providers in Korea, *Health Policy and Planning*, 18(1): 84–92.
Kwon, S. (2003c) Pharmaceutical reform and physician strikes in Korea: separation of drug prescribing and dispensing, *Social Science and Medicine*, 57(3): 529–38.
Kwon, S. (2003d) Health and health care in Korea, *Social Indicators Research*, 62/63: 171–86.
Ministry of Health and Welfare (2000) *Evaluation of the 3rd-Year Pilot Programme on DRG-Based Payment*. Seoul: MoHW (in Korean).
Ministry of Health and Welfare (2002) *National Health Expenditure*. Seoul: MoHW (in Korean).
Ministry of Health and Welfare and Korea Institute for Health and Social Affairs (1999) *'98 Survey of Health and Nutrition*. Seoul: MoHW/KIHASA (in Korean).
National Health Insurance Corporation (1999) *Internal Report*. Seoul: NHIC (in Korean).
OECD (2003) *OECD Health Data 2003*. Paris: Organization for Economic Cooperation and Development.
World Health Organization (2000) *The World Health Report 2000 – Health Systems: Improving Performance*. Geneva: WHO.

4

TAIWAN
Tung-liang Chiang

Population 2002	2.5 million
Ethnic composition 2002	Taiwanese (including Hakka) 84%, mainland Chinese 14%, Aborigine 2%
Capital city	Taipei
Live births per woman 2002	1.34
Infant mortality rate per 1000 live births 2002	5.4
Life expectancy at birth 2002 (male/female)	73.0/79.0 years
Total health expenditure as a percentage of GDP 2002	6.1%
Government health expenditure as a percentage of total health expenditure 2002	65%
Total health expenditure per capita 2002 (US$ PPP)	776
Practising physicians per 1000 population 2002	1.4
Health system	Public health: National Health Department, 25 county and city health bureaus, and 368 township and district health stations. Personal health funding: national health insurance (social insurer). Provision: largely by private sector.

Political system	Multi-party democratic regime headed by popularly elected president and unicameral legislature.

Source: Republic of China Department of Health (2003)

INTRODUCTION

Taiwan, formerly known as Formosa, is located in the western Pacific about 160 kilometres off China's southeast coast, midway between Japan and the Philippines. In 2002, Taiwan had a population of 22.5 million, with a density of 620 persons per square kilometre. Taiwan was returned to China at the end of the Second World War, following 50 years of Japanese colonization. The government of the Republic of China, led by the Kuomintang, relocated to Taiwan in 1949 when mainland China fell to the Communists. Taiwan was subsequently ruled by an authoritarian regime until the lifting of martial law in 1987, and is currently a political democracy.

Taiwan's achievements in economic development in the last half of the twentieth century mean it is often referred to as an 'economic miracle' (Kuo *et al.* 1981). Its gross national product per capita increased from US$145 in 1951 to US$12,900 in 2002. Importantly, income distribution in Taiwan has also improved – in 2002, the ratio of income share of the richest 20 per cent to that of the poorest 20 per cent was 6.4, compared with 20.3 in 1952. Together with economic development, Taiwan has witnessed a demographic transition. The crude birth rate in Taiwan declined sharply from a peak of 50 per 1000 in 1951 to 11 per 1000 in 2002. The crude death rate also declined from 12 per 1000 in 1951 to a bottom of 5 per 1000 in the mid-1970s, but increased slightly to 6 per 1000 in 2002 due to population ageing. In 2002, there were 2 million people aged 65 and over, representing 9.0 per cent of the total population.

In addition to being an 'economic miracle', Taiwan has also achieved a 'health miracle'. Since the 1950s, mortality has declined remarkably among all age groups. The improvement is especially significant in infant mortality, which decreased from 45 per 1000 in 1952 to 5 per 1000 in 2002. Accordingly, life expectancy at birth in Taiwan has increased for males and females, respectively, from 57 and 61 years in 1952 to 73 and 79 years in 2002. Along with the decline in death rates, Taiwan has experienced an epidemiological transition. In the early 1950s, the leading causes of death in Taiwan were infectious diseases, including gastroenteritis, pneumonia, tuberculosis, nephritis, bronchitis and malaria. These shortly gave way to non-infectious diseases. By the beginning of the twenty-first century, non-infectious diseases (such as cancers, strokes, heart disease, hypertension diseases, diabetes mellitus) and accidents had become the dominant health problems in Taiwan.

This chapter reviews the progress and performance of Taiwan's health care system from a health policy perspective in the above changing social context. It first discusses the evolution of public health administration, the dynamic relationship between modern Western medicine and traditional Chinese medicine, the development of health care resources and universal health insurance in Taiwan. Then the chapter analyses three major issues challenging Taiwan's health care system: equity in access to health care, macro-economic efficiency and micro-economic efficiency. Finally, the chapter considers future directions for health care reform in Taiwan.

EVOLUTION OF PUBLIC HEALTH ADMINISTRATION

Government is essential in the health policy process. Yet before the twentieth century, the Taiwan government barely played any role in the organization, financing and delivery of public health services. Since then, public health administration in Taiwan has had three important periods of development: under the police system (1895–1945), under the Provincial Health Department (1945–71) and under the national Department of Health (1971 to present).

The first period began with the establishment of a public health office a few months after the Japanese government took over Taiwan in 1895. The health conditions in Taiwan were still in the age of pestilence and famine when Japan attacked the island. According to Japanese records, only 515 people were wounded and 164 killed in battle, but 26,094 fell sick and 4642 died from communicable diseases such as malaria and cholera. With the large numbers of soldiers and workers succumbing to the epidemics, the Japanese government immediately set up a public health office under the governor-general to take charge of communicable disease control, environmental sanitation and public hospitals. Nevertheless, the public health office was abolished after the military administration was replaced by the civil administration in 1896, and the police system took over public health administration in Taiwan until the end of Japanese colonization.

The second period of public health administration commenced after the Second World War, and was characterized by the development of a public health network. In 1945, the government of the Republic of China resumed control of Taiwan and established the Taiwan Provincial Administration Office, under which public health administration was taken over by a newly created Department of Health. In 1947, following the replacement of the Taiwan Provincial Administration Office by the Taiwan Provincial Government, the Taiwan Provincial Health Department was founded to be responsible for public health administration. Importantly, by the late 1950s, the provincial government had established a comprehensive public health network (one health bureau for each county and city, and one health station for each township and district) to facilitate the operation of public health programmes, including malaria eradication, tuberculosis control, immunization, maternal and child health, family planning and health inspection.

The third period commenced in 1971 with the establishment of the Department of Health under the national cabinet, the Executive Yuan. After the central government relocated to Taiwan in 1949, the national Department of Health was downsized as one section of the Ministry of the Interior. Consequently, the Taiwan Provincial Health Department was fully authorized to take charge of public health administration in Taiwan. However, when Taipei City was elevated to the status of municipality (equivalent to province) in 1967, the Department of Health, Executive Yuan, was created assuming responsibility for determining health policies, formulating health programmes, and supervising and coordinating public health activities at all levels of government. In 1999, the Department of Health, Executive Yuan, took over the Taiwan Provincial Health Department due to the downsizing of the Taiwan Provincial Government.

Figure 4.1 presents the schematic structure of current public health administration in Taiwan. At national level, the Department of Health is the highest health authority consisting of four bureaus (medical affairs, pharmaceutical affairs, food sanitation and health planning), nine subordinate agencies (including the Centre for Disease Control, the Bureau of Health Promotion, the Bureau of National Health Insurance, and the Committee on Chinese Medicine and Pharmacy) and 34 public hospitals. At municipality level, two health bureaus are responsible for planning and implementing public

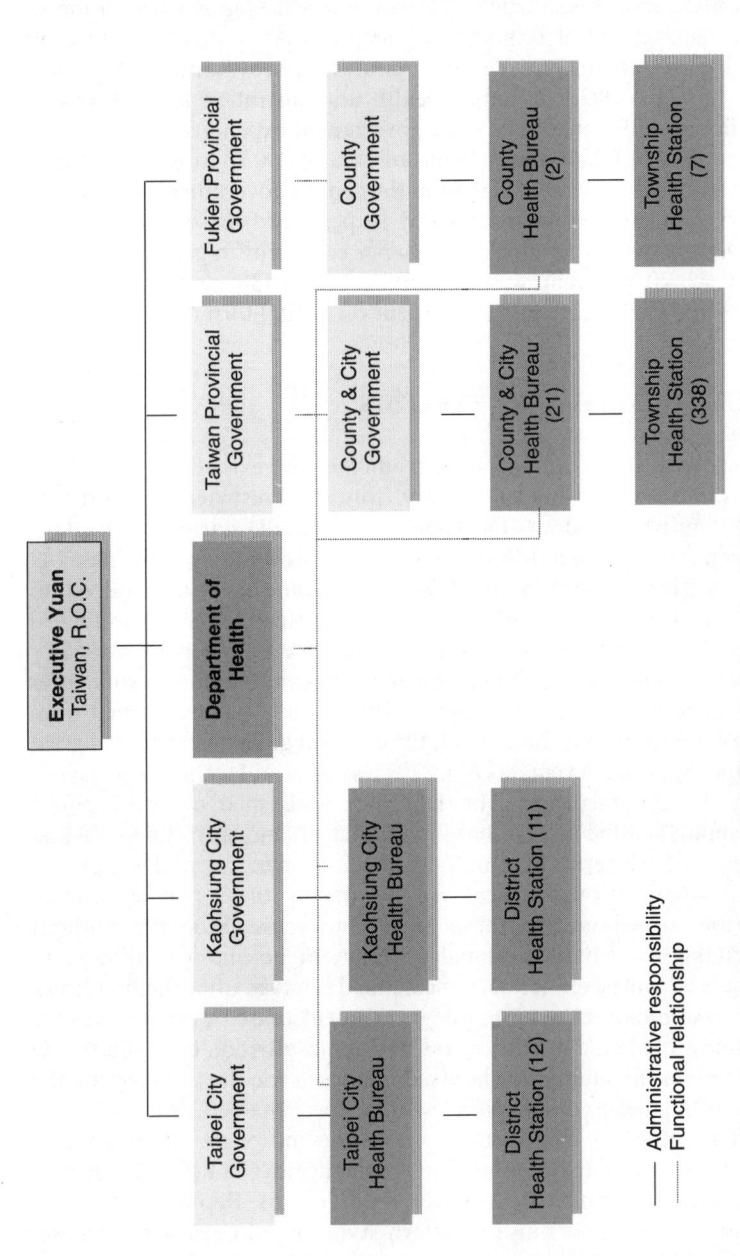

Figure 4.1 Schematic structure of public health administration in Taiwan.

health programmes through 23 district health stations in addition to the management of 14 municipal hospitals. At county and city level, 23 health bureaus provide public health services through 345 health stations. In 2002, the public health administration spent NT$44.2 billion, or 1.9 per cent of total government expenditures, in Taiwan (Republic of China Department of Health 2003). In terms of funding sources, 66 per cent was from the central government, 15 per cent from municipal governments and 19 per cent from county and city governments. As to allocation, 20 per cent went to general administration, 20 per cent was for public health, 38 per cent went on personal health care and 21 per cent on capital formulation.

DUAL HEALTH-CARE SYSTEMS

Chinese medicine and Western medicine have existed side by side in Taiwan since the first missionary from the Presbyterian Church of the United Kingdom, Dr James L. Maxwell, started his medical practice in Tainan in 1865 (Chiang 1988). However, over the past 140 years, Chinese medicine and Western medicine have not blended into a unified system of health care, but have instead led to a hierarchical pluralistic structure within Taiwan's health care system (Lee 1982).

The dominance of Chinese medicine began to diminish soon after Japan took over Taiwan (Chiang 1988). First, having learned from the experience of its homeland, the colonial government placed great value on the achievements of modern science and technology, including Western medicine. The Japanese established not only public hospitals staffed by Western-style doctors, but also Taiwan's first school of Western medicine. In total, 2797 medical students graduated from various medical schools during the Japanese colonial period, of whom two-thirds were Taiwanese. Secondly, without permission from the colonial government no-one was allowed to practise Chinese or Western medicine. However, after the first licensure examination in 1901, the government ceased examinations for Chinese medicine practitioners. With time, attrition caused a steady decline in the number of licensed Chinese-style doctors, and by the end of Japanese colonization less than 150 remained.

The return of Taiwan to China at the end of the Second World War was a turning point for Chinese medicine (Chi 1994). Unlike the colonial government, the government of the Republic of China granted licences not only to Western-style doctors but also to Chinese-style doctors. As a result, the number of licensed Chinese-style doctors in Taiwan sharply increased to more than 1500 in the early 1950s and has kept growing. Regrettably, many Chinese-style doctors, passing the licensure examination through self-study or by apprenticeship, never received any formal medical education.

The Taiwan government has actively supported Western medicine over Chinese medicine. First, in terms of training resources, there are today four public schools and seven private schools offering professional training programmes for Western-style doctors, as opposed to only two private schools for Chinese-style doctors. Secondly, Western-style doctors have directed and staffed health departments and public hospitals at various levels of the government. Thirdly, social health insurance schemes did not formally include Chinese medicine in their benefit packages until the introduction of universal health insurance in 1995. Accordingly, Western medicine has continued to flourish and dominate in Taiwan. For instance, in 2002, the average number of visits to Western-style doctors per capita was 12.1, compared with 1.3 visits to a Chinese-style doctor (Republic of China Bureau of National Health Insurance 2003).

HEALTH-CARE WORKFORCE AND ORGANIZATIONS

There are various types of licensed health care professionals in Taiwan, including Western-style doctors, Chinese-style doctors, nurses, midwives, pharmacists, dentists, physical, occupational and speech therapists, and medical laboratory and radiology technicians. For all types of health care workers, except physicians, no formal educational programmes existed in Taiwan during the Japanese colonial period (Chiang 1988). At present, there are 20 universities, 10 junior colleges and 5 senior vocational schools offering various programmes for different health professionals (Republic of China Ministry of Education 2003). Most of the schools were established in the 1950s and 1960s. In 2002, there were more than 20,000 graduates from health profession schools: 1085 in Western medicine; 215 in Chinese medicine; 19,106 in nursing; 1690 in pharmacy; 321 in dentistry; 1771 in medical technology; 552 in medical radiology; and 557 in physical, occupational and speech therapy.

With the expanding capacity of health profession schools, the active health care workforce in Taiwan has increased substantially (see Table 4.1). Between 1960 and 2002, for instance, the number of physicians increased by 6.5 times to 31,511, the number of Chinese medicine practitioners by 2.4 times to 4040, the number of nurses by

Table 4.1 Health care resourcing and financing indicators, 1960–2002

	1960	1980	1990	2000	2002
Health care resources					
Physicians per 1000 population	0.5	0.7	1.0	1.3	1.4
Hospital beds per 1000 population	0.7*	3.2**	4.1	5.1	5.3
% Public hospital beds	71.3*	53.3**	42.7	35.1	35.0
Health care financing					
% Population insured	6.3	16.0	47.3	96.5	97.1
Per capita health spending (US$)	NA	78	330	669	669
Health spending as % of GDP	NA	3.3	4.2	5.4	6.1
% Public health spending	NA	31.3	50.8	64.5	65.0

Sources: Chiang (2003a), Republic of China Council for Economic Planning and Development (2003), Republic of China Department of Health (2003)
* 1961; ** 1982; NA = not available

53.9 times to 79,931, the number of pharmacists by 8.4 times to 11,579 and the number of dentists by 11.3 times to 9206. In 2002, there were 140 physicians, 18 Chinese medicine doctors, 355 nurses, 51 pharmacists and 41 dentists per 100,000 population. Thus, Taiwan no longer has a health care workforce shortage, particularly among nurses and pharmacists (National Health Research Institute 2001).

At present, more than 160,000 health care personnel work in various health care organizations in Taiwan. Hospitals, which employ about two-thirds of health care personnel, have become the most important sector of health care organization. The number of hospitals in Taiwan increased from 174 in 1961 to a peak of 913 in 1988, and then declined to 610 in 2002. However, the average number of beds per hospital increased from 45 to 196 during the same period, reflecting in part a sharp decline in the number of hospitals with fewer than 50 beds. Accordingly, the number of hospital beds per 1000 population continued to increase from 0.7 in 1961 to 5.3 in 2002.

The ownership profile of hospitals has changed over time. Public hospitals were dominant during the period of Japanese colonization but, after the Second World War, the number of private hospitals outgrew public hospitals. At present, about 10 per cent of hospitals are public and 90 per cent are private. Of the public hospitals, 40 per cent are owned by the central government, 22 per cent by local governments and 38 per cent by the military and veterans administration. Although fewer in number, the public hospitals tend to be larger, constituting 35 per cent of the total hospital beds in Taiwan in 2002. In practice, most hospitals in Taiwan are independent and keenly compete for patients regardless of ownership and size.

In 2002, alongside the hospitals, there were 9287 Western-style clinics, 2601 Chinese-style clinics, 5730 dental clinics, 6397 dispensaries and 664 long-term care facilities in Taiwan. Most clinics are solo practice; less than 20 per cent are partnerships or group practices. Up until 1997, when an amendment of the Pharmaceutical Affairs Law became effective and enforced a separation policy, private practitioners both prescribed and dispensed drugs for their patients. Subsequently, most private practitioners have chosen to employ pharmacists to fill their prescriptions. Accordingly, in 2002, 6099 pharmacists worked in clinics, in addition to 5480 pharmacists in hospitals and 6990 in dispensaries. There is barely any cooperation among dispensaries, clinics and hospitals.

UNIVERSAL HEALTH INSURANCE

Under considerable domestic political pressure, the Taiwan government launched a compulsory national health insurance on 1 March 1995 (Chiang 1997a). Since then, social health insurance has replaced direct household payments and government budgets as the major source of personal health care financing. The National Health Insurance scheme provides comprehensive health care benefits, with moderate cost sharing, and is financed mainly by payroll tax. In 2002, it covered more than 97 per cent of the total population and paid for 57 per cent of national health expenditure, while direct household payments and government budgets accounted for 31 and 8 per cent, respectively.

Before the introduction of national health insurance, the Taiwan government had been passive in removing financial barriers to health care. The Labor Insurance introduced in 1950 was the first social insurance in Taiwan, but did not offer health care benefits until 1956. In 1958, the government launched the Government Employees' Insurance, which also provided health care benefits. However, by the early 1980s, there were only two social insurance schemes covering less than 20 per cent of the population, while all public hospitals and clinics charged for health services as if they were private providers.

Meanwhile, some prominent economists in Taiwan began to advocate social welfare as a means to social stability, although their primary concern remained economic development. Thus, in 1984, the Council for Economic Planning and Development (CEPD) organized a comprehensive planning task force to review Taiwan's social welfare programmes. Two years later, the task force completed an integrated planning report on social welfare and recommended phasing in a universal health insurance scheme by the year 2000.

However, with the rapid growth of political participation in Taiwan, the target year of 2000 seemed too long to wait. In the early 1980s, political participation broadened from the local to the national level and led to the founding of the Democratic Progressive Party in 1986. As the first opposition party, the Democratic Progressive Party fiercely attacked the ruling Kuomintang on the issue of political freedom as well as social policies including national health insurance. In response, the government implemented a farmers' health insurance on a trial basis in 1986, but political pressure was so strong that, before long, the farmers' health insurance became mandatory for all farmers. In 1989, the government finally announced that 1995 was to be the new target year for national health insurance implementation.

Nine years on from its launch, the National Health Insurance scheme has become the most popular social welfare programme in Taiwan. In a broad sense, Taiwan shares the same objectives of health care reforms as all industrialized countries (OECD 1995). As stated in the CEPD report of the national health insurance plan, Taiwan has identified three objectives: (1) to provide equal access to adequate health care for all citizens to improve the health of the people; (2) to control health care costs at a socially affordable level; and (3) to promote the efficient use of health care resources (Republic of China Council for Economic Planning and Development 1990). The following sections discuss whether Taiwan's health care system has achieved these objectives.

EQUITY IN ACCESS TO HEALTH CARE

Access to health care refers to the potential and actual entry of a given population to the health care delivery system (Andersen *et al.* 1983). Equity implies reducing or eliminating differentials that are not only unnecessary and avoidable, but also unfair and unjust (Whitehead 1990). As far as the issue of equity is concerned, underpinning Taiwan's health care system is an aim to bring the geographic and socioeconomic differentials in access to health care down to the lowest level possible.

The availability of physicians, the supply of hospital facilities and the coverage of health insurance are three major indicators of potential access to health care. The geographic distribution of physicians in Taiwan was almost entirely left up to market forces until the group practice centres programme was implemented in 1983 (Chiang 1995). Under this programme, the government began to assign physicians who had received medical scholarships to serve in rural areas. Nevertheless, the programme was too limited to countervail powerful market forces, and not all communities have equitably enjoyed the rapid growth in the physician workforce. For example, between 1984 and 1998, the national physician-to-population ratio increased from 0.7 to 1.2 per cent and the number of townships with a physician-to-population ratio below 1 : 3000 decreased from 197 to 143. However, the Gini coefficient of the township physician supply increased from 0.42 to 0.47, indicating no improvement in the geographic distribution of physicians in Taiwan (Huang *et al.* 2001).

Unlike the physician workforce, the Taiwan government has paid a great deal of attention to the geographic distribution of hospital facilities (Chiang 2003a). Public hospitals used to play the major role in providing inpatient services in Taiwan, and the government had undertaken to secure at least one public hospital for each county and city, and set up military and veteran hospitals. In 1978, the government even attempted to establish a public hospital-based medical care network, but it failed in part due to the rapid growth of the private hospital industry. In 1985, the government initiated another medical care network programme to improve the geographic distribution of health care resources, this time involving both public and private health sectors. Under the new medical care network programme, Taiwan was divided into 17 medical care regions and hospitals were classified into three groups as medical centre, regional hospital and district hospital, and a regulatory policy of 'certificate of need' was implemented. Yet, market forces have remained powerful in determining the geographic distribution of hospital facilities in Taiwan; at present, regrettably, 5 of 17 medical care regions still do not have a regional hospital.

The National Health Insurance scheme to date has been the most important policy for improving potential access to health care in Taiwan. Regardless of age, sex, family income, place of abode or health status, all citizens must compulsorily take part in the scheme.

In 2002, the Supreme Court further ruled that no-one in Taiwan could be denied access to care because of an inability to pay premiums. Furthermore, on political rather than economic considerations, the benefits of national health insurance are comprehensive. They include ambulatory care, inpatient care, emergency care, prescription drugs, X-ray and laboratory tests, rehabilitation, treatment for mental illness, dental care, traditional Chinese medicine, certain preventive services and limited home care. Finally, patients are completely free to choose between health care providers, and there is no rationing of care in Taiwan.

Actual or realized access to health care is important, and can be evaluated through various utilization rates. The geographic differentials in realized access to health care in Taiwan have diminished at an accelerating pace, except in mountainous areas and on offshore islands. Thus, Chu *et al.* (2000) found that the availability of physicians no longer had a bearing on the use of physician services by individuals. On the other hand, cross-border use of health services has increased rapidly in part due to great improvements in transportation. For example, Hong *et al.* (1998) found that, for the medical care regions with no regional hospital, cross-border admission had substantially increased in the 10 years after implementation of the new medical care network programme.

Socioeconomic differentials in realized access to health care mainly reflect financial difficulties. National health insurance has significantly reduced differentials in realized access to health care. Following a cohort sample of 1211 adults over a 9-month period after the inauguration of national health insurance, Cheng and Chiang (1997) found that among those who were hitherto uninsured, the probability of using physician services and hospital care increased by 69 per cent and 145 per cent, respectively. Thus, the National Health Insurance scheme brought the hitherto uninsured up to par with those who previously had social health insurance.

Have the poor benefited from national health insurance? The answer seems positive. For example, the ratio of national health insurance payments to premiums contributed for the bottom 20 per cent of households was 1.75 in 1998, compared with 1.16 and 0.96 for the middle 20 per cent and top 20 per cent of households, respectively (Chiang 2000). However, in terms of total health care expenses, the middle social class benefited most. For instance, between 1994 and 1998, the growth rate of health care expenses per household for the middle 20 per cent of households was 64.5 per cent, compared with 24.5 per cent and 33.5 per cent for the bottom 20 per cent and top 20 per cent of households, respectively (Chiang 2000). Because the bottom 20 per cent of households had the lowest growth rate, the socioeconomic differentials in health care expenses have continued to widen at a slow pace.

MACRO-ECONOMIC EFFICIENCY

Macro-economic efficiency implies that a health care system should consume an 'appropriate' share of GDP (OECD 1995). Taiwan paid no attention to the issue of macro-economic efficiency until escalating health care spending became a recognized problem in the 1980s. From 1980 to 1994, health care spending in Taiwan increased at an average rate of 14.5 per cent from NT$50 billion to NT$318 billion (Chiang 2003b). After adjusting for population size, per capita health care spending increased from NT$2805 to NT$15,124 during the same period. Because health care spending increased more rapidly than GDP, the share of health care spending in GDP rose from 3.3 per cent in 1980 to 4.9 per cent in 1994 (see Table 4.1 for more details on expenditure growth).

With the rapid growth of health care spending, the Labor Insurance, the Government Employees' Insurance and the Farmers' Health Insurance all ran into large deficits in the 1980s, but were unable to raise their premium rates for political reasons. The government was greatly concerned with the financial situation of social health insurance. Thus, when the Council for Economic Planning and Development organized the National Health Insurance Planning Task Force in 1988, one of the main issues to be addressed was 'can Taiwan afford a national health insurance?' In reply, the task force recommended all payments be made through a single-payer system with a global budget (Chiang 1997a). Following the recommendation, in 1995, the government established the Bureau of National Health Insurance under the Department of Health as the only purchaser and consolidated all existing social health insurance programmes into one single national scheme.

After the implementation of national health insurance, health care spending increased markedly at a rate of 16.4 per cent in 1995 and 9.8 per cent in 1996, mainly due to the large-scale expansion of the insured population and generous rise in the fee schedule (Chiang 2003b). However, this effect did not last long, and from 1996 to 2002 the rate of increase in health care spending dropped to 6.4 per cent. Lu and Hsiao (2003) attributed such an effective management of health spending inflation to the single-payer system with a uniform fee schedule. The Bureau of National Health Insurance did not implement global budgeting until 5 years after the National Health Insurance scheme commenced; this was phased in beginning in 1998 into the dental sector and then in 2002 into the hospital sector.

In 2002, Taiwan spent a total of NT$591 billion on health care, representing 6.1 per cent of GDP. Is 6.1 per cent an 'appropriate' share? In most OECD counties, the percentage of GDP spent on health care has been relatively stable at about 7–9 per cent since the 1990s (Anderson and Hussey 2001). Thus, by the benchmark of OECD countries, one might suggest that Taiwan's health care system is underfunded (Cheng 2003). Yet, health care spending as a proportion of GDP depends on how much is spent on health care as well as the extent to which the economy is growing. For instance, in recent years, Taiwan has experienced a severe economic crisis; the rate of increase in GDP in Taiwan was −1.62 per cent in 2001 and only 2.55 per cent in 2002. If GDP continued increasing at an average rate of 9.1 per cent as in the 1990s, the share of health care spending should have declined to 5.4 per cent in 2001 and 5.2 per cent in 2002.

The spending increases raise the issue of increasing the premium rate of national health insurance, which pays for two-thirds of national health care spending, in step with the growth in payments. National health insurance payments have outstripped revenues since 1998 and, at first, large cash reserves accumulated during the first 3 years were used to cover the deficits. By the end of 2001, the cash reserve dwindled to less than one month's payments, and the Department of Health called to raise the premium rate from 4.25 to 4.91 per cent to save the National Health Insurance scheme from imminent bankruptcy. However, politicians and the public opposed this proposal and insisted that the Bureau of National Health Insurance should give priority to eliminating widespread waste, fraud and system abuse (Cheng 2003). The Department of Health finally pushed through a premium rate increase to 4.55 per cent in September 2002. In return, the public satisfaction rate declined sharply from 79 per cent in May to 60 per cent in November 2002 (Republic of China Bureau of National Health Insurance 2004).

MICRO-ECONOMIC EFFICIENCY

Micro-economic efficiency refers to the efficient use of health care resources. Since the advent of national health insurance, Taiwan has managed to contain rising health care costs. For example, between 1996 and 2000, the annual average growth rate of real health care spending was only 4.0 per cent, and after adjusting for ageing and population growth per capita volume-intensity increased at an average rate of 0.5 per cent (Chiang 2003b). Yet, simply slowing down the growth rate of health care spending does not imply the efficient use of health care resources; several vital signs indicate that the National Health Insurance scheme probably undermined efficiency.

First, the excessive use of ambulatory care by the insured remains a critical problem. Before implementation of national health insurance, social health insurance schemes were notorious for extremely high utilization of physician services. For example, the number of annual physician visits (not including visits to Chinese-style doctors and dentists) per capita per year was over 12 among the insured population in 1994 (Chiang 2003a). One popular explanation was that the insured had no incentives to be prudent, since they paid nothing but a token registration fee for each visit. For that reason, the national health insurance institutionalized a basic co-insurance rate of 20 per cent for ambulatory care and extra co-payments for heavy users and those who seek primary care from regional hospitals and medical centres without referral (Chiang 1997a). Yet, according to Cheng and Chiang (1997), the cost-sharing measures did not affect the utilization pattern of the newly insured or the previously insured; for the previously insured, utilization rates of physician services even rose slightly. At present, the average number of annual physician visits per capita in Taiwan still exceeds 12 (Republic of China Bureau of National Health Insurance 2003), compared with 5–7 visits for the majority of OECD countries (Anderson and Hussey 2001). Surprisingly, the physician-to-population ratio of Taiwan is less than half the OECD median.

Secondly, the acute-bed occupancy rate of hospitals in Taiwan has continued to fall. According to primary data from the National Hospital Surveys of 1994 and 2000, the acute-bed occupancy rate of hospitals decreased from 72.9 per cent in 1994 to 62.3 per cent in 2000. Importantly, the lower the accreditation level, the faster the decrease of the acute-bed occupancy rate: medical centres by 7.3 per cent, regional hospitals by 15.7 per cent, district teaching hospitals by 23.7 per cent and district non-teaching hospitals by 34.5 per cent. Why did the acute-bed occupancy ratio of hospitals decrease following the implementation of national health insurance, which has greatly increased demand for inpatient care? The paradox lies in the rapid expansion of the hospital industry. Between 1994 and 2000, the number of acute hospital beds in Taiwan increased by 12.8 per cent from 61,284 to 69,124. And the higher the accreditation level, the faster the increase of acute hospital beds: medical centres by 48.9 per cent, regional hospitals by 38.8 per cent, district teaching hospitals by −3.4 per cent and district non-teaching hospitals by −21.9 per cent.

Thirdly, the medical ecology of Taiwan has become unbalanced. In recent years, medical centres and regional hospitals, often referred to as 'big hospitals' in Taiwan, have been providing more and more health care services as referral systems barely exist. According to the Bureau of National Health Insurance (2004), between 1996 and 2000 the number of outpatient and inpatient claims from big hospitals increased by 47.2 per cent and 24.6 per cent, respectively. In contrast, the number of outpatient claims from district hospitals and clinics together increased by only 11.3 per cent, and the number of inpatient claims from district hospitals even declined by 4.8 per cent. An analysis of the impact of change in claim mix by the accreditation level of hospitals on health care costs revealed that, during the period 1996–2000, the expansion of big hospitals was responsible for about 30 per cent of the growth of health care spending in Taiwan (Chiang 2003b). Yet, the expansion of the hospital industry has further hampered the geographic distribution of private practitioners. Liu and Chiang (2004) found that where the hospital industry expanded rapidly, the number of office-based private practitioners increased slowly.

Finally, as noted by Cheng (2003), the issue of health care quality needs closer attention. The Taiwan government has undertaken structural approaches, including medical education, licensure, specialty certification and hospital accreditation, to improve the quality of health care. Hospital accreditation as a comprehensive mechanism plays an extremely important role. The first hospital accreditation programme initiated in 1978 applied only to teaching hospitals, but since the late 1980s all hospitals have been subject to accreditation under the medical care network programme (Huang 1995). However, the process by which health care is delivered determines quality and, in this, there remains considerable space for improvement in Taiwan. For example, outpatient care has been characterized by short visits, many prescriptions and frequent follow-up visits (Peabody *et al.* 1995), and hospitals have increasingly compensated physicians based on revenue productivity: the number of patients seen, procedures performed, laboratory tests ordered, drugs prescribed, and so on (Cheng 2003). This makes it not only difficult for hospitals to improve the quality of health care provided to individual patients, but is also the cause of systemic quality problems. For instance, some big hospitals were the major source of the SARS outbreak in Taiwan in 2003 (Lee *et al.* 2003). Accordingly, the Bureau of National Health Insurance in recent years has initiated a variety of quality monitoring and assurance programmes, using information technology and payment incentives to move providers towards greater accountability for quality. Particularly noteworthy is an innovative experiment with payments based on clinical outcomes – the so-called fee-for-outcomes approach (Cheng 2003).

CONCLUSIONS

Overall, Taiwan has made significant progress in the pursuit of equitable access to health care without causing a macro-economic crisis, but there are also urgent calls for reducing the waste of health-care resources and improving the quality of health care. Why has Taiwan's health care system had trouble in achieving micro-economic efficiency? First, the National Health Insurance scheme, offering comprehensive benefits and paying for health care on a basis of fee-for-service, provides no incentives for patients and providers to be prudent in the use of health care resources. Secondly, rising health care costs are not the problem; it is poor quality. However, the Taiwan government has paid more attention to cost containment than to quality improvement. Thirdly, because big hospitals in Taiwan are more attractive to patients and get higher payments from the National Health Insurance scheme, the hospital industry in recent years has expanded rapidly (Chiang 2003a). Accordingly, competition among big hospitals, small hospitals and clinics has become more intense. These facts suggest that Taiwan should develop a new health insurance market to meet the challenge of efficient use of health care resources (Chiang 2003a). The new health insurance market should include five key elements: an equalization fund, risk-adjusted capitation, health management organizations, open enrolment and outcome management, as illustrated in Figure 4.2. However, such a market raises a variety of issues that require consideration.

First, there exists the trade-off between equity and efficiency in a traditional health insurance market, as demonstrated in the United States. To prevent such a trade-off, a new health insurance market as proposed above would need to institutionalize an equalization fund to replace the Bureau of National Health Insurance (Chang and

```
                    ┌─────────────┐
                    │ Equalization│
                    │    Fund     │
                    └─────────────┘
                     ↗           ↖
          Income-related      Risk-adjusted
             premium           capitation
           ↗                              ↖
  ┌─────────────┐  Open enrolment   ┌─────────────┐
  │             │   & report card   │   Health    │
  │ Subscribers │ ←───────────────→ │ Management  │
  │             │                   │Organizations│
  │             │     Outcomes      │             │
  └─────────────┘    management     └─────────────┘
```

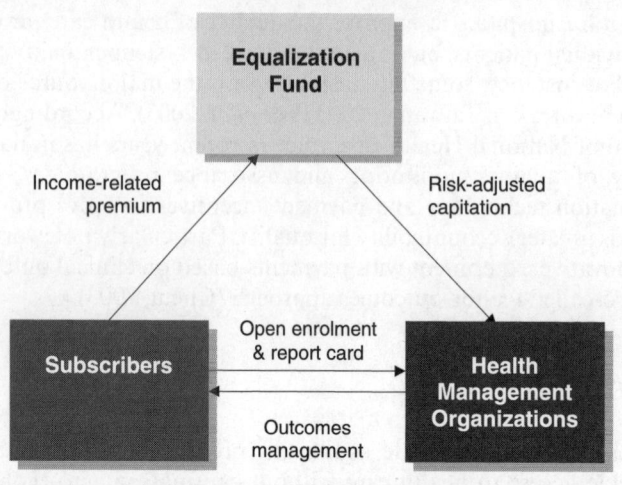

Figure 4.2 A model of the new health insurance market.

Chiang 1998; van de Ven 2000). The equalization fund would be better in the hands of central government for the spirit of social solidarity. Through an equalization fund, the insured pay premiums in accordance with their ability to pay, as with the National Health Insurance scheme, while health management organizations are able to collect risk-adjusted capitation payments. A health management organization is a non-profit cooperative of various levels of health-care providers; any qualified health management organization has an obligation to welcome all subscribers, who are free to leave following the principle of open enrolment.

Secondly, learning lessons from managed care in the United States, the National Health Insurance scheme should put quality improvement before cost containment (Brook 1997; Chiang and Hu 2001). The health insurance market outlined in Figure 4.2 is characterized by decentralization through people's choice. To facilitate people making choices, the equalization fund has to actively provide information concerning the structure and performance of health management organizations, via a so-called 'report card' (Eddy 1998). One of the important pieces of information in the report card should be the extent to which a health management organization has improved the health status of the enrolled. It is hoped that, through people's choice and the report card, health management organizations will compete to achieve the best health outcomes (Ellwood

1988); the backlash against managed care experienced in the United States should not occur, while the health insurance market would move towards purchasing for the health of the population in Taiwan (Kindig 1998).

Taiwanese health care reform has an unfinished agenda. The new health insurance market proposal was first presented in public at a seminar on the second anniversary of national health insurance (Chiang 1997b), followed by a series of symposiums and a draft amendment of the National Health Insurance Law submitted to the Legislative Yuan in 1999. However, the idea of a new health insurance market made various stakeholders extremely cautious; in particular, disadvantaged groups viewed this as the privatization of the National Health Insurance scheme, while private practitioners and small hospitals were afraid that they would eventually be subsumed by large hospitals. The draft amendment was sidelined due to the political pressure of the upcoming presidential election in 2000. After the presidential election, the new administration advocated purchasing health as a guiding principle for health policy in Taiwan (Lee 2000) and a review committee was established to examine the National Health Insurance scheme. One year later, the committee completed an assessment report and the development of a new health insurance market remained one of the major recommendations (National Health Insurance Review Committee 2001). However, the Department of Health decided not to hastily initiate any major health care reform; instead, a planning task force was organized to contemplate 'generation 2 (G2) national health insurance' (The Generation 2 National Health Insurance Planning Task Force 2003, 2004). Whatever form G2 national health insurance will take, many challenges lie ahead.

REFERENCES

Andersen, R.M., McCutcheon, A., Aday, L.A. *et al.* (1983) Exploring dimensions of access to medical care, *Health Service Research*, 18: 49–74.

Anderson, G. and Hussey, P.S. (2001) Comparing health system performance in OECD countries, *Health Affairs*, 20(3): 219–32.

Brook, R.H. (1997) Managed care is not the problem, quality is, *Journal of the American Medical Association*, 278: 1612–14.

Chang, R.E. and Chiang, T.L. (1998) Risk adjustment: a key to efficiency and equity in the health insurance market, *Chinese Journal of Public Health (Taipei)*, 17: 373–80 (in Chinese).

Cheng, C.M. (2003) Taiwan's new national health insurance programme: genesis and experience so far, *Health Affairs*, 22(3): 61–76.

Cheng, S.H. and Chiang, T.L. (1997) The effect of universal health insurance on health care utilization, *Journal of the American Medical Association*, 278: 89–93.

Chi, C. (1994) Integrating traditional medicine into modern health care systems: examining the role of Chinese medicine in Taiwan, *Social Science and Medicine*, 39: 307–21.

Chiang, T.L. (1988) Health care delivery in Taiwan: progress and problems, *Chinese Journal of Public Health (Taipei)*, 8: 75–90.

Chiang, T.L. (1995) Deviation from carrying capacity for physicians and growth rate of physician supply: the Taiwan case, *Social Science and Medicine*, 40: 371–7.

Chiang, T.L. (1997a) Taiwan's 1995 health care reform, *Health Policy*, 39: 225–39.

Chiang, T.L. (1997b) Reforming the National Health Insurance: a preliminary proposal. Paper presented at the *Symposium on the National Health Insurance: Review and Prospect*, the Capital Foundation, the Health and Welfare Foundation, Taipei, Taiwan, 1 March.

Chiang, T.L. (2000) Taiwan's universal health insurance: What has been achieved? What hasn't? Where to go? Paper presented at the *International Symposium on the National Health Insurance System*, Korea Health and Welfare Forum, Seoul, Korea, 9 June.

Chiang, T.L. (2003a) *Health Care Policy in Taiwan*, 2nd edn. Taipei: Chu-Liu Book Co. (in Chinese).

Chiang, T.L. (2003b) Analysis on trends for health care expenditures in Taiwan, *Taiwan Journal of Public Health*, 21: 157–63 (in Chinese).

Chiang, T.L. and Hu, T.W. (2001) Managed care: US experiences and lessons for Taiwan, *Chinese Journal of Public Health (Taipei)*, 19: 340–55 (in Chinese).

Chu, C.L., Hsueh, Y.S. and Chiang, T.L. (2000) Does the supply of physicians affect the use of ambulatory services by the insured? Findings from the 1994 Taiwan health interview survey, *Chinese Journal of Public Health (Taipei)*, 19: 381–8 (in Chinese).

Eddy, D.M. (1998) Performance measurement: problems and solutions, *Health Affairs*, 17(4): 7–25.

Ellwood, P.M. (1988) Shattuck Lecture: outcomes management, *New England Journal of Medicine*, 318: 1549–56.

Hong, W.H., Cheng, S.H., Chang, R.E. and Chiang, T.L. (1998) Change in the proportion of cross-region admissions in Taiwan, *Chinese Journal of Public Health (Taipei)*, 16: 388–94 (in Chinese).

Huang, P. (1995) An overview of hospital accreditation in Taiwan, Republic of China, *International Journal of Health Planning and Management*, 10: 183–91.

Huang, W.Y., Chang, R.E. and Chiang, T.L. (2001) Changing geographic distribution of physicians in Taiwan, 1984–1998, *Journal of Medical Education (Taipei)*, 5: 13–20 (in Chinese).

Kindig, D.A. (1998) Purchasing population health: aligning financial incentives to improve health outcomes, *Health Service Research*, 33: 223–42.

Kuo, S.W.Y., Ranis, G. and Fei, J.C.H. (1981) *The Taiwan Success Story: Rapid Growth with Improved Distribution in the Republic of China, 1952–1979*. Boulder, CO: Westview.

Lee, M.L. (2000) The future directions of health policy in Taiwan, *Mingsheng Daily*, 13 May.

Lee, M.L., Chen, C.J., Su, I.J. *et al.* (2003) Severe acute respiratory syndrome – Taiwan, 2003, *Morbidity and Mortality Weekly Report*, 52: 461–6.

Lee, R.P. (1982) Comparative studies of health care systems, *Social Science and Medicine*, 16: 629–42.

Liu, J.H. and Chiang, T.L. (2004) The relationship between the expansion of the hospital industry and the growth of office-based physician manpower in sub-medical regions in Taiwan, *Taiwan Journal of Public Health*, 23: 32–6.

Lu, J.F. and Hsiao, W.C. (2003) Does universal health insurance make health care unaffordable? Lessons from Taiwan, *Health Affairs*, 22(3): 77–88.

National Health Insurance Review Committee (2001) *National Health Insurance Assessment Report*. Taipei: NHRI (in Chinese).

National Health Research Institute (2001) *Policy Recommendations for Health Care Workforce in Taiwan – Summary*. Taipei: NHRI (in Chinese).

OECD (1995) *New Directions in Health Care Policy*. Paris: Organization for Economic Cooperation and Development.

Peabody, J.W., Yu, J.C., Wang, Y.R. and Bickel, S.R. (1995) Health system reform in the Republic of China: formulating policy in a market-based health system, *Journal of the American Medical Association*, 273: 777–81.

Republic of China Bureau of National Health Insurance (2003) *National Health Insurance Statistics 2002*. Taipei: Bureau of National Health Insurance.

Republic of China Bureau of National Health Insurance (2004) NHI Summary Statistics (available at: http://www.nhi.gov.tw/01intro/statistic/s20.htm; accessed 16 January 2004).

Republic of China Council for Economic Planning and Development (1990) *The Report of National Health Insurance Plan (the CEPD Report)*. Taipei: Council for Economic Planning and Development.

Republic of China Council for Economic Planning and Development (2003) *Taiwan Statistical Data Book, 2003*. Taipei: Council for Economic Planning and Development.

Republic of China Department of Health (2003) *Health and Vital Statistics, Vol. 1: General Health Statistics, 2002*. Taipei: Department of Health.

Republic of China Ministry of Education (2003) *Educational Statistics of the Republic of China 2003*. Taipei: Ministry of Education.

The Generation 2 National Health Insurance Planning Task Force (2003) *Annual Report to Executive Yuan 2002*. Taipei: Department of Health, Executive Yuan.

The Generation 2 National Health Insurance Planning Task Force (2004) *Annual Report to Executive Yuan 2003*. Taipei: Department of Health, Executive Yuan.

van de Ven, W.P.P.M. (2000) Risk adjustment in competitive health plan markets, in A.J. Culyer and J.P. Newhouse (eds) *Handbook of Health Economics*, Vol. 1A. Amsterdam: Elsevier.

Whitehead, M. (1990) *The Concepts and Principles of Equity and Health*. Unpublished document #EUR/ICP/RPD 414. Copenhagen: WHO Regional Office for Europe.

5

AUSTRALIA
Stephen Duckett

Population 2003	20 million
Ethnic composition 2001	Indigenous population 2.2%, overseas born 0.1%
State populations 2001	New South Wales 33.8%, Victoria 24.8%, Queensland 18.8%, South Australia 7.7%, Western Australia 9.8%, Tasmania 2.4%, Northern Territories 1%, Australian Capital Territory 1.6%
Remoteness 2001	Major cities 65.9%, inner regional areas 20.6%, outer regional areas 10.5%, remote 1.8%, very remote 1.1%
Capital city	Canberra
Live births per woman 2003	1.75
Infant mortality rate per 1000 live births 2001	5.3
Life expectancy at birth 2001 (male/female)	77.0/82.4 years
Total health expenditure as a percentage of GDP 2001	9.3%
Government health expenditure as a percentage of total health expenditure 2001–2002	68.8%
Total health expenditure per capita 2001 (US$ PPP)	2513

Practising physicians per 1000 population 2000	2.5 (67% male, 33% female)
Health system	Mixed public, private; Commonwealth – State
Political system	Federation, cabinet-dominated parliamentary democracy

Source: Australian Social Trends, Australian Bureau of Statistics (2003, Catalogue 4102.0)

INTRODUCTION

Health services in Australia perform well against criteria of equity, efficiency, quality and accountability (Duckett 2004). With health expenditure at around 9.3 per cent of GDP, Australia stands in the mid-range of OECD countries. This chapter describes the health status of the Australian population, outlines the health care financing system, and discusses the three main elements of health care provision: hospitals, medical services and pharmaceuticals.[1]

HEALTH STATUS

Overall, Australians report good health. In the National Health Survey of 2001 (Australian Bureau of Statistics 2002), 81.2 per cent of adults aged 18 years and over reported their health was good, very good or excellent. However, despite this positive rating, 78 per cent were experiencing a long-term condition (6 months or more). The most common long-term conditions were: long- or short-sightedness (29.7 per cent of population), back pain (20.8 per cent), hay fever (15.5 per cent) and asthma (11.6 per cent). The life expectancy of Australians is comparable to that of residents in other developed countries.

Illness and sickness are unevenly distributed in the population, with people in lower socioeconomic status groups experiencing more ill health (McClelland and Scotton 1998; House 2001), and these socioeconomic differences appear to be worsening (Hayes *et al.* 2002). Walker and Abello (2000) have shown that people on low income report, on average, 40–50 per cent more long-term conditions than the rest of the population, while Korda *et al.* (2002) have shown that, among working adults, professionals had the best self-reported health and blue-collar workers the worst. In recent Australian studies, Morrell *et al.* (1998) have shown a strong association between unemployment and ill health, as have Mathers and Schofield (1998), with the direction of causation probably from unemployment to ill health. The health of Aboriginal and Torres Strait Islander people is significantly worse than that of other Australians: the indigenous population has an age-standardized death rate at least twice that of the non-indigenous population, with a male indigenous person aged 35–44 years almost six times more likely to die than a non-indigenous male of the same age. The same trends are reflected in differences in self-reported health status, recent illnesses and long-term conditions. Although infant mortality rates per 1000 live births for Aboriginal populations are declining, they are still three times greater than those for non-Aboriginal Australians (Mathews 1997). Birth weights for Aboriginal infants are considerably lower than those for non-Aboriginal infants.

Australia spends about 0.4 per cent of GDP on community and public health activities (5 per cent of total health expenditure). 'Public health' is still a relatively neglected area of health policy in Australia, with responsibility primarily vested in the states (and territories) with national coordination via the National Public Health Partnership and some specific Commonwealth initiatives. National programmes generally focus on specific diseases or 'risk factors' rather than adopting a more integrated approach. Specific national programmes have been developed for breast screening, tobacco control, HIV/AIDS, immunization, and so on. Commonwealth funding to the states for these programmes is incorporated in public health outcome funding agreements that incorporate specific performance indicators covering the included programmes.

FINANCING

Australia spent A$66.6 billion on health services in 2001–2002, principally on recurrent expenditure; total capital expenditure (and capital consumption) was less than A$4 billion in that year. Over one-third (35 per cent) of recurrent expenditure is spent on hospitals, with a further 7 per cent on high-level residential care (i.e. nursing homes; expenditure on low-level residential care or hostels is classified under the System of National Accounts as welfare expenditure). About 18 per cent of all expenditure is spent on medical services, with a further 14 per cent on pharmaceuticals.[2]

94 Comparative health policy in the Asia-Pacific

Because of Australia's universal health insurance system, Medicare, over two-thirds of total health expenditure is from government, with the Commonwealth being responsible for 48 per cent of expenditure and state and local government for 22 per cent. The balance of expenditure comes from out-of-pocket expenses by consumers (20 per cent), with a further 8 per cent being mediated through health insurance funds and 4 per cent from other sources (see Figure 5.1 for an outline of flows of funds for hospital and medical services).

The distribution of sources of funds is variable across the health sector; for example, most public hospital expenditure is by government, either Commonwealth or state (see Figure 5.2). Expenditure on nursing homes and medical services also comes mainly from the Commonwealth government, while private hospital, dental services and other health profession funding comes from individuals – either via health insurance or as out-of-pocket expenditure. These significantly different shares in funding responsibilities have implications

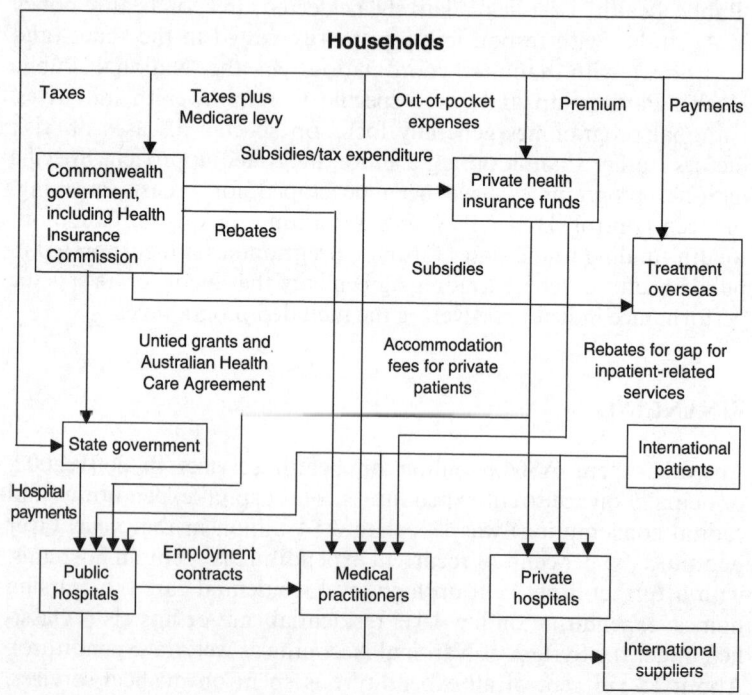

Figure 5.1 Funding flows for hospital and medical services in Australia.

Australia 95

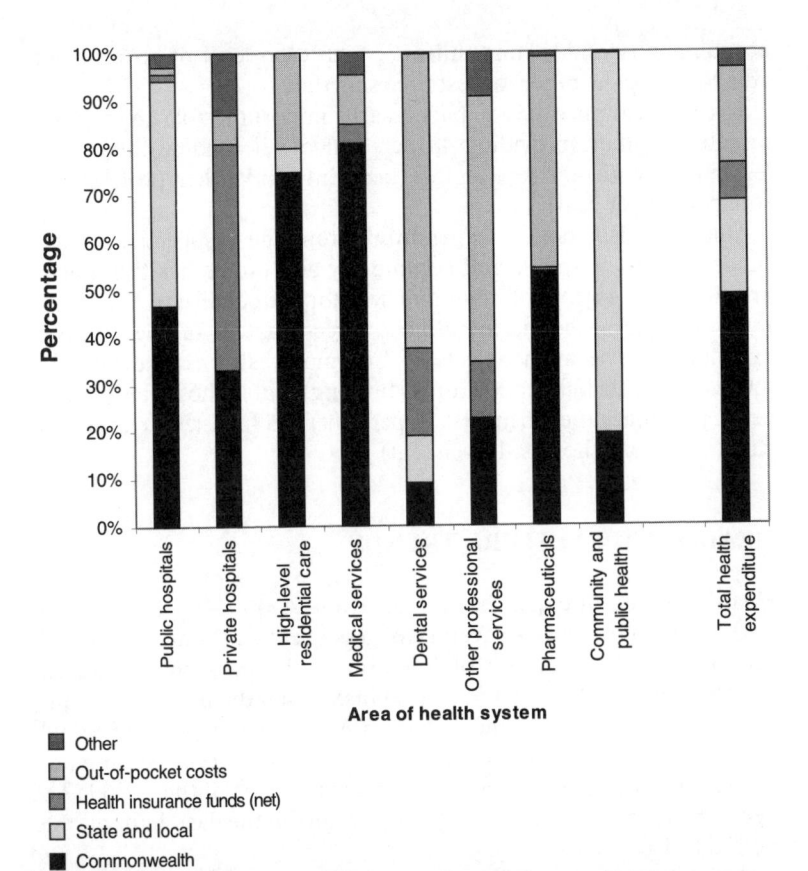

Figure 5.2 Relative proportions of recurrent health expenditure, 2001–2002. *Source*: Australian Institute of Health and Welfare (2003).

for policy. The Commonwealth government clearly dominates nursing home care (high-level residential care), where it provides 75 per cent of funds, and medical services (80 per cent). Policy response to issues that arise in these areas is clearly a Commonwealth government responsibility. The same is true in pharmaceuticals, where funding is derived from either the Commonwealth government (54 per cent) or consumers (45 per cent). In contrast, public hospital funding responsibility is shared equally between the Commonwealth and state governments; state governments dominate funding for community and public health services (80 per cent). The areas of shared funding responsibilities can cause problems of accountability and 'blame shifting', with each level of government able to blame the other for resource shortfalls.

Health insurance has a particularly important role in funding private hospitals (providing 48 per cent of all funding) and, to a lesser extent, dental services (19 per cent) and other professional services (12 per cent).

One can also look at expenditure from the perspective of the funder. Public hospitals and community and public health services are the main objects of state and territory expenditure: these two items together account for almost three-quarters of their health expenditure. The main objects of Commonwealth expenditure are medical benefits (30 per cent of its funding), public hospitals (26 per cent), pharmaceutical benefits (16 per cent) and high-level residential care (i.e. nursing homes, 10 per cent).

HEALTH EXPENDITURE TRENDS

Health expenditure per head rose from A$1904 in 1991–92 to A$3397 in 2001–2002, an average of 6 per cent per annum. Most of this increase was because of inflation in the economy. However, health spending per capita increased faster than the rest of the economy. In real terms, spending rose from A$2357 per capita to A$3292 (2000–2001 dollars), an average increase of 3.4 per cent per annum. There was a slower real growth rate in the first part of the period (2.8 per cent from 1992–93 to 1997–98) than in the last half of the period (4.1 per cent).

A significant feature of health expenditure patterns in Australia is the instability in funding shares between Commonwealth and state governments over the period 1975 to 1985 (see Figure 5.3). This period covered the introduction of Medibank in 1975, when the Commonwealth's role and funding increased significantly and the state share concomitantly decreased. This policy initiative was slowly dismantled under the Fraser government,[3] when the Commonwealth share decreased and the states' share increased. With the reintroduction of Medicare in 1984, the Commonwealth and state roles again reversed. The state share has marginally declined from the early 1990s level of around 25 per cent to 22 per cent in 2001–2002, with a marginal increase in the Commonwealth share over the same period from 42 per cent to 46 per cent.

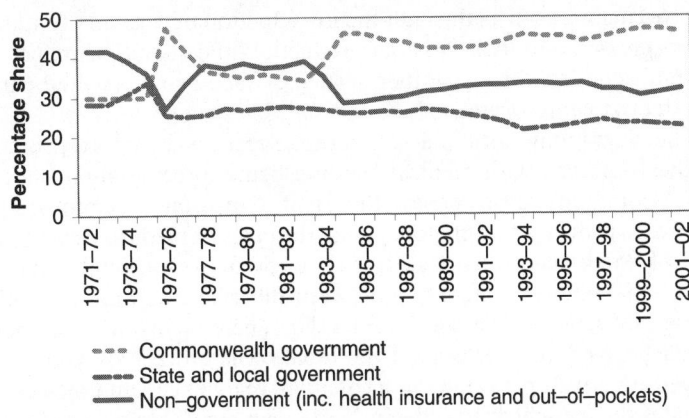

Figure 5.3 Relative share of total health expenditure, 1971–72 to 2001–2002. *Source*: Australian Institute of Health and Welfare (2003)

MEDICARE

Medicare is an important part of the health policy landscape in Australia because it provides the mechanism for financing two key provider groups: hospitals and doctors. The principal objective of Medicare is to remove (or reduce) financial barriers to access to health care for all Australian residents.

Historically, hospitals developed as a state responsibility and the Commonwealth's hospital Medicare policies are thus implemented via the states. The Commonwealth government has entered into agreements with each state that provide for Commonwealth funds to be provided to the states for hospital services. In return for this funding, the states agree to abide by a number of conditions, including: to provide a network of hospital services and to allow all consumers to be able to access inpatient services in these hospitals as 'public patients' free of any cost.

The agreements provide that states are responsible for the full marginal cost of any increase in hospital budgets during the term of the agreement. Conversely, states accrue the full benefit of any reduction in hospital budgets over this period. Commonwealth Medicare funding is formula-driven during the course of an agreement, with the formula being unrelated to actual hospital budgets, adjusting only for exogenous factors such as population growth and ageing. This places strong incentives on states to achieve efficiency improvements, such as through the introduction of case-mix funding of hospitals (Duckett 1996) and a reduction in demand, or reducing hospital budgets through other strategies such as across-the-board 'productivity improvements'.

The Commonwealth plays a more direct role with respect to medical services, with medical funding being directly administered by a Commonwealth agency, the Health Insurance Commission. Medicare provides for rebates against the costs of medical care at the rate of 85 per cent of a scheduled fee for out-of-hospital services with a maximum per item gap between the rebate and the schedule fee of A$57.10 (November 2002 levels). There is also a safety net: Medicare pays 100 per cent of the rebate when total gap payments exceed A$319.70 per family in a calendar year. The Commonwealth updates the fee schedule and gap limits on a regular basis. Medicare also pays a rebate of 75 per cent of the scheduled fee for medical services provided to private inpatients (with no maximum gap).

Doctors can send their bill to the Health Insurance Commission through a process known as 'bulk' or 'direct' billing, in which case the medical practitioner must accept the rebate in full settlement of the account with no patient co-payment.[4] Alternatively, doctors can bill patients and there is then no limit on fees that may be charged; patients then obtain a rebate from the Health Insurance Commission for the relevant percentage of the government schedule fee.[5]

Health insurance funds are generally not allowed to cover any charges by medical practitioners above the schedule fee. This policy was designed to place financial pressure on doctors to influence their fee-charging behaviour. However, since 1996, insurers may make contractual arrangements (known as medical purchaser provider agreements) with doctors providing services to (private) hospital inpatients to pay rebates above the schedule fee. Medicare is funded from general taxation. However, Australia's income tax laws provide for a 'Medicare levy', currently 1.5 per cent of taxable income. Differential low-income thresholds (below which no levy is payable) are set for individuals, single parents and couples. Couples and families with a combined income over A$100,000 who do not have health insurance that provides cover for hospital care are liable to a levy surcharge of a further 1 per cent of taxable income. (The single person cut-off is A$50,000.)

The Medicare levy is not intended to cover the full cost of Commonwealth health expenditure (or, indeed, total expenditure on health) but rather was introduced as a financing measure to raise additional revenue to pay for the introduction of Medicare in 1984.

The levy is not a 'hypothecated' tax; that is, Medicare levy collections are not specifically allocated to the health portfolio, although the need to increase health spending is often used as a political justification for increasing the levy. The levy is thus simply another tax that flows into the pool of funds from which Commonwealth expenditure derives. In 1999–2000, total revenue from the Medicare levy was A$4.2 billion, representing about 16 per cent of total Commonwealth health expenditure.

Direct billing (more commonly known as bulk billing) increased each year from the introduction of Medicare up to 1996, when it peaked at around 80 per cent for all general practitioner services across Australia (see Figure 5.4). The subsequent decline in direct billing to the contemporary level of under 70 per cent of general practitioner services has been politically contentious and evinced government and opposition policy responses. The government's proposals (submitted in two rounds, the first having been rejected by the Senate in late 2003) undercut Medicare's universality, placing incentives on medical practitioners to bulk bill concession card holders and services to children.[6]

HEALTH INSURANCE

Patterns of private health insurance largely reflect changes in government and national health policy. Before the introduction of

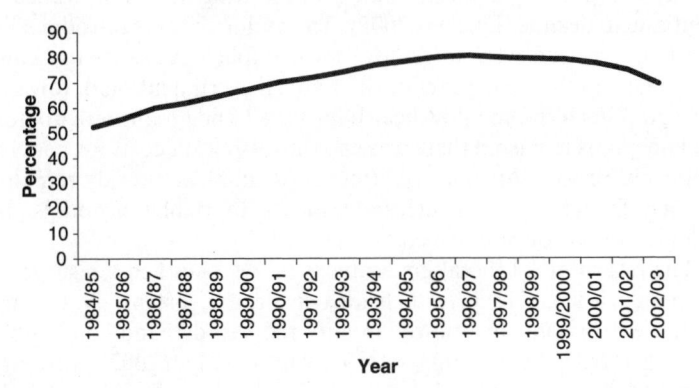

Figure 5.4 Percentage of general practitioner attendances bulk billed, 1984–85 to 2002–2003. *Source*: Australian Government Department of Health and Ageing (2004).

Medicare in 1984, health insurance accounted for about 20 per cent of all health expenditure. Immediately after the introduction of Medicare (1984–85), the health insurance share of expenditure declined precipitately to 8.8 per cent of health expenditure, with a slight increase in the intervening period to its current (2001–2002) level of 8 per cent of expenditure. The proportion of the population with health insurance declined up to the late 1990s, despite the introduction of significant tax rebate incentives to take out private health insurance (Hall *et al.* 1999). The introduction of 'Life Time Cover' led, in 1999, to an increase in health insurance.

As Figure 5.5 shows, the proportion of the population with private health insurance has been declining since the 1970s, with a steeper decline associated with the introduction of universal health insurance in 1984. There has been a differential rate of decline in the prevalence of insurance across different population groups, leading to a change in the composition of the insured population. Middle-income families were more likely to drop insurance relative to high-income and low-income families, and younger families were more likely to drop insurance relative to older families (Schofield *et al.* 1997).

For much of the 1970s, health funding policy was in a state of flux with frequent gyrations of policy, as the then Fraser government used health policy as an instrument of economic policy and repeated attempts to induce greater take-up of private health insurance (Duckett 1979, 1980, 1984; Scotton 1980; Gray 1996). The Labor government from 1984 to 1996 provided some stability to health policy and pursued a passive policy of allowing health insurance to continue to decline (Duckett 2003). The major changes introduced in the Labor period were to remove most implicit subsidies to health insurance (in the early years of the Labor government) and, towards the end of its term, to allow health insurers to negotiate with doctors and hospitals to ensure there were no out-of-pocket costs for patients following private inpatient treatment. An implicit subsidy remains, as bed-day charges for private patients in public hospitals are significantly below average cost.

The return of a Liberal government in 1996 marked a resurgence of policy interest in private health insurance, ostensibly because increased private insurance might reduce demand on public hospitals (Duckett and Jackson 2000; Vaithianathan 2002). Although the new government introduced a rebate/subsidy for health insurance in its first budget, this did nothing to reverse the decline in the proportion of the population with insurance, and was followed by a

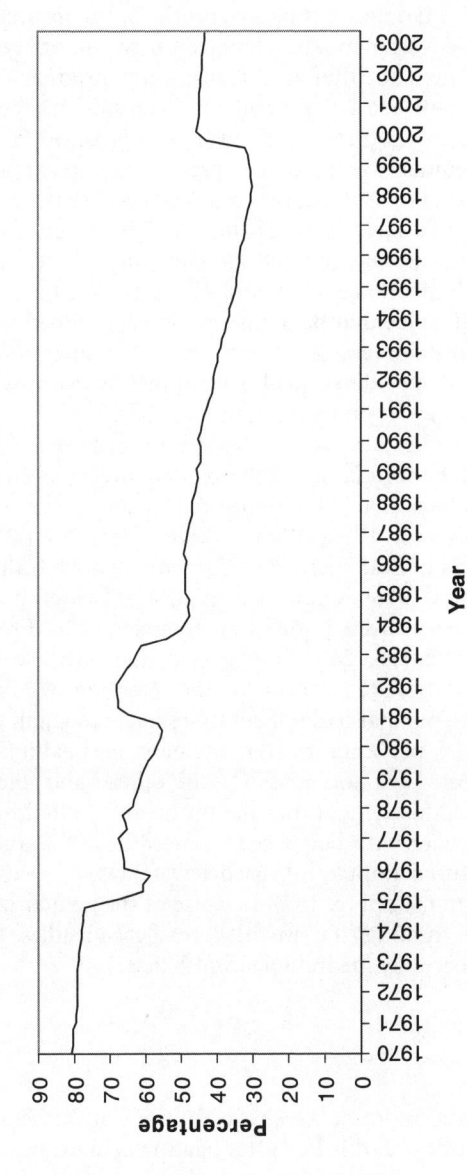

Figure 5.5 Percentage of population with private health insurance, for the month of September 1970–2003. *Source*: Australian Government Private Health Insurance Information Council (2004).

more generous rebate/subsidy scheme introduced in 1999. Partly in response to the higher drop-out rate in younger families, and the consequent risk of a deteriorating age profile of the insured population, in 1999 the government also changed the regulatory controls on funds to allow them to offer health insurance products with premiums varying with age of entry in the insurance market. People who first take out health insurance over the age of 30 face a 2 per cent per annum cumulative increase in premiums (capped at 65); thus a person who first takes out insurance at 35 faces a 10 per cent higher premium than would have applied if they had taken out insurance at age 30. This latter policy (known as Life Time Cover) led to an increase in health insurance to around 45 per cent of the population (Butler 2002), but since that peak insurance has declined to stand at around 43 per cent in June 2003 and recent health insurance data show that the risk profile of health insurance is again worsening, with younger people dropping out (Butler 2002).

A number of studies have shown that health insurance is unevenly distributed in the population: the insured are wealthier, better educated and older than the uninsured (Cameron *et al.* 1988; Cameron and Trivedi 1991; Willcox 1991; Burrows *et al.* 1993; Australian Bureau of Statistics 1994; Cameron and McCallum 1996; Hopkins and Kidd 1996; Schofield *et al.* 1997). Evidence about the risk profile of the insured population is mixed. The Productivity Commission (1999: 196, 244–6) suggested that 'adverse selection' – that is, disproportionate recruitment and retention of contributors with health problems that make them more likely to claim benefits – accounted for 17 per cent of the increase in health insurance premiums between 1990 and 1995. On the other hand, the Productivity Commission also noted that the probability of holding health insurance was higher with better self-assessed health status (p. 195) and that the insured population used fewer hospital bed-days per capita than the uninsured (p. 187). Because of the greater take-up of health insurance among the wealthy, rebates/subsidies to health insurance are inherently inequitable (Smith 2001).

HOSPITALS

Hospitals are without doubt the key institutions of the health sector, accounting for over one-third of total health expenditure, as well as playing a dominant role in professional education. Table 5.1 provides a brief summary of Australian hospital services.

Table 5.1 Summary of hospital services and use

Provision (2001–2002)	1306 hospitals (57 per cent public) with 78,868 beds (65 per cent public) provided 23 million bed-days (70 per cent public) to 6.4 million inpatients (62 per cent public); 246 hospitals were day procedure centres; 47.6 per cent of public and 59.9 per cent of private hospital patients were treated on a same-day basis
	Public hospitals, which account for 57 per cent of all hospitals, are generally larger (mean 69 beds) than private hospitals (mean 49 beds)
	The average length of stay for all patients was 3.6 days; for patients who stayed overnight it was 6.5 days
	Public hospitals provided 39.5 million outpatient occasions of service, including 5.7 million occasions of service in emergency departments
Resourcing (2000–2001)	Hospitals cost A$20 billion to run
	Public hospitals cost A$16.3 billion to run, A$3059 per patient treated or A$749 per patient day
	Public hospitals employed 192,187 equivalent full-time staff, 44 per cent of whom were nurses

Australia has 4.0 acute beds per 1000 population. There are substantial differences between the states in hospital provision, in terms of the relative role of the private sector (36 per cent of all beds in Victoria being in private hospitals compared with 30 per cent in New South Wales). Almost 50 per cent of beds in Tasmania are in private hospitals, in part reflecting the fact that one of the state's major public hospitals was privatized in the 1990s. There are also differences in overall level of provision between the states. South Australia has a bed-to-population ratio of 4.9 beds per 1000 population, 32 per cent higher than the Victorian provision of 3.7. The different level of provision is also associated with different levels of utilization: South Australia has a separation rate[7] of 352.7 per 1000 population (age-standardized) and bed-day utilization of 1310 per 1000 population, being 4 per cent and 12 per cent above Victorian levels, respectively.

Just over half of all hospital separations in 2001–2002 did not involve an overnight stay. The 'same-day' proportion was slightly higher in private hospitals (53 per cent; 60 per cent of all separations from private facilities, taking into account day procedure facilities) than public hospitals (48 per cent).[8] The same-day proportion varies between states: 42 per cent of separations from New South Wales public hospitals are same-day compared with 53 per cent from Victorian public hospitals. In contrast, 62 per cent of separations from private facilities in New South Wales are same-day, compared with 60 per cent in Victoria.

Although the proportion of beds in larger private hospitals that are able to deal with more complex procedures is higher than it was a decade ago, the average complexity of cases treated in private hospitals is still less than in public hospitals. In 2001–2002, the average 'DRG cost weight' (a measure of complexity derived from the mix of patients classified according to their diagnosis-related roup (DRG), and the DRG average cost) was 9 per cent lower in private hospitals than in public hospitals (0.91 compared with 0.99).

Although Medicare has eliminated financial barriers to hospital care access, there are still time barriers to access in the form of public hospital waiting lists. Waiting list management is now essentially the responsibility of individual hospitals, although a number of states have introduced penalty/incentive plans and payments to reward good (or, more accurately, penalize bad) performance on managing patients with extended waits.

Quality of care has been a quiescent policy issue for most of the last decade. There was a flurry of activity in the mid-1990s with the release of the Quality in Australian Health Care Study (Wilson *et al.* 1995), which showed that about one in every six admissions to hospital was associated with an adverse event, although this rate was subsequently revised down to one in every ten (Runciman *et al.* 2000; Thomas *et al.* 2000). Even this revised rate is, of course, unacceptable and this led to the formation of the Australian Council on Safety and Quality in Health Care, whose intention is to:

- provide national leadership in system-wide approaches to quality improvement in health care;
- develop a coherent plan for improving the quality of health care services; and
- facilitate action by appropriate organizations and agencies in priority areas.

The Council's priority areas are supporting health care professionals to deliver safer patient care; improve data and information; involve consumers; redesign systems of health care to facilitate a culture of safety; and build awareness and understanding of health care safety. The Council can thus be seen to be adopting a facilitatory, systems-change approach to its task.

Trends in inpatient provision

Since 1986, there has been a substantial decline (by almost 50 per cent) in the number of public acute hospital beds per capita, with the number of private acute beds being relatively stable. The decline in public provision has been a result of specific government policies to reduce bed provision, particularly in rural areas. Despite the reduction in beds per capita, there has been a 45 per cent increase in separations per capita (20 per cent in public hospitals, 135 per cent in private hospitals). Thus, despite the decline in health insurance prior to 1999, the private sector has not experienced a reduction in demand.

The dramatic increase in separation rates also reflects the growth of private day procedure centres. Since 1982–83, length of stay has almost halved (from 6.9 to 3.9 days in 2001–2002). However, this decline masks contributing factors. The reduction in average length of stay has occurred principally because of the significant increase in the proportion of day-only patients. Very long-stay patients are also staying in hospital for a shorter period. Both these trends have been facilitated by improvements in medical technology (for example, shorter-action anaesthetic agents and flexible endoscopy). Most states regulate the number of private hospital beds, and bed licences are tradable commodities. Thus, although there has been a redistribution of private beds, few have been closed. The reduction in private hospital provision per capita has been caused principally by an increase in the population. Per capita provision of private hospitals in non-metropolitan areas has increased, partly reflecting reductions in population, but also the development of new private hospitals in major rural centres. Private hospitals have also experienced substantial growth (as reflected in increased admissions per 1000 population) with the increase principally occurring through day procedure activity (also occurring in the public sector) and, to some extent, increased occupancy rates for multi-day cases. About 55 per cent of all private hospitals are for-profit, and this sector of the industry is expanding. Over the period 1996–97 to 2000–2001, the number of beds in for-profit hospitals increased by 15 per cent, while beds in not-for-profit hospitals declined (by 3 per cent). Separations from for-profit hospitals increased faster than those from not-for-profit hospitals (41 per cent versus 13 per cent).

MEDICAL SERVICES

There are over 50,000 registered medical practitioners in the medical labour force, 90 per cent of whom are in clinical practice. Of those in clinical practice, 45 per cent are primary care practitioners and 34 per cent specialists, with the rest hospital-based non-specialists and trainees. General practitioners manage a range of problems (see Figure 5.6).

Utilization of medical services has increased since the reintroduction of Medicare. In 1984–85, there was an average of 7.2 services per head of population; by 2002–2003 this had risen to 11.1 per head. There are significant differences in per capita use between the states. For example, in 2002–2003 people resident in New South Wales used an average of 11.85 Medicare services per head compared with 11.2 in Victoria and South Australia and 10.1 in Western Australia. People resident in the Northern Territory used only 6.3 Medicare services per head. This is partly the result of the younger population in the territory, but is also the result of alternative ways of funding Medicare services, especially for Aboriginal and Torres Strait Islander peoples.

The Commonwealth government publishes an annual fee schedule for the Medicare scheme. The schedule lists medical services and procedures and defines the rebate that will be payable by the government for these services. Most items listed on the schedule are surgical procedures, pathology investigations or diagnostic imaging procedures. Most of the expenditure on Medicare benefits, however, is for 'attendances'.

Fee-for-service payments provide a strong encouragement to increase activity, with relatively weaker incentives for other desirable aspects of primary care provision (Gosden *et al.* 2001). A fee-for-service model is implicitly based on a 'professional' paradigm, where an individual professional has a relationship with a patient for which there is an individual payment. This is not the dominant situation in general practice today. Group practices are more common than solo practice and large for-profit chains are increasing their share of the general practice market (Catchlove 2001).

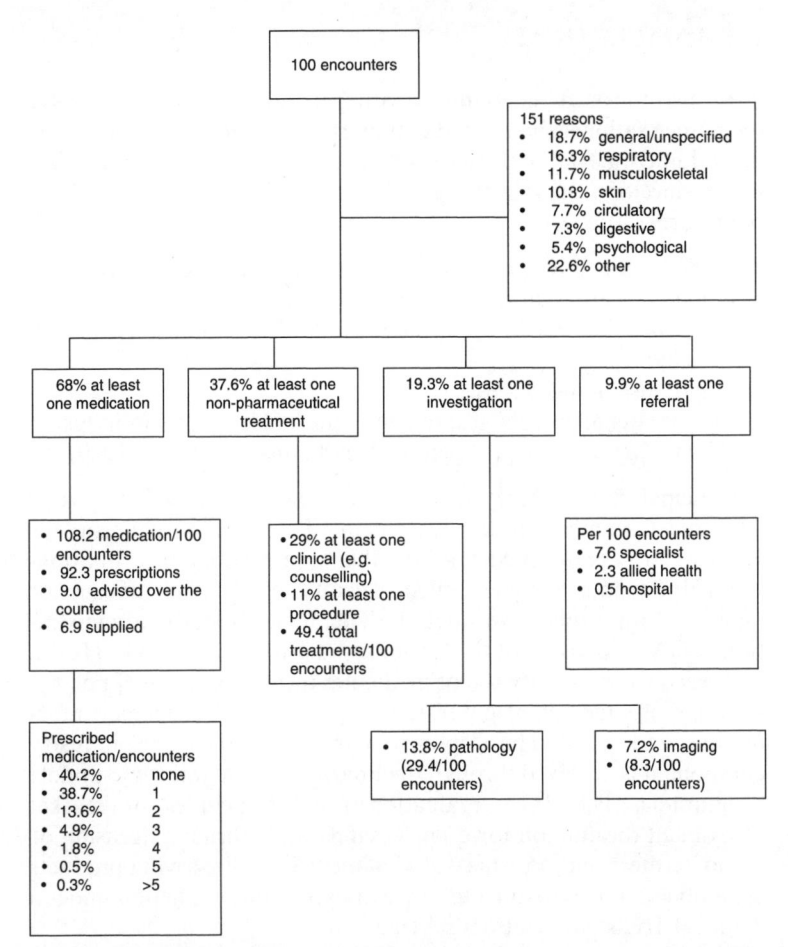

```
                    ┌─────────────────┐
                    │  100 encounters │
                    └─────────────────┘
                             │
                             │        ┌──────────────────────────────────┐
                             ├────────│ 151 reasons                      │
                             │        │  • 18.7% general/unspecified     │
                             │        │  • 16.3% respiratory             │
                             │        │  • 11.7% musculoskeletal         │
                             │        │  • 10.3% skin                    │
                             │        │  •  7.7% circulatory             │
                             │        │  •  7.3% digestive               │
                             │        │  •  5.4% psychological           │
                             │        │  • 22.6% other                   │
                             │        └──────────────────────────────────┘
```

68% at least one medication	37.6% at least one non-pharmaceutical treatment	19.3% at least one investigation	9.9% at least one referral
• 108.2 medication/100 encounters • 92.3 prescriptions • 9.0 advised over the counter • 6.9 supplied	• 29% at least one clinical (e.g. counselling) • 11% at least one procedure • 49.4 total treatments/100 encounters	• 13.8% pathology (29.4/100 encounters) • 7.2% imaging (8.3/100 encounters)	Per 100 encounters • 7.6 specialist • 2.3 allied health • 0.5 hospital

Prescribed medication/encounters
- 40.2% none
- 38.7% 1
- 13.6% 2
- 4.9%   3
- 1.8%   4
- 0.5%   5
- 0.3%   >5

Figure 5.6 General practice activity, 2000–2001. *Source*: Derived from Britt *et al.* (2001).

Doctors working for these chains are changing their behaviour and self-perception (White 2000) and are exposed to ethical risks (Fitzgerald 2001). The increasing role of for-profit chains, motivated to ensure a return on equity, calls into question whether uncapped fee-for-service payments, extensively subsidized by government, provide the appropriate reward mechanism for the emerging industry structure.

PHARMACEUTICALS

Over two-thirds of encounters with general practitioners involve recommendations about medication (Britt *et al.* 2001). Australia has adopted a National Medicines Policy to guide pharmaceutical policy development (Harvey and Murray 1995). Key planks of the policy are:

- timely access to the medicines that Australians need, at a cost to individuals and that the community can afford;
- medicines that meet appropriate standards of quality, safety and efficacy;
- quality use of medicines;
- the maintenance of a responsible and viable medicine industry. (Commonwealth Department of Health and Aged Care 1999)

Principal responsibility for the National Medicines Policy rests with the Commonwealth government. The main mechanism for ensuring access to medicines is the Commonwealth's Pharmaceutical Benefits Scheme (PBS). Quality, safety and efficacy of medicines are regulated through the Therapeutic Goods Administration (TGA), a division of the Commonwealth Department of Health and Aged Care. Quality use of medicines involves a range of policies in terms of educational programmes, provision of consumer information, and so on. The responsible and viable medicines industry component is achieved through the pharmaceutical industry support programme. The TGA evaluation process includes pre-market assessment (evaluation for quality, safety and efficacy), licensing of manufacturers and post-market vigilance. Some life-saving products for individual or experimental use can bypass this regulation under a 'Clinical Trials Notification' scheme.

The Pharmaceutical Benefits Scheme was introduced on 1 July 1948 but relatively few prescriptions were provided under this scheme because of opposition from the medical profession. The Liberal government elected in 1949 altered the scheme (with effect from 4 September 1950), introducing a list of 139 'life-saving and disease-preventing drugs' that were provided free of charge to the whole community (Sloan 1995). Since then, the range of drugs covered by the scheme has increased dramatically and, by August 2003, the scheme covered 601 generic products, available in 1469 forms or strengths and marketed as 2602 different brands. Some of these items are restricted – that is, they require some form of authority to prescribe them (over and above medical registration).

The authority scheme is not well received by doctors and is seen as bureaucratic and not to be evidence-based (Liaw *et al.* 2003).

Patient co-payments are structured separately for the general population and concession cardholders. There are three main classes of concession cardholders: Commonwealth seniors health cardholders, health care cardholders and the pensioners concession cardholders. About 8 million concession cards were on issue in 2003 (just over one-third of the total population), about 25 per cent to age pensioners, about 25 per cent to recipients of the parenting payment, with the balance spread across about 60 different income support payments. Initially, the Pharmaceutical Benefits Scheme involved no patient co-payment, but a 50 cent co-payment was introduced for general beneficiaries on 1 March 1960. A co-payment for concession cardholders of A$2.50 per prescription was introduced on 1 November 1990. The co-payment amounts are indexed for inflation and, by 2003, the co-payment for concessional beneficiaries had increased to A$3.70 per prescription and for general beneficiaries to A$23.10. The Pharmaceutical Benefits Scheme provides some protection from the cumulative impact of these co-payments through a 'safety net threshold'. For cardholders, this is set at 52 times the co-payment: if concession cardholders require more than 52 prescriptions in any one year, they can obtain a safety net card that entitles them to further prescriptions without any co-payment.

When a pharmaceutical is listed on the Pharmaceuticals Benefit Scheme under more than one brand name, pharmacists may dispense 'generically' identical forms of the drug unless specifically directed not to do so by the prescribing medical practitioner on the prescription form. If generic equivalents are available, the scheme will only pay for the least costly product and the consumer meets any additional costs for a specific brand name alternative in addition to the co-payments described above. An additional co-payment is available if other pharmaceuticals in the same therapeutic class are deemed to be equivalent, and an exemption on clinical grounds has not been granted for that patient. This policy, known as 'Therapeutic Group Premiums', applies only to items in three therapeutic groups: H2-receptor antagonists, calcium channel blockers and ACE inhibitors.

The generic substitution policy is facilitated by a government requirement that, where computer software used by medical practitioners to generate prescriptions for the Pharmaceutical Benefits Scheme has a default preferred drug, it defaults automatically to the generic form of a drug rather than a proprietary form of the drug. As at May 2002, 293 products had a brand premium, with the premium ranging from one cent to A$79.48. Over 30 million prescriptions had been dispensed with a brand premium, being about 50 per cent of all prescriptions covered by the brand premium policy. (For a fuller discussion of generic drug policy, see Löfgren 2002.)

Expenditure on pharmaceutical benefits has increased exponentially since the start of the programme, with particularly rapid growth in expenditure on drugs used by pensioners and concession cardholders. Importantly, 73 per cent of government pharmaceutical benefits prescription expenditure is for concession cardholders, and therefore shifting costs to consumers can have deleterious equity effects, especially since an increased co-payment will have an impact on both 'essential' and 'discretionary' drugs (McManus *et al.* 1996).

Expenditure on pharmaceuticals has been growing faster than the economy as a whole in recent years. Since the late 1970s, pharmaceutical expenditure has grown from 0.6 per cent of GDP to 1.1 per cent in 2000–2001. Expenditure on the Pharmaceutical Benefits Scheme is the fastest-growing component of health expenditure, growing at 15–20 per cent per annum. If the current rates of growth continue, expenditure on the scheme will exceed that on public hospitals by 2007–2008 and on all hospitals by 2010–2011 (for the impact of different growth scenarios on PBS expenditure, see Walker *et al.* 1998).

The decision to list an item on the Pharmaceutical Benefits Scheme can lead to commitment of significant government expenditure and, since 1993, has involved a decision not only about whether the drug is an effective complement to existing items on the scheme, but also an assessment of whether the drug is cost-effective. The legislation to require cost effectiveness analysis was passed in 1987; draft guidelines on how listing submissions were to incorporate cost-effectiveness analysis were published in 1990, with definitive guidelines in 1992. These are updated regularly (see www.health.gov.au/pbs/general/pubs/guidelines).

The guidelines provide that a drug will be listed on the Pharmaceutical Benefits Scheme if:

- it is needed for the prevention or treatment of significant medical conditions not already covered, or inadequately covered, by drugs in the existing list and is of acceptable cost-effectiveness;

- it is more effective or less toxic (or both) than a drug already listed for the same indications, and is of acceptable cost-effectiveness; or
- it is at least as effective and safe as a drug already listed for the same indications and is of similar or better cost-effectiveness.

Under the cost-effectiveness arrangements, the pharmaceutical manufacturer needs to present cost-effectiveness data to the Pharmaceutical Benefits Advisory Committee (PBAC: Henry 1992; Harris 1994; Mitchell 1996; Hailey 1997; Hill et al. 1997; Salkeld et al. 1999). Australia was the first country to incorporate economic evaluation formally in decision-making processes about subsidizing drugs, and is still at the forefront of policy in this area (Dickson et al. 2003). However, the operation of PBAC and the economic evaluation policies of the Pharmaceutical Benefits Scheme have not been without controversy. Early in 2001, for example, in a controversial move, the government restructured the membership of PBAC to include a person with strong industry links. This initiative was believed to be in response to industry pressure to water down the emphasis on economic evaluation followed by the committee and was seen in the public debate as weakening PBAC (Goddard et al. 2001). These fears do not appear to have translated into reality and economic evaluation still seems to be a central component of the listing recommendations (Aroni et al. 2003). Government need not accept PBAC recommendations and there is also evidence to suggest that it might have been more generous in price negotiations than economic considerations may have warranted (Richardson 2003).

The purchasing arrangements for pharmaceuticals covered under the Pharmaceutical Benefits Scheme involve a government-agreed price (90 per cent of which is for the supplier, 10 per cent for the wholesaler). The government also undertakes post-marketing surveillance to ensure that the volumes of listed drugs are close to those predicted in the cost-effectiveness analyses and other submissions on which the pricing negotiations were based. This post-market surveillance does not always appear to be effective (Richardson 2003).

Historically, the government has been able to use its monopsonistic purchasing strength to achieve lower prices relative to those paid in international markets. The ability to do this appears to be weakening as other countries establish schemes similar to the Pharmaceutical Benefits Scheme and monitor international pricing negotiations (Löfgren 1998). However, Bessell et al. (1999) have documented an example where the market price rose when the product was deleted from the Pharmaceutical Benefits Scheme.

PBS pricing decisions have significant implications for profit that pharmaceutical manufacturers obtain from selling their products in Australia. The success of the scheme in restraining prices has attracted the ire of the US pharmaceutical manufacturing industry (Lokuge and Denniss 2003). International comparison of pricing is difficult, in part because of the existence of discounting arrangements in several countries. Prices in Australia are certainly substantially less than prices in the USA, but are similar to prices in other countries.

There are significant differences in price relativities for different types of drugs. The differences between new and innovative pharmaceuticals are much higher than for all pharmaceuticals, suggesting that the Australian purchasers (particularly those involved in setting prices under the Pharmaceutical Benefits Scheme) are not able to extract the same price discounts for newer drugs relative to older preparations.

Because listing under the Pharmaceutical Benefits Scheme provides a significant marketing boost (by reducing the effective price faced by consumers to the co-payment), government is in a strong position to negotiate over prices. However, where a pharmaceutical company has a new medication significantly superior to others, or which is unique, it can threaten to rely on consumers paying the full price for the drug rather than accept a lower price from government. In these circumstances, consumers are likely to place significant pressure on government to list the product.

POLICY CHALLENGES

Australia's hospital policy framework has been remarkably stable over the last quarter of a century, with systems for funding hospital care established and embedded. Significant changes have occurred in support for private health insurance, with ideologically driven changes introduced by the current Coalition government. Controversial changes in medical services funding are currently before Parliament.

These policy changes are in part the result of the three critical cleavages that shape Australian health policy: an emphasis on universalism versus selectivism; public versus private provision; and Commonwealth versus state responsibilities. One of these cleavages is primarily structural (Commonwealth versus state), one is about values and value conflict (universalism versus selectivism), and the third (public versus private) involves both value and structural issues.

Parts of the Australian health care system are based on universalist principles (e.g. all Australians are entitled to access public hospitals without charge, all are eligible for the private health insurance rebate), but a number have selectivist elements (for example, patient contribution levels for the Pharmaceutical Benefits Scheme are based on different income levels). Medicare was founded on universalist principles – that all Australians are entitled to both the public hospital and medical services elements of Medicare. However, the universalist nature of Medicare was brought into question in 2003 when the Commonwealth Liberal-National Party government, in response to the decline in bulk billing, responded with policies that were selectivist in nature. These policies provided incentives to general practitioners to bulk bill only pensioners and health care cardholders rather than all patients. This policy was presumably predicated on the view that bulk billing should be only for a targeted group.

The second cleavage is about public versus private provision. Although almost one-third of Australian health expenditure is from private sources, a much higher percentage of service delivery is by private business, including private practitioners. The dominance of private provision has both positive and negative aspects, the relevance of which can vary over time, different locations and types of services. A competitive private market is assumed to ensure that consumers have greater choice, the services will be more responsive to their needs and that less responsive services will be squeezed out of the market. The reality, of course, does not always accord with theoretical prescriptions. In rural areas, for example, private practitioners may be monopoly providers and may not be as responsive to consumers as market theory based on perfect competition would predict. Monopoly providers can charge higher prices, evidenced in the health sector by higher out-of-pocket costs for medical services in rural Australia.

In terms of hospital services, private providers will focus on niche markets where their ability to make a profit is maximized. Thus, the private sector will be responsible for more profitable services and/or clients who are expected to be relatively less expensive. A system where revenue or profit is the organizing principle and basis for service provision decisions may lead to different priority choices, different access and a different mix of services than one planned or organized on the basis of need.

The Australian mix of a public and private system also means that planning for services is quite complex. Although planning for public services is typically about maximizing 'social welfare' or responding to need subject to political constraints, private services are provided in response to market conditions and opportunities. The significance of private providers means that the principal planning mechanism in much of the health sector is via financial incentives. Financial incentives are necessarily crude and apply to all participants in the market and do not necessarily allow sophisticated and targeted responses to need.

Private provision axiomatically entails creation of property rights for private providers. Interest groups emerge to protect those property rights and associated income streams. Protection of property rights, income streams and growth potential does not necessarily lead to the best organization of health services. Market-based organization is designed to ensure services are responsive only to those able to participate in the market.

Private providers also organize against threats to their market share. The development of community health services in Australia in the mid-1970s, for example, was vigorously opposed by the organized medial profession representing the interests of private medical practitioners. The Australian Medical Association feared that the (public) community health services would threaten independent private medical practitioners' practice and acted both nationally and locally to stymie their development.

Private provision is often associated with an emphasis on selectivity rather than universalism as the underlying value or organizing principle for service provision. Market-based solutions typically require individuals to have significant income to purchase services and almost inevitably lead to differential access. An anomaly in terms of Australian provision is that private provision of hospital services is underwritten by public funding through the 30 per cent health insurance rebate. Here, public funds are used to promote and ensure better access for those with health insurance.

The third major cleavage is a structural one: the different responsibilities exercised by Commonwealth and state governments. The Commonwealth government has principal responsibility in areas such as medical services, pharmaceuticals and aged care, while states have management and policy responsibility for hospital services and public health. This inevitably means there are interface problems between related services. Over the last few years, for example, there has been vociferous political debate where state health ministers have argued that the Commonwealth is under-providing aged care services (particularly residential aged care) and that, as a result, hospital beds are occupied inappropriately by long-staying elderly patients who would be better placed in residential aged care. This 'bed blockage', in turn, is seen as denying access to beds for acute patients (also likely to be elderly). Interface problems also occur between primary medical care and hospitals and again in recent years has led to criticisms that inadequacies of the primary medical care system (in particular the decline in bulk billing) have increased demand on hospital emergency services. Accusations abound about cost-shifting (where state or Commonwealth develop services to shift costs from one level of government to the other) and blame-shifting (where the state or Commonwealth blames political problems in their policies on the other).

The disjointed responsibility in primary care (Commonwealth funding of general medical practitioners, state responsibility for publicly provided primary care and a large private sector under-pinned by private health insurance regulated by the Commonwealth) has led to occasional calls for more integrated funding, particularly through the creation of area-based purchasing (Peacock and Segal 2000; Richardson 2001; Segal *et al.* 2002). The benefits of such moves are generally only postulated in theoretical terms and have not received widespread political support. Policy scepticism in this area may be because of the results of the Coordinated Care Trials, a large-scale policy innovation of the mid-1990s which tested the benefits of funds pooling and integrated care management. The Trial evaluation found that adding a 'care coordinator' was valued by patients, but did not lead to measurable improvements in health or well-being compared with control groups (Commonwealth Department of Health and Aged Care 2001). Furthermore, savings from improved coordination could not fund the care coordinator's role.

In reality, the problems of Commonwealth and state relations mainly relate to opportunity costs: that services could be improved if there were better continuity of care between services that are the principal responsibility of the alternate level of government. These opportunity costs are only in part a product of government structures. They are also driven by lack of imagination and confidence at both levels of government. Their lack of synoptic abilities (Lindblom 1965) means they tend to neglect developing policy responses and organizational arrangements that are outside their normal purview and lie within the policy responsibility of the other level of government. For example, it may be economically efficient for a state government to subsidize private general practitioners to provide preventive services, but such a policy may not be considered because private medical practice is seen as a Commonwealth government responsibility. However, strategies based on private general practice tend not to be among the policy options considered by state governments.

CONCLUSIONS

The three cleavages inhibit development of strategies for improving the efficiency, equity and quality of health care services in Australia. The public–private division is likely to remain a fundamental feature of health care services. However, it is possible to contemplate the development of improved financial incentives to strengthen equity, and ensure that the private system is used for public good by enhancing its ability to respond to consumers and to ensure that the services provided by the private sector are appropriately designed to fit within a broader range of needs.

In terms of the value conflict between universalism and selectivism, this may emerge from time to time as different political parties gain ascendancy. In broad general terms, the Labor Party is more likely to promote universalist policies and has a stronger policy commitment to the underlying universalist principles of Medicare than the Liberal-National Party. Even under a Liberal-National Party government, the strong reaction to its retreat from universalist policies suggests that the political costs of pursuing selectivism remain high.

With respect to Commonwealth–state division, cooperative action between different levels of government should always be possible, but relies on goodwill between the two levels of government. This cooperative action could facilitate a major reduction of policy impediments to improved services.

Despite these problem areas, it is important to recall that the Australian health system is one that is relatively efficient, relatively equitable and provides high-quality services. The improvements required, therefore, are more in the nature of marginal changes to improve the organizational arrangements and policy settings, rather than a need for a fundamental system redesign.

NOTES

1 More detailed analysis of the functioning of the Australian health care system in these and other areas can be found elsewhere (Duckett 2004). This chapter also draws on that publication.
2 Expenditure on medical services and pharmaceuticals includes in-hospital and community expenditure.
3 The Fraser government served from 1975 to 1983. For a review of health policy in this period, see Duckett (1984).
4 Although a medical practitioner who bulk bills generally only receives 85 per cent of the schedule fee, this discount was originally seen as providing compensation for reduced administrative costs and elimination of bad debts. The discount is now seen as too great (e.g. the advent of widespread use of credit cards has also acted to reduce cash collection costs and bad debts and in 2004 increased rebates were announced for some bulk billed services; see note 6).
5 Deeble (1999) provides a good review of trends in Medicare services and expenditure.
6 An additional rebate of A$5 is paid in metropolitan areas, A$7.50 additional in rural areas and Tasmania.
7 A separation is a discharge, death or transfer.
8 Typical same-day cases include simple elective procedures and investigations, such as endoscopies, chemotherapy and renal dialysis.

REFERENCES

Aroni, R., de Boer, R. and Harvey, K. (2003) The Viagra affair: evidence as the terrain for competing 'partners', in V. Lin and B. Gibson (eds) *Evidence-Based Health Policy*. South Melbourne, VIC: Oxford University Press.

Australian Bureau of Statistics (1994) *Australian Social Trends: Apparent Determinants of Private Health Insurance*. Catalogue No. 4102.0. Canberra, ACT: ABS.

Australian Bureau of Statistics (2002) *National Health Survey 2001: Summary of Results*. Catalogue No. 4364.0. Canberra, ACT: ABS.

Australian Bureau of Statistics (2003) *Australian Social Trends*. Catalogue No. 4102.0. Canberra, ACT: ABS.

Australian Government Department of Health and Ageing (2004) *Medicare Statistics: March Quarter 2004*, Canberra (available at: http://www.health.gov.au/ haf/medstats/index.htm; accessed 27 May 2004).

Australian Government Private Health Insurance Information Council (2004) Website (available at: http://www.phiac.gov.au/statistics/index.htm; accessed 27 May 2004).

Australian Institute of Health and Welfare (2003) *Health Expenditure Australia 2001–02*. Canberra, ACT: AIHW.

Bessell, T.L., Hiller, J.E. and Sansom, L.N. (1999) 'Pharmacist only' medicines, *Australian and New Zealand Journal of Public Health*, 23(6): 661–2.
Britt, H., Miller, G., Knox, S. *et al.* (2001) *General Practice Activity in Australia 2000–01*. Australian Institute of Health and Welfare General Practice Series No. 8. Catalogue No. GEP 8. Canberra, ACT: AIHW.
Burrows, C., Brown, K. and Gruskin, A. (1993) Who buys health insurance? A survey of two large organizations, *Australian Journal of Social Issues*, 28(2): 106–23.
Butler, J.R.G. (2002) Policy change and private health insurance: did the cheapest policy do the trick?, *Australian Health Review*, 25(6): 33–41.
Cameron, A.C. and McCallum, J. (1996) Private health insurance choice in health: the role of long-term utilization of health services, in *Economics and Health: 1995*. Sydney, NSW: School of Health Services Management, University of New South Wales.
Cameron, A.C. and Trivedi, P.K. (1991) The role of income and health risk in the choice of health insurance: evidence form Australia, *Journal of Public Economics*, 45: 1–28.
Cameron, A.C., Trivedi, P.K., Milne, F. and Piggott, J. (1988) Microeconometric model of the demand for health care and health insurance in Australia, *Review of Economic Studies*, 55: 85–106.
Catchlove, B.R. (2001) The why and the wherefore, *Medical Journal of Australia*, 175: 68–70.
Commonwealth Department of Health and Aged Care (1999) *National Medicines Policy*. Canberra, ACT: Production Unit, Parliamentary and Access Branch.
Commonwealth Department of Health and Aged Care (2001) *The Australian Coordinated Care Trials: Final Technical National Evaluation Report on the First Round of Trials*. Canverra, ACT: Commonwealth Department of Health and Aged Care.
Deeble, J. (1999) Medicare: Where have we been? Where are we going?, *Australian and New Zealand Journal of Public Health*, 23(6): 563–70.
Dickson, M., Hurst, J. and Jacobzone, S. (2003) *Survey of Pharmacoeconomic Assessment Activity in Eleven Countries*. OECD Health Working Papers No. 4. Paris, OECD.
Duckett, S.J. (1979) Chopping and changing Medibank part 1: implementation of a new policy, *Australian Journal of Social Issues*, 14: 230–43.
Duckett, S.J. (1980) Chopping and changing Medibank part 2: an interpretation of the policy making process, *Australian Journal of Social Issues*, 15: 79–91.
Duckett, S.J. (1984) Structural interests and Australian health policy, *Social Science and Medicine*, 18(11): 959–66.
Duckett, S.J. (1996) The new market in health care: prospects for managed care in Australia, *Australian Health Review*, 19(2): 7–21.
Duckett, S.J. (2003) Making a difference in health care, in S. Ryan and T. Bramston (eds) *The Hawke Government: A Critical Perspective*. North Melbourne, VIC: Pluto Press.

Duckett, S.J. (2004) *The Australian Health Care System*, 2nd edn. South Melbourne, VIC: Oxford University Press.
Duckett, S.J. and Jackson, T. (2000) The new health insurance rebate: an inefficient way of assisting public hospitals, *Medical Journal of Australia*, 172(9): 439–44.
Fitzgerald, P.D. (2001) The ethics of doctors and big business, *Medical Journal of Australia*, 175: 73–5.
Goddard, M., Henry, D. and Birkett, D.J. (2001) Securing the future of the Pharmaceutical Benefits Scheme, in G. Mooney and A. Plant (eds) *Daring to Dream: The Future of Australian Health Care*. Bentley, W.A: Black Swan Press.
Gosden, T., Forland, F., Kristiansen, I.S. et al. (2001) Impact of payment method on behaviour of primary care physicians: a systematic review, *Journal of Health Services Research and Policy*, 6(1): 44–5.
Gray, G. (1996) Reform and reaction in Australian health policy, *Journal of Health Politics, Policy and Law*, 21(3): 587–615.
Hailey, D. (1997) Australian economic evaluation and government decisions on pharmaceuticals, compared to assessment of other health technologies, *Social Science and Medicine*, 45(4): 563–81.
Hall, J., De Abreu Lourenco, R. and Viney, R. (1999) Carrots and sticks – the fall and fall of private health insurance in Australia, *Health Economics*, 8(8): 653–60.
Harris, A.H. (1994) Economic appraisal in the regulation of pharmaceuticals in Australia: its rationale and potential impact, *Australian Economic Review*, 2nd Quarter: 98–105.
Harvey, K. and Murray, M. (1995) Medicinal drug policy, in H. Gardner (ed.) *The Politics of Health: The Australian Experience*. Maryborough: Churchill Livingstone.
Hayes, L.J., Quine, S., Taylor, R. and Berry, G. (2002) Socio-economic mortality differentials in Sydney over a quarter of a century, 1970–94, *Australian and New Zealand Journal of Public Health*, 26(4): 311–17.
Henry, D. (1992) Economic analysis as an aid to subsidization decisions: the development of Australian guidelines for pharmaceuticals, *PharmacoEconomics*, 1(1): 54–67.
Hill, S., Henry, D., Pekarsky, B. and Mitchell, A. (1997) Economic evaluation of pharmaceuticals: what are reasonable standards for clinical evidence – the Australian experience, *British Journal of Clinical Pharmacology*, 44: 421–5.
Hopkins, S. and Kidd, M.P. (1996) The determinants of the demand for private health insurance under Medicare, *Applied Economics*, 28: 1623–32.
House, J.S. (2001) Understanding social factors and inequalities in health: 20th century progress and 21st century prospects, *Health and Social Behavior*, 43: 125–42.
Korda, R.J., Strazdins, L., Broom, D.H. and Lim, L.L.-Y. (2002) The health of the Australian workforce: 1998–2001, *Australian and New Zealand Journal of Public Health*, 26(4): 325–31.

Liaw, S.-T., Pearce, C.M., Chondros, P. *et al.* (2003) Doctors' perceptions and attitudes to prescribing within the Authority Prescribing System, *Medical Journal of Australia*, 178: 203–6.

Lindblom, C.E. (1965) *The Intelligence of Democracy: Decision Making through Mutual Adjustment*. New York: Free Press.

Löfgren, H. (1998) The Pharmaceuticals Benefit Scheme and the shifting paradigm of welfare policy, *Australian Health Review*, 21(2): 111–23.

Löfgren, H. (2002) *Generic Drugs: International Trends and Policy Developments in Australia*. Working Paper No. 10. Melbourne, VIC: Centre for Strategic Economic Studies, Victoria University of Technology.

Lokuge, K. and Denniss, R. (2003) *Trading in our Health System? The Impact of the Australia–US Free Trade Agreement on the Pharmaceutical Benefits Scheme*. Discussion Paper No. 55. Canberra, ACT: The Australia Institute, Australian National University.

Mathers, C.D. and Schofield, D.J. (1998) The health consequences of unemployment: the evidence, *Medical Journal of Australia*, 168: 178–82.

Mathews, J.D. (1997) Historical, social and biological understanding is needed to improve Aboriginal health, *Recent Advances in Mibrobiology*, 5: 257–84.

McClelland, A. and Scotton, R. (1998) Poverty and health, in R. Fincher and J. Nieuwenhuysen (eds) *Australian Poverty: Then and Now*. Melbourne, VIC: Melbourne University Press.

McManus, P., Donnelly, N., Henry, D. *et al.* (1996) Prescription drug utilization following patient co-payment changes in Australia, *Pharmacoepidemiology and Drug Safety*, 5: 385–92.

Mitchell, A. (1996) Update and evaluation of Australian guidelines: government perspective, *Medical Care*, 34(12): DS216–DS225.

Morrell, S.L., Taylor, R.J. and Kerr, C.B. (1998) Unemployment and young people's health, *Medical Journal of Australia*, 168: 236–40.

Peacock, S. and Segal, L. (2000) Capitation funding in Australia: imperatives and impediments, *Health Care Management Science*, 3: 77–88.

Productivity Commission (1999) *Inquiry Report*, No. 4 Canberra, ACT: Ausinfo.

Richardson, J. (2001) A GODS analysis of Medicare: goals, obstacles, deficiencies, solutions: or, in what form should we adopt managed care, in G. Mooney and A. Plant (eds) *Daring to Dream: The Future of Australian Health Care*. Bentley, WA: Black Swan Press.

Richardson, J. (2003) *Financing Health Care: Short Run Problems, Long Run Options*. CHPE Working Paper No. 138. Melbourne, VIC: Monash University Press.

Runciman, W.B., Webb, R.K., Helps, S.C. *et al.* (2000) A comparison of iatrogenic injury studies in Australia and the U.S.A. II: Reviewer behaviour and quality of care, *International Journal for Quality in Health Care*, 12(5): 379–88.

Salkeld, G., Mitchell, A. and Hill, S. (1999) Pharmaceuticals, in G. Mooney and R. Scotton (eds) *Economics and Australian Health Policy*. St Leonards: Allen & Unwin.

Schofield, D., Fischer, S. and Percival, R. (1997) *Behind the Decline: The Changing Composition of Private Health Insurance in Australia, 1983–95*. Discussion Paper No. 18. Canberra, ACT: National Centre for Social and Economic Modelling, University of Canberra.

Scotton, R.B. (1980) Health insurance: Medibank and after, in R.B. Scotton and H. Ferber (eds) *Public Expenditures and Social Policy in Australia*. Melbourne, VIC: Longman Cheshire.

Segal, L., Donato, R., Richardson, J. and Peacock, S. (2002) Strengths and limitations of competitive versus non-competitive models of integrated capitated fundholding, *Journal of Health Services Research and Policy*, 7(suppl. 1): S1:56–S1:64.

Sloan, C. (1995) *A History of the Pharmaceutical Benefits Scheme 1947–1992*. Canberra, ACT: Commonweath Department of Human Services and Health.

Smith, J. (2001) Tax expenditures and public health financing in Australia, *Economic and Labour Relations Review*, 12(2): 239–62.

Thomas, E.J., Studdert, D.M., Runciman, W.B. *et al.* (2000) A comparison of iatrogenic injury studies in Australia and the U.S.A. I: Context, methods, casemix, population, patient and hospital characteristic', *International Journal for Quality in Health Care*, 12(5): 371–8.

Vaithianathan, R. (2002) Will subsidising private health insurance help the public health system?, *The Economic Record*, 78(242): 277–83.

Walker, A. and Abello, A. (2000) *Changes in the Health Status of Low Income Groups in Australia, 1977–78 to 1995*. Discussion Paper No. 52. Canberra, ACT: National Centre for Social and Economic Modelling, University of Canberra.

Walker, A., Percival, R. and Harding, A. (1998) *The Impact of Demographic and Other Changes on Expenditure on Pharmaceutical Benefits in 2020 in Australia*. Discussion Paper No. 31. Canberra, ACT: National Centre for Social and Economic Modelling, University of Canberra.

White, K.N. (2000) The state, the market, and general practice: the Australian case, *International Journal of Health Services*, 30(2): 285–308.

Willcox, S. (1991) *A Health Risk? Use of Private Insurance*. Background Paper No. 4. Melbourne, VIC: National Health Strategy Unit.

Wilson, R.M., Runciman, W.B., Gibberd, R.W. *et al.* (1995) The Quality in Australian Health Care Study, *Medical Journal of Australia*, 163: 458–71.

6

JAPAN
Naoki Ikegami

Population 2003	127.2 million
Ethnic composition 2001	Japanese (98.9%), others (1.1%)
Capital city	Tokyo
Live births per woman 2003	1.38
Infant mortality rate per 1000 live births 2001	3.1
Life expectancy at birth 2001 (male/female)	78.1/84.9 years
Total health expenditure as a percentage of GDP 2001	8.0
Government health expenditure as a percentage of total health expenditure 2002	77.9
Total health expenditure per capita 2001 (US$ PPP)	2131
Practising physicians per 1000 population 2000	1.9
Health system	Ministry of Health, Labor and Welfare; national social insurance
Political system	Bicameral, cabinet-dominated parliamentary democracy

Source: National Institute of Population and Social Security Research (2003); OECD (2003)

INTRODUCTION

Japan has the second largest economy in the world and its population of 127 million is the ninth largest. Power has been concentrated at the central level but there has been a move to shift more power to the 47 prefectures and 3000 municipalities. Japan's macro health indices of life expectation at birth and infant mortality are the best in the world, while the percentage of the GDP devoted to health expenditure is 7.4 per cent, among the lowest in the major developed countries (OECD 2003). This impressive record may partly be explained by the fact that less demand is placed on the system in terms of crime, illicit drug use, numbers of traffic accidents and rates of HIV/AIDS compared with most developed countries (Campbell and Ikegami 1998). The comparative equality in income distribution may also be a contributing factor. The health care system deserves credit for achieving universal coverage without explicit rationing or waiting lists. An intriguing question, addressed in this chapter, is why the per capita numbers of renal dialysis, CAT (computer-aided tomography) and MRI (magnetic resonance imaging) equipment are the highest in the world with such relatively low levels of expenditure (OECD 2003).

This chapter focuses on three key aspects of the Japanese health system. The first is the country's history as a developmental state. When Japan started to import Western culture in the latter half of the nineteenth century, the state had to take a leading role. Social institutions such as hospitals, medical schools, social insurance, and so forth were transplanted to an alien soil that led to their unique development under the auspices, but not necessary the direct control, of the government. The second is the incremental nature of the system's development. There has been no major restructuring, despite the unitary parliamentary government structure, and the fact that the same political party has been in power almost continuously for half a century. The third is that of the fee schedule: the price set by the government for all services and drugs covered by health insurance. The fee schedule not only provides the link between the delivery and the financing systems but, through its fine-tuned manipulation, has also served as the most effective mechanism for containing costs and implementing government policy. These three aspects warrant taking a historical perspective to understand the system and evaluate how well the country will be able to meet the current challenges of a rapidly ageing society and stagnant economy.

HEALTH-CARE DELIVERY SYSTEM

The indigenous system

Japan had a well-established network of practitioners in Chinese medicine by the middle of the eighteenth century. Chinese medicine took a holistic approach, focusing on the need to restore the balance between the two opposing forces of *yin* and *yang* within the body. Medication was the main treatment, to the extent that Chinese medicine practitioners were often known as apothecaries. Payment was theoretically made only for the cost of the drugs, since it was regarded as morally unacceptable to accept fees for performing a humane service. Once when a practitioner sued a patient for non-payment, the municipal government of Edo (present-day Tokyo) came out with a verdict strongly condemning the plaintiff: the official view was that practitioners in medicine should not demand payment. However, the unstated quid pro quo was that patients were expected to pay according to their ability, and therefore munificently if they had the means. This norm served a useful purpose for the government: it was absolved of the responsibility of providing public assistance for medical care because the practitioner's duty to provide services and the patient's obligation to pay were not directly connected.

Medical practice was an exception to the rigidly divided society of that time because it was open to all classes and there was competition based on skill. Practitioners recognized a hierarchy among themselves, with those appointed as personal physicians to the feudal lord being ranked the highest. Despite the austere rule of not demanding payment from the patients, many practitioners were able to become quite wealthy. Indeed, it could be said that de-emphasizing money was part of their strategy to advance their position in society, because if it became explicit that they depended on the practice of medicine for their livelihood, they would be seen as having the same low rank as an artisan. It was as scholars possessing knowledge of medicine that they would rank highly, because such skills were esteemed in Confucian teaching as they fulfilled the sacrosanct filial duty of maintaining the health of one's parents.

Compared with Western nations, there was little development of guilds and professional identity among medical practitioners in Japan, and there was also very little provision of institutional care for the sick and indigent either by religious organizations or by government. The selfless practice of philanthropy was not a religious duty for the popular Buddhist and Shinto sects, nor was it a secular duty under the Confucian ideology favoured by the rulers, which emphasized practical ethics. Care of the ill, disabled and elderly was regarded as the responsibility of the family.

From the Meiji era to the end of the Second World War

With the inauguration of the Emperor Meiji in 1868, the government embarked on a policy of rapid Westernization. The early years, in particular, were characterized by wholesale and enthusiastic adoption of Western ideas and institutions. In health care, the first edicts issued in 1875 proclaimed that in the future only Western medicine would be given official recognition, and eventually all practitioners would have to sit for a national licensing examination. In retrospect, these edicts were very radical compared with the development of medical care in other non-Western countries. However, the Meiji leaders soon realized that they had to be more realistic. For one thing, little public money could be allocated to health care because the country was facing foreign aggression and internal discord: available resources had to be invested in defence and building the industrial infrastructure. Moreover, to grant licences only to physicians trained in Western medicine would mean that existing practitioners would be deprived of their livelihood, and most of the population would be denied service access.

Compromises were therefore inevitable. First, most available resources were put into one medical school, the University of Tokyo. The students were taught by German professors at the same high standard as in Germany. After completing their training, they were appointed as faculty at other schools. Later in the century, some of these schools were given university status, but others (including most of the private ones) remained at the vocational-school level. This pattern led to a difference in status among the physicians that in some ways reconstituted the hierarchical structure of the previous period. Indeed, many thought that university hospital professors behaved exactly like retainers of feudal lords, if not like the lords themselves. The second compromise occurred in 1882, the year before medical licences were to be granted only to those who had studied Western medicine. The government 'grandfathered-in' the existing practitioners of Chinese medicine – and even their sons – so they could continue to practise indefinitely.

Thus, the pattern of medical practice was transformed to the Western model, but the basic structure of the indigenous system was left intact. However, in one area – hospitals – it was necessary to adopt a completely new method of delivering care. As noted earlier, before the Meiji era there were virtually no public or religious institutions that could serve as nuclei for hospitals. This institution therefore developed quite differently than in the West. For example, hospitals had no association with care for the indigent (in fact, hospitals were the first to introduce regular fees because they were not constrained by the old rule of not demanding payment from patients). Another major difference was that since Japan had no tradition of community-based philanthropic activities, the task of establishing hospitals was taken on by the government on the one hand or by individual physicians on the other.

Hospitals in Japan were, therefore, built for several specific purposes. The first was for teaching and research. Since Western medicine could not be taught without studying patients, hospitals had to be built along with medical schools. The second was for the Army and Navy. The several rebellions and wars of the Meiji era created a pressing need for hospitals to treat combat-related diseases and injuries. The third type was established by the local governments for quarantine of communicable and venereal diseases. The fourth type, to become the most common, was built by private practitioners as extensions to their offices. In all four cases, the hospital was regarded as very much the doctor's workshop, and the physician as the director carried both clinical and administrative responsibilities. Hospitals, therefore, failed to develop an identity independent from physicians.

The independence of hospitals was further weakened by control over their medical staff by the professors of prestigious medical schools. Physicians were rotated at the whim of the professor within the closed network of the university clinical department and its affiliated hospitals. Although this arrangement developed partly as a result of the acute shortage of physicians – hospital founders had to beg the professors to send physicians – it fitted very well with the vertical structure of Japanese society. Hierarchical relations were formed among physicians within the close-knit, family-like network in each clinical department, presided over by the patriarchal figure of the professor. The strength of these vertical relationships made the development of professional organizations difficult. As a result, practice patterns tended to differ even within the same university if the physicians did not belong to the same clinical department. Another problem was that hospital physicians tended to be more concerned with research than with clinical medicine because their career advancement depended on the approval of the professor. Young physicians concentrated on obtaining the research degree of Doctor of Medical Science, which came to be regarded as a mark of professional competence by the public because there was no formal system of accreditation for specialists.

Despite the tensions inherent in this hierarchical system, most physicians were relatively satisfied. Attaining a senior position in a prestigious hospital was denied to anyone not a graduate of the elite medical schools, but to the vast majority of physicians, hospital appointments were only a temporary stage in their careers. Even the most elite graduates expected eventually to go into private practice, where a high income was almost guaranteed because of the continued shortage of trained physicians. Doctors no longer had access to hospital facilities once they became private practitioners, but those who wanted to continue to perform surgical operations or provide inpatient care could do so by building small hospitals next to their offices. The most successful of these continued to expand until they rivalled the large hospitals in the public sector. There was, thus, a continuum from physicians' offices to small hospitals to large hospitals. There was also not much distinction between specialists and general practitioners. Those who went into open practice continued to regard themselves as specialists, but in fact they mostly provided primary care.

The general public did not see much change in medical care. Most went on seeing private practitioners and were treated mainly with medication obtained directly from the physician. People seldom visited hospitals, and even when they were hospitalized (except in military hospitals), nursing care continued to be provided primarily by family members who would bring in bedding and prepare meals. Nurses were trained almost solely for the purpose of assisting physicians. However, it is important to observe that the government eventually did succeed in changing the basis of medical practice from Chinese to Western medicine. Unlike other Asian countries, independent schools or formal qualifications in Chinese medicine were not allowed to co-exist. Moreover, this transition was achieved with minimal cost and social disruption. It was only when the war with China in the 1930s brought pressure from the Army to improve the health conditions of conscripted men that the government changed its style of gradual adjustment. In 1942, virtually all major hospitals, except university hospitals, were nationalized and placed under the newly created Japan Medical Corporation (Nippon Iryodan). As well as managing existing regular hospitals and building new ones, the Corporation was given the responsibility of building more tuberculosis sanatoria (tuberculosis was the main cause of death at that time) and improving access to health care in rural areas.

Post-war development

Japan's defeat in the Second World War led to the disbanding of the Japan Medical Corporation, which in effect closed a road that might have led to a system like the British National Health Service. This decision came in part from the American Occupation authorities' traditional hostility towards socialized medicine itself, but in a more general sense as part of the overall policy of dismantling the top-down controls of the war years. The Americans had strong ideas about how the Japanese medical care system should be reconstructed as part of their efforts to 'democratize' the entire fabric of Japanese society. However, their efforts were at best only partially successful.

In medical education, the two-tiered system of university and vocational schools was abolished, but the hierarchical structure with the University of Tokyo at the top remained intact. The professors of clinical departments maintained their control within the encompassing networks of affiliated hospitals. Efforts to improve nursing conditions had only limited success, while those to introduce professional hospital administrators failed so that clinical doctors continued to be directors. In 1948, as the first step towards the closing down of sub-standard small hospitals, inpatient facilities were divided into 'hospitals', with at least 20 licensed beds, and 'clinics with beds' or physicians' offices having less than 20 beds. The length of stay was limited to 48 hours in the latter, but after pressure from the Japan Medical Association this exclusion was made meaningless by adding the clause, 'unless unavoidable for medical reasons'. A drive to prohibit doctors from dispensing was also thwarted.

Thus, the structure of the delivery system remained essentially unchanged. Despite the huge expansion of hospitals in the post-war period, their role as actors in the health policy arena has continued to be marginal, as that of specialist organizations. The power of private-practice physicians increased under the charismatic leadership of Taro Takemi, who served as the President of the Japan Medical Association from 1958 to 1982. Even today, the Association is the sole provider organization that the Ministry of Health, Labor and Welfare negotiates with in all aspects of health policy.[1] Advances in technology together with heightened expectations of patients did not lead to the death-knell of small hospitals and the 'clinics with beds' because of the influx of long-stay geriatric inpatients, which led to their survival as de facto nursing homes. As a result, nearly half of all hospital inpatients in Japan are now 65 or older, and one-third of these have been hospitalized for over a year. Of the 6 per cent of the population 65 and over institutionalized, 4 per cent are in hospitals.

The present system

Virtually all physicians' offices are solo practices, professing some specialty but essentially providing primary care. About a third of these practices have up to 19 beds for inpatient care. The majority of hospitals are owned and operated by individual physicians, and nearly all started as expansions of clinics. The remainder are in the public sector or are owned by quasi-public organizations such as the Red Cross. However, since these hospitals are subsidized for their capital costs, they tend to provide most high-tech care. Yet, they also maintain large outpatient departments and most of their patients come without referrals as there is no gatekeeping in the system. This unrestricted access to even tertiary hospitals means that there are no waiting lists for outpatient consultations. Although there are complaints about the long waiting time in hospitals, patients are seen on the same day. The delivery system is still weighted towards outpatient care, so that Japan has one of the highest rates of physician visits and the one of the lowest rates of hospital admissions among advanced industrialized countries (OECD 2003). Waiting lists for inpatient care are limited to a few prestigious hospitals, and patients who cannot wait are referred to their affiliated hospitals. Public attention is presently focused on the quality rather than the quantity or rationing of care. In particular, medical errors have caught the attention of the media and forced hospitals to be more open with patients. Partly due to the lack of formal mechanisms for investigating medical errors, hospitals must report serious cases to the police as abnormal deaths. The number of such reports from hospitals has increased from 12 in 1997 to 117 in 2002.[2] Physicians have come to realize that prior reporting of serious errors would be their best policy to prevent future litigations. The number prosecuted has declined from 59 in 2000 to 16 in 2002 (Nikkei 2003).

National hospitals are now required to report serious medical errors to the regional offices, while all university main hospitals must offer consultation services to patients on medical errors. In addition, the Ministry has come up with a plan to establish agencies for this purpose in each prefecture. On the other hand, there has not been much progress in meeting the broader need for more peer evaluation. Since most hospital doctors are appointed by the university clinical department chairs, certification as specialists and the formal process of training have lagged. Although two-thirds of doctors are now certified as specialists, half of them have been 'grandfathered in' based on their experience. A hospital accrediting organization was created in 1997 with funds provided by the Ministry of Health, the Japan Medical Association and other provider organizations. About 10 per cent of all hospitals are now accredited and the survey results have become available on the web (see www.jcqhc.or.jp).

Frustration about the lack of accountability has led to two movements. One is to allow investor-owned hospitals to enter the market, which has been pushed by economists and business leaders in the Regulation Reform Council. They have not met with much success and the door has only been opened to high-tech services provided outside of public health insurance. The other is to transfer national and local government hospitals into public corporations. Because of the strong resistance by the community and labour unions, changes have remained largely cosmetic.

HEALTH-CARE FINANCING SYSTEM

Development of social insurance

Health insurance in Japan began with coverage of government (including military) personnel and employees in a few paternalistic private companies from the late nineteenth century. The Factory Law of 1911 established a compulsory Workman's Compensation system. Then, in 1922, the Health Insurance Act was legislated (implementation was delayed until 1926 because of the Tokyo earthquake). This initially covered only blue-collar workers, representing 3 per cent of the population. The motives lay in pre-empting labour unrest and improving industrial productivity. An unusual feature was that blue-collar workers in small firms were covered at the same time as large-firm employees. The reason was not political demand, but probably administrative convenience because small-firm employees were also covered by the same worker's compensation system. In any case, since small firms did not have the management capability or large enough pools to manage their own systems, the government had to provide health insurance for them directly. This role of the government as one among a variety of providers of health insurance, rather than just as a coordinator of direct providers on the one hand or as the sole provider on the other, is the most distinctive element of the Japanese health insurance system even today. It was more an accidental result of the situation of the time than a deliberate strategy, but in the post-war period it led to the Ministry of Health and Welfare taking the lead among insurers (for example, in bargaining with providers), rather than the associations of large firms or of local government carriers.

As Figure 6.1 shows, the Japanese population covered by these employment-based systems increased rapidly as the Japanese economy became organized for war. Employee health insurance coverage was extended to white-collar employees, and to dependents, in 1941. However, the far larger number of farmers presented more difficult problems. They had no employers to contribute, and indeed no wages from which to deduct their own contributions. Grass-roots medical cooperatives had been founded in a growing number of villages in the 1920s and 1930s, and the national government in 1938 officially supported (and subsidized) rural health care with passage of the Citizens' Health Insurance Act (Higuchi 1974).[3]

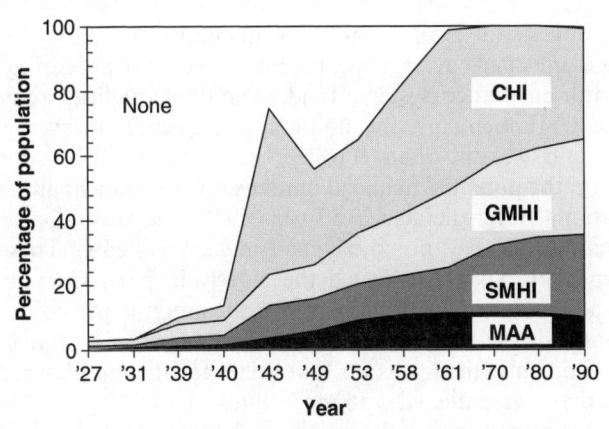

Figure 6.1 Growth in the percentage of population covered by health insurance in Japan. CHI = citizen's health insurance, GMHI = government-managed health insurance, SMHI = society-managed health insurance, MAA = Mutual Aid Association. From Campbell and Ikegami (1998).

Again, the motive for the new health insurance system was hardly compassion. The proximate reason was that the military had become concerned about the physical condition of recruits and, by extension, of potential mothers of recruits. The number of localities participating in Citizens' Health Insurance (CHI) grew slowly until the war with China intensified, when the system was expanded dramatically by the government. By 1943, more than 70 per cent of the Japanese population was covered by some form of mandated health insurance. However, financial problems towards the end of the war, and in the immediate post-war period, caused many localities to drop out and the covered population fell to under 60 per cent by 1948.

Achieving universal coverage and equity

As the economy recovered, more and more localities re-established CHI programmes. Together with growth in employment-related health insurance, the expansion of these community-level programmes – spurred by increasing government subsidies – led to nearly 90 per cent coverage of the population by the late 1950s. This meant covering the remainder would not be too radical a jump, while at the same time political pressures for universal coverage had built up. The socialist and conservative parties had been unified in 1955, and the two new parties both vied for votes in the subsequent elections by calling for 'health insurance for all'. The necessary legislation was passed in 1958 for full implementation by 1961. However, although universal coverage was the biggest step towards an egalitarian health insurance system, fundamental inequalities remained. Because CHI members, the non-employed, were on average less healthy and wealthy than enrollees in employment-based health insurance, the potential financial burdens on government at the local and national level dictated a 50 per cent co-payment for services (while employees had no co-payment in their systems). These high out-of-pocket expenses affected the elderly in particular, most of whom at that time were receiving no meaningful pensions at all. Statistics indicate that the use of medical facilities by old people, inpatient or outpatient, was far lower than for the middle-aged even though they were afflicted with more illness.

This inequality was substantially redressed in the early 1970s, which, not by coincidence, was another period of intense political party competition. In the period conventionally called the 'dawn of the welfare era', the largest co-payments were reduced to 30 per cent, and the 'catastrophic' cap on out-of-pocket costs was introduced on the same basis for all health insurance systems. Most dramatically, in 1972, a new programme of 'free' medical care for the elderly – coverage from general revenues of the entire co-payment for most people aged 70 and over (plus the bedridden from age 65) – was established by the national government.

These early 1970s reforms marked the high point of the first form of cross-subsidization, in which the general population paid various proportions of the health care costs of needier people by means of direct payments from tax revenues. These egalitarian reforms had their intended effect. The less well off in general, and older people in particular, began going to the doctor much more often. Not so intended was the development that a sizeable number of the elderly also moved into hospitals, since they now could get custodial long-term care at virtually no cost to themselves or their families. The cost of the government subsidy for old-age medical care accordingly rose sharply, more than doubling in the second half of the 1970s to reach nearly one trillion yen or nearly 10 per cent of total health spending by 1980. Giving 'free' medical care to the elderly became the most visible symbol for conservatives of public spending going out of control. It was inevitable, then, that health care in general and the programme for the elderly in particular would become targets of the 'administrative reform' austerity campaign that got underway in the early 1980s. This resulted in the Health Care for the Elderly Law (passed in 1982 and implemented in 1983), which led to health plans with less than the national average of elderly contributing more to the national pool to pay for their medical care, and the introduction of a token co-payment for the elderly.

Although the immediate financial problem was solved for the time being, the 1982 Act left untouched the issue of whether custodial care should be financed by health insurance. The underlying public resentment of the coverage of such services was one of the driving forces for the implementation of the public long-term care insurance in 2000. The details of the new social insurance programme are beyond the scope of this chapter (see Campbell and Ikegami 2000), but suffice it to say that long-term care, which had been provided by both the health and social services, was unified. In community care, the visiting nurse service and home-helpers came to be paid out of one budget at the municipal level with the amount of benefit set according to the individual's eligibility level. However, in institutional care, the transfer of hospital long-term care beds to the new insurance was incomplete so that a significant proportion continued to be paid by health insurance.

The present system

Virtually all residents in Japan are compulsorily covered either by the health plan provided by their employer or by the municipality where they reside if they are self-employed or pensioners. Dependents are covered by the plan of the household head. These plans can be grouped into three tiers, each enrolling about a third of the population, according to the extent to which they rely on subsidies. The first tier consists of plans established by the public sector, the Mutual Aid Association and by large companies, society managed health insurances. The second tier is a single plan managed by the Ministry of Health, Labor and Welfare, the government managed health insurance, for those employed in small to medium-sized companies. The third tier consists of plans established by municipalities, the citizen's health insurance, for those who are self-employed and pensioners. Despite major differences in their risk pool and revenue structure, the benefits are essentially the same, irrespective of the tier, and all have free access to virtually all medical facilities. Japan's remarkably egalitarian system is a result of the following mechanisms. The first is having no choice of plans and making the premium rate a fixed ratio of income to all those enrolled in the same plan. Given the still primitive state of risk-adjusting, this is an effective means to prevent adverse selection and cream-skimming. The second is the subsidies provided by the national government to plans in tiers two and three, which insure people with comparatively low incomes. The third is the central pooling fund to finance the care for the elderly towards which all plans must contribute the sum that they would have paid in benefits if their elderly enrolment was at the national average.[4] For example, a plan having an elderly enrolment of 2 per cent with expenditures amounting to US$30 million must contribute US$210 million because the national average is 14 per cent, which is seven times the plan's ratio.

However, the financing system has been under strain from two sources. The first is the ageing of the population and consequent increases in the contribution rate to the pooling fund.[5] Contribution rates have risen so that they compose nearly 40 per cent of the expenditures in 2001 (Iryou Hoken Seido Kenkyukai 2003) and are the main reason why premium rates have had to be increased. The second source is the stagnant economy. Employees laid-off move out of the first and second tier into the third tier. Since the national government must subsidize half the health expenditures of the third tier, increases in those covered by this tier lead to increases in subsidies that must be appropriated from taxes.[6] Furthermore, due to a decline in income, the ratio of households insured in the third tier who are either waived from paying premiums or are refusing to pay premiums increased to 45 per cent in 2002. The resulting decrease in premium revenue has forced many municipalities to increase subsidies from their own tax revenue to fill the deficit.

The combination of the ageing society and the stagnation in the economy forced the government, in July 2002, to legislate stop-gap austerity measures. The premium rate in the government managed health insurance was increased from 7.2 to 8.2 per cent,[7] and the personal co-payment rate for employees, which had been increased from 10 to 20 per cent in 1998, was further increased from 20 to 30 per cent. Meanwhile, that for the elderly was increased from a flat sum to a fixed rate of 10 per cent (20 per cent for those with high income),[8] and prices in the fee schedule were lowered (see next section). However, these measures do not address the fundamental issue of rising premiums due to increased contributions to the pooling fund for the elderly, or the need for more subsidies from taxes to plans in the third tier, which are both due to differences in the age and income of those who are enrolled. Another aspect that has drawn insufficient attention is the fact that many plans have become too small for risk pool purposes. As companies have downsized, nearly half of the 1600 society managed health insurances (large corporations) now have members of less than 3000 (excluding dependents, thus the number enrolled would be about double). Of the 3000 municipality-based citizen's health insurance plans, the percentage with less than 3000 insured has increased from 10 per cent in 1965 to 36 per cent in 2000 as their inhabitants have migrated to the large cities (Iryou Hoken Seido Kenkyukai 2003). The obvious solution would be for them to merge, and the Ministry of Health, Labor and Welfare proposed the prefecture as the unit for doing so, but since no two plans have the same age and income structure, this would lead to an increase in the premium rate for one of the two parties. Thus, little progress has so far been made.

Current reform plans

To address these structural issues, in December 2002 the Ministry of Health, Labor and Welfare made two reform proposals. One called for cross-subsidization among all health plans so that the age and income differences of those enrolled could be adjusted, and for the eventual merging of all plans into a single tiered financing system on a prefectural basis. The other proposal called for the creation of an independent health plan for all people over 75 towards which they would be expected to pay higher premiums. The reason why the latter was also proposed was because the strain coming from financing medical care for elders has been the main focus of public grievances as contributions to the pooling fund have increased (which are more visible than the subsidies financed through taxes in tiers two and three). There was also opposition towards cross-subsidization between plans for the employed (in the first and second tiers) and the self-employed (in the third tier) because the latter tend to under-report their income. Thus, those employed would pay a disproportionate share of expenditure as premiums are based on declared income.

The proposal to create an independent plan for the elderly has three major problems. The first is how to finance it. If it relies on contributions from other plans, then there will be little real change from the present system. If it is to be financed entirely by taxes, then it would lead to tax increases, which would be impractical, given the current economic climate. Levying more from elders would also be impractical because the reason why about one-fifth of the elderly are currently not paying premiums is due to their low incomes that qualify them as dependents of their children. Consequently, any increases in the threshold would yield only very marginal gains in revenue. Second, both the prefectural and municipal governments have emphatically opposed becoming responsible for such a plan, as it is very likely to run a deficit. Third, there is risk of under-financed, sub-standard care for the elderly if a separate plan were to be created.

However, the government and ruling coalition parties did not give much consideration to these caveats. The cabinet approved a compromise reform plan in March 2003, which called for creation of an independent insurance plan for those over 75, but also for cross-subsidization among plans for the costs of those in the 65–74 age range. Cross-subsidization was limited to the latter because, as pensioners, their income would be transparent for the purposes of levying premiums. Since this compromise retains the independent plan for those 75 and over, it faces the same problems and is one reason why it would be difficult to legislate and implement.

Matching population needs with expenditures

The link between population needs and expenditures is not clear because employment-based insurance plans are organized at national level with premium rates uniform throughout the nation. Thus, those living in prefectures with low utilization of health care are in effect subsidizing the expenditures of those living in prefectures with high utilization. For the employed in the government managed health insurance, the prefecture with the highest per capita expenditure in 2000 was 1.4 times that of the lowest (Iryou Hoken Seido Kenkyukai 2003). Even in the case of the citizen's health insurance managed by municipalities, the national government subsidizes on average half their expenditures by taxes, so money is again transferred from the low to the high utilization areas. Some of the differences may be justified by the level of morbidity and mortality, but expenditure is strongly correlated to the availability of resources. If health insurance plans can be restructured on a prefectural basis, the disparity in premium rates, after adjusting for age and income of the enrolled, could focus attention on the need to achieve a better match of population needs with expenditures. The regional health plan, which is at present restricted to limiting the number of hospital beds, could be utilized to more rationally allocate capital investment.

The fact that a population health perspective has not been taken in allocating resource does not mean that prevention has been neglected. On the contrary, Japan has one of the most elaborate health-screening programmes in the world, at schools and workplaces (for those employed) and in the community (for those not employed).[9] The popularity of screening is due to the following. First, the successful eradication of tuberculosis after the Second World War engendered an optimistic view of the effectiveness of screening among both the general public and professionals. Second, once a national network of public health centres had been established for this purpose, new missions had to be found once tuberculosis ceased to be a major hazard. Third, preventive health is one of the few services where insurance plans are given a free hand in Japan. Those with ample funds, such as society managed health insurance societies that enrol those who are relatively young and with high incomes, offered elaborate screening programmes that had a demonstration effect on others. The effectiveness, let alone the cost-effectiveness of these programmes, has never been rigorously evaluated, while it is left to the individual to seek treatment should they be notified that they have any health problems.

THE UNIFYING FEE SCHEDULE

Basic structure of the fee schedule

The present fee schedule ultimately derives from the fee-for-service payment used by office-based physicians when the Health Insurance Act was implemented in 1926. The fees were set at a low level from the start, 20 per cent below customary charges of that period. Dispensing was the most important component, so much so that the basic unit was based on the fee for a day's dosage of an average drug. These aspects have been retained in its basic structure. That is, fees have been kept at a low level so that they are about a quarter of the amount in the USA using purchasing parity prices. Drugs are still a key component, though down from 39 per cent in 1980 to 20 per cent of all medical expenditures financed by social insurance. About 60 per cent of all prescriptions continue to be dispensed at physicians' offices or hospitals, not independent pharmacies. Although decreased, profits can still be derived from dispensing. Structurally, hospitals continue to be paid in exactly the same way as office-based physicians. No explicit mechanisms for reimbursing capital expenditures or administrative costs exist, so that they have to be financed from providing the listed services after their direct costs have been deducted. Doctors practising in hospitals receive fixed salaries, in a similar way to the staff employed by solo practitioners.

The fee schedule plays a key role in linking the delivery and financing systems, and has been the principal means for achieving cost containment. As Figure 6.2 shows, it acts as the single valve that controls the money flowing from all insurance plans to all providers, except for subsidies to public sector hospitals. If fees are increased, the valve is loosened and more money flows to the providers. The amount of money that can be billed directly to patients is also strictly restricted to the statutory co-payment rate: extra payment is confined to private room charges and new technology still under development.[10] The only other source of revenue is the direct subsidies from the national and local governments that go to public sector hospitals.

However, the fee schedule can only regulate price and not volume. Since payments are made on a fee-for-service basis, physicians and hospitals can increase volume to meet their target incomes. How has it been possible to restrain their revenue-maximizing behaviour? First, for most surgical operations and high-tech new procedures, the fees are set so low that providing these services would result in a net

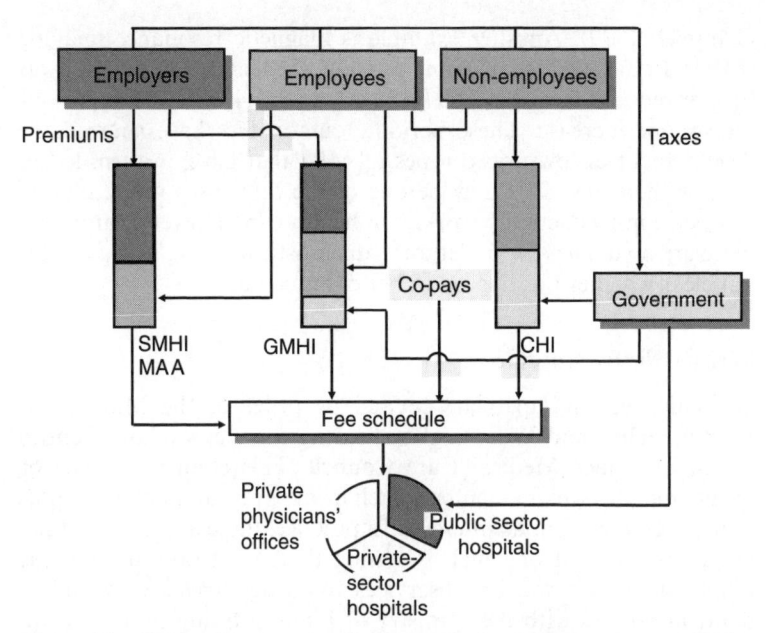

Figure 6.2 Flow of money in the Japanese health care system. CHI = citizen's health insurance, GMHI = government-managed health insurance, SMHI = society-managed health insurance, MAA = Mutual Aid Association. From Campbell and Ikegami (1998).

loss. However, these services are provided because physicians find them professionally rewarding and their salary is not linked to the profits they may bring to the hospital. Most of the surgical operations requiring general anaesthesia are provided in public sector hospitals, where financial constraints are weaker because costs are subsidized by the government.

Second, when the fee schedule is revised, rather than adjusting for inflation with an across-the-board conversion factor, as is common elsewhere, the items are individually altered. In particular, fees for procedures that show inappropriately large increases in volume will actually be reduced. For example, the fees for laboratory tests and diagnostic imaging have been continuously lowered, whether directly, through 'bundling' (per unit fees are lowered as the number of tests increases), or through restrictions on the number of times that can be billed within a calendar month. As a result, despite major advances in technology for diagnostic tests between 1979 and 1993, their average unit costs have remained the same (Ikegami and

Campbell 1999). Another example is magnetic resonance imaging (MRI). In the 2002 fee schedule revision, the fee for a head MRI was further reduced from ¥16,600 (US$151) to ¥11,400 (US$100), to offset volume increase. These periodic cuts in fees have spurred the development of low-priced types of MRI that have, in turn, led to volume increases. This may be one of the rare cases where market competition has actually worked in health care. However, although there are no queues for undergoing diagnostic imaging in Japan, it is not clear whether this has led to better outcomes.

Revising the fee schedule

Officially, fees in Japan are revised by order of the Minister of Health, Labor and Welfare after hearing the views of the Central Social Insurance Medical Care Council. This council consists of twenty members, eight members each from payers and providers plus four to represent public interests. In practice, there are three distinct processes, the first of which is setting the global rate: the volume weighted revision rate for all services and drugs. This is essentially a political process with the Ministry of Finance trying to hold down the rate while the Japan Medical Association lobbies to increase the rate. Because a quarter of health expenditure is financed from the national budget, the global rate has to be set to coincide with the next year's budget. In particular, the subsidies to the government managed health insurance provide a direct link because they are set at a fixed percentage of its expenditures, and because this plan is directly managed by the Ministry of Health, Labor and Welfare.

The second process is to set the global revision rate for drugs based on the current market-price survey. The government researches the current wholesale price of each medication through a survey of providers and on-site inspections at distributors. It normally finds these prices have been lowered since the previous survey because of competition to sell to providers. The fee schedule price then is lowered to a fixed percentage above the average 'market' price. This percentage has been progressively lowered from 15 per cent in 1990 to the present 2 per cent. Independent of this survey, prices of new drugs that had sales greater than the estimates made by the manufacturers are unilaterally lowered.

The third step is to appropriate the remainder of the global rate among the over 3000 service items listed in the fee schedule. This process is one of heated negotiations between the Ministry of Health, Labor and Welfare and the Japan Medical Association, each trying to pursue its policy goal. The impact of the revisions on each individual item on the global rate can be estimated from the national claims data survey that shows the volume of each. At the end of the day, the sum of the net effect of each item revision should equal the global rate. However, because the survey sample is limited, there is considerable discretion in revising each item within which the Ministry tries to decrease, and the Japan Medical Association tries to increase, the fee. However, the two parties agree on most policy goals such as discouraging hospitals, especially large ones, from providing outpatient services, by lowering the fees for initial and repeat consultations for hospitals so that they are *less* than those for physicians' offices.

Close attention is also paid to changes in the relative economic standings of providers: hospitals versus office-based physicians, inpatient versus outpatient care, internists versus surgeons, and so forth. If a technological or social trend has disproportionately affected one category for the better or worse, various fees can be adjusted to bring them back into balance. For example, the fee for paediatric consultations was raised when a low birth rate meant fewer young patients. This balancing principle inhibits rapid changes and minimizes conflict. It keeps important constituents from becoming too dissatisfied and, if dissatisfied, allows them to hope to do better in the subsequent fee-revision process 2 years later. Equally important, the incremental nature of the revision has allowed those who had a large share initially to better maintain their original share, to the advantage of the private practitioners who form the backbone of the Japan Medical Association.

Current issues in the fee schedule

For the first time in history, the global rate for services was decreased by 1.3 per cent in the 2002 revision. Formerly, the reduction in drug prices was sufficient to finance an increase in the service fees. Together with the reduction in the number of physician visits due to co-payment increases, this has led to an unprecedented real decrease in total expenditures in 2002.[11] A shrinking pie makes reconciliation among providers more difficult. In April 2002, delegates re-elected the President and Chair of the Japan Medical Association by a relatively narrow margin. The rank and file questioned the value of continuing to make political donations towards the ruling Liberal Democratic Party as its Diet (parliament) members, who had been endorsed by the Association, were unable to overturn the decision to reduce service fees. At the same time, the Ministry of Finance was still not satisfied by the cost containment achieved because the decline in expenditures was more than offset by the decline in premium revenue for the government managed health insurance.

These strains have increased the pressure to move away from the present basic principle of fee-for-service towards a more inclusive payment system. This has led to the introduction of the Diagnosis and Procedure Combination (DPC) in April 2003, and its full implementation in July of that year in the 80 university main hospitals and the two national centres, one for cancer and the other for cardiovascular diseases. The DPC differs from the United States' DRG (diagnosis-related group) in the following aspects:

- The 2552 DPC groups were designed by expert panels of physicians on clinical grounds. Of these, rates were set for 1860 that had enough cases and that had variations on claims amounts within reasonable range. Payment by DPC constitutes about 90 per cent of the total number of admissions, with the remaining patients continuing to be reimbursed on a fee-for-service basis.
- A per-diem rate is set for each DPC group instead of a per hospitalization rate.
- The per-diem rate differs by the length of stay set for each DPC, with lower rates as the length of stay becomes extended, and also by each hospital.[12]
- Surgical fees and procedures fees that are higher than ¥10,000 (US$90) are excluded and are reimbursed on a fee-for-service basis.

These measures were introduced to cushion the effect of introducing the new system. It was judged to be impractical to move to a uniform rate because of the wide variations even among these tertiary hospitals: for example, the average length of stay varied twofold (longest 29.1, shortest 15.8 days). The use of the DPC-based payment may, in due course, be expanded to other hospitals. However, the application will remain limited because hospitals must meet basic standards in their medical records; at present, only 10 per cent of all hospitals use ICD coding (Ministry of Health, Labor and Welfare 1999).

In contrast to the gradual expansion of inclusive payment in the acute sector, the long-term care sector may move more rapidly. About one-fifth of hospital beds are already excluded from fee-for-service payments, and are paid according to a flat per-diem rate for long-term care. It turned out that the flat rate acted as a disincentive to admit heavy care or sub-acute patients. One of the objectives of the new public long-term care insurance system, which was introduced in April, 2000, was to deal with this problem by transferring long-term care hospital beds from health to long-term care insurance, where fees vary by level of disability (Campbell and Ikegami 2000, 2003). However, relatively few beds have been transferred primarily because the municipalities, as long-term care insurers, did not want these costly patients unloaded into their system. Consequently, the proportion of long-term care patients paid by health insurance has declined only marginally. Moreover, such hospitals lack any incentive to admit heavy care or sub-acute patients. Since there is a general consensus for reform in this area, a case-mix based system is likely to be introduced within a few years that should have more impact on providers, as many hospitals provide long-term and sub-acute care in Japan.

CONCLUSIONS

The most striking feature of Japan's health care system is the extent to which the original structure has remained intact: it is dominated by private practitioners in solo practice, a workplace-based social insurance system and a fee-for-service payment regulated by a fee schedule. However, two-thirds of doctors are now employed in hospitals, over half of all health expenditures are financed by tax subsidies and cross-subsidization through the pooling fund for the elderly, and inclusive payments have been introduced to the payment system. On the one hand, it could be said that the system has adjusted flexibly to change, and Japan has been spared the disrupting restructurings driven mainly by the ideological commitment of politicians and untested theory of academics that have occurred periodically in other countries. On the other hand, the incremental adjustments have resulted in a complicated and fragmented system that appears to have no principles. In particular, if a visitor to Japan were to visit a hospital, the consultation would give an impression of being in a time-slip. It remains to be seen whether the demand for more accountability from the public and the recent revisions in the fee schedule will lead to substantial changes in provider behaviour. The policy of 'muddling through' appears to have had some success in the past. Whether the mixture as before will serve equally well in the future is hard to predict but is the most likely scenario.

NOTES

1 In 2001, the Ministry of Health and Welfare was merged with the Ministry of Labor to become the present Ministry of Health, Labor and Welfare.
2 The two medical errors that received the widest media coverage were an operation carried out by mistake on another patient, and the cover-up of errors occurring during a heart operation, both in university hospitals. The latter incident was disclosed by investigations by the patient's family and leaks from the hospital staff. Reports from these sources to the police totalled 9 in 1997 and 64 in 2002.
3 Kokumin Kenko Hoken Ho, the usual translation is 'National' Health Insurance. The programme was organized on a voluntary basis in each village. Once established, if two-thirds of the inhabitants became covered, it was made compulsory for all.
4 There are, strictly speaking, two pooling funds. One for those aged 65–74, who are retirees from plans in tiers one and two, and another for all those aged over 75. Contributions are made based on a similar principle so that employment-based plans are under their combined burden.
5 The percentage of the population 65 and over has increased from 7.1 per cent in 1970 to 18 per cent in 2001 and is projected to reach 29.6 per cent in 2030 (National Institute of Population and Social Security Research 2003).
6 The proportions of revenue were 53 per cent premiums, 32 per cent taxes (24 per cent national, 8 per cent local) and 15 per cent patient co-payment in 2000 (Iryou Hoken Seido Kenkyukai 2003).
7 The basis for levying premiums was changed from the standard monthly wage to all-income, including bonus payments. Thus, the new rate of 8.2 per cent of all-income would be the equivalent of 9.5 per cent of monthly wages under the former method of calculation.
8 These co-payment rates are applicable up to the catastrophic ceiling, which is about US$700 per month for those with average income, after which it becomes 1 per cent.
9 Screening programmes include blood tests for diabetes and liver diseases, and screening for lung, stomach, uterus and breast cancers. Japan also has public health programmes in health promotion and education, health visits by public health nurses and targeted programmes in areas such as nutrition.
10 There is very little private medicine outside of public insurance. Economists and business leaders who sit on the Economic and Fiscal Committee within the Cabinet Office have called for allowing balance billing but their views have been ignored.
11 Total expenditures decreased also in 2000 but this was the result of transferring services to the public long-term care insurance.
12 For each DPC, the average length of stay for all 82 hospitals is calculated. For hospital days within the shorter 25 percentile, the per-diem

rate is increased 15 per cent, then somewhat below the basic rate until the mean, followed by a further 15 per cent reduction until twice the standard deviation, after which it will revert to fee-for-service.

REFERENCES

Campbell, J.C. and Ikegami, N. (1998) *The Art of Balance in Health Policy – Maintaining Japan's Low-cost, Egalitarian System*. Cambridge: Cambridge University Press.

Campbell, J.C. and Ikegami, N. (2000) Long-term care insurance comes to Japan, *Health Affairs*, 19(1): 26–39.

Campbell, J.C. and Ikegami, N. (2003) Japan's radical reform of long-term care, *Social Policy and Administration*, 37(1): 21–34.

Higuchi, T. (1974) Medical care through social insurance in the Japanese rural sector, *International Labor Review*, 109(3): 251–74.

Ikegami, N. and Campbell, J.C. (1999) Health care reform in Japan: the virtues of muddling through, *Health Affairs*, 18(3): 56–75.

Iryou Hoken Seido Kenkyukai (Research Group on Health Insurance) (2003) *2003 Medemiru Iryouhoken Hakush* (Graphic White Paper on Health Insurance). Tokyo: Gyousei.

Ministry of Health, Labor and Welfare (1996, 1999) *Iryou Shisetsu Chousa* (Survey of Medical Facilities). Tokyo: Kousei Toukei Kyokai, 1998, 2001.

National Institute of Population and Social Security Research (2003) *Population Statistics of Japan, 2003*. Tokyo: NIPSSR.

Nikkei (Nihon Keizai Shimbun) (2003) Rapid increase in the reporting of 'medical errors', Nikkei, 21 May 21 (in Japanese).

OECD (2003) *OECD Health Data 2003*. Paris: Organization for Economic Cooperation and Development.

7

SINGAPORE
Michael Barr

Land area 2002	685.4 km^2
Population 2002	3.38 million
Ethnic composition 2002	Chinese 76.5%, Malays 13.8%, Indians 8.1%, others 1.6%
Live births per woman 2003	1.24
Infant mortality rate per 1000 live births 2002	2.9
Life expectancy at birth 2002 (male/female)	76.8/80.6 years
Total health expenditure as a percentage of GDP 2001	3.63%
Government health expenditure as a percentage of total health expenditure 2001	25%
Total health expenditure per capita 2001 (US$ PPP)	993
Practising physicians per 1000 population 2002	1.448
Health system	Complicated system of state and private funding and provision, along with state-managed medical savings accounts, state-managed catastrophic insurance and state-funded subsidy schemes

Political system	Single-chamber parliament dominated by the Prime Minister and Cabinet; ruled by the People's Action Party since 1959. Tightly controlled dominant-party system.

Sources: Ministry of Health (2004a), Ministry of Manpower (2004)

INTRODUCTION

Singapore is home to four million people, of whom over three million are citizens of the republic. This small island-state hosts a multiracial population that enjoys a First World standard of living including a world-class medical system. When Singapore achieved self-government in 1959, it inherited from the British an expanding but inadequate public health service (Tan 1991) in which hospitals and government health clinics were free or charged nominal fees, and private doctors and clinics operated independently of the government. The People's Action Party government left the colonial inheritance substantially in place until the mid-1980s, concentrating on extending the delivery of services and using the public health system as a tool to reduce the birth rate. Then, in 1984, the government implemented two revolutionary reforms based upon corporatization of hospitals and the introduction of medical savings accounts. These two initiatives have transformed the face of the Singapore health system, making it something of a celebrity among its peers.

This chapter looks at the history of Singapore's health policy, focusing in particular on the period since 1984. It also places the present arrangements in the broader context of national health and fitness programmes.

HISTORY AND POLITICS

Poised on the southern tip of the Malayan peninsula, Singapore's modern history began with the arrival of the British in 1819, though before that it was already an integral part of the Johore-Riau Sultanate as a base for pirates and traders. Since the middle of the nineteenth century, the population has been predominantly ethnic Chinese, with substantial minorities of Malays and Indians. Since independence in 1965, the young nation has moved from being mixed rural–urban, to completely urban and mostly working class (1970s), to the current state of being completely urban and mostly middle class. Despite this trend of upward mobility, poverty still exists and has been growing in recent years, with perhaps 10 per cent of the population living in grinding poverty and another 20–30 per cent struggling to keep up with Singapore's high cost of living.[1]

Although Singapore holds clean elections every 5 years for a single-chamber parliament, there is no serious pretence that opposition parties are given a fair chance to compete with the ruling People's Action Party. The government takes the cultivation of the electorate very seriously, but anyone who poses a serious challenge to the government's rule or its ideology is cut down using one or more of a wide choice of tools at the government's disposal.

HEALTH CARE: 1959–84

The story of Singapore's public health system up to 1984 is basically a simple one of the expansion and improvement of services, and the concurrent improvement of the population's health. This was a direct consequence of the island moving from reliance upon the goodwill of the British to independent rule by an energetic nationalist leadership. The island achieved self-government in 1959 and independence in 1965.[2] By 1974, there were 14 hospitals (up from 9 in 1960) and 26 outpatient dispensaries (up from 13 in 1959), while maternal and child health clinics increased from 49 in 1959 to 64 in 1965. The doctor–patient ratio improved dramatically from 1 : 2573 in 1960 to 1 : 972 in 1985 (Lim 1989).

Yet, despite these systematic improvements, the expansion of hospitals did not keep up with the population increase and the ratio of hospital beds per person worsened from 1 : 229 in 1960 to 1 : 259 in 1985 (Lim 1989). The demographic pressure of a high birth rate – which in 1965 was being fuelled by a crude birth rate of 30 per 1000 population (Saw Swee-Hock 1991) – was adversely affecting fields such as education and housing, as well as health care.[3] This pressure drove the Singapore government to use the expanding health system and other mechanisms to reduce the birth rate through the promotion of contraception, sterilization and abortion, the latter two of which were legalized in 1969.[4] Health considerations of individual mothers and children became secondary in this quest, which was pursued relentlessly by the official Family Planning and Population

Board. No stone was left unturned in the pursuit of a 'Stop at Two' campaign, including the manipulation of confinement charges to make a third birth in a hospital prohibitively expensive, and financial and even workplace incentives to encourage sterilization after two children (Saw Swee-Hock 1991). Combined with the usual social effects of educating the female population and improving the standard (and cost) of living, the programme was wildly successful. In fact, it was so successful that Singapore now faces the prospect of a greying population.

REFORMS OF 1984

By the early 1980s, the health system was already a point of pride for the government, which was evidenced by the then Health Minister Goh Chok Tong's declaration that 'We have a hospital system which we can be proud of. It stands up to comparison with the best in the world' (Goh Chok Tong 1982a). Yet, in 1982, the government foreshadowed a wholesale health revolution that was implemented in one motion two years later. The reforms were focused primarily on the hospital sector, and were designed to increase industrial efficiency and curb increasing costs by forcing fiscal responsibility onto stakeholders: onto hospitals by devolving financial responsibility onto their boards rather than the Ministry of Health, and onto patients by insisting on substantial co-payments (fees) from newly created medical savings accounts called Medisave.

According to the Ministry of Health (2004a), the financing philosophy of the resultant health care delivery system is based on: 'individual responsibility, coupled with Government subsidies to keep basic health care affordable. Patients are expected to pay part of the cost of medical services which they use, and pay more when they demand a higher level of services. The principle of co-payment applies even to the most heavily subsidised wards to avoid the pitfalls of providing "free" medical services'.

The 'Singapore system' is a continually evolving effort to reconcile the Singapore government's aversion to welfare with the reality that, for both economic and political reasons, it must ensure the provision of health services to the whole population, including low-income earners and the poor. In fact, the Singapore system developed as an explicit reaction to the perceived failures of 'social and health welfare' in Europe and the United States – a perception premised more on ideological preconceptions than on empirical data. In November

1981, on the eve of the move to introduce medical savings accounts, Prime Minister Lee Kuan Yew (1981) told a meeting of government MPs: 'Subsidies on consumption are wrong and ruinous ... for however wealthy a nation, it cannot carry health, unemployment and pension benefits without massive taxation and overloading the system, reducing the incentives to work and to save and care for one's family – when all can look to the state for welfare. ... Social and health welfare are like opium or heroin. People get addicted, and withdrawal of welfare benefits is very painful' (p. 8).

It is of some importance to realize that Medisave was not a 'progressive' attempt to ameliorate the effects of a *laissez-faire* health system, but a bold attempt to introduce market forces into government-funded health care. Under the previous system, hospital care was free and government clinics were subsidized directly by the government. Furthermore, there was no immediate funding problem with the old system. Although per capita costs in simple dollar terms had been increasing by 11 per cent per annum (Hsiao 1995), health costs as a proportion of GDP had been falling steadily since 1960 (Toh Mun Heng and Low 1991). Even the government's share of overall health costs had dropped slightly by the early 1980s, being 68 per cent in 1980, down from 70.1 per cent in 1970 (Blank and Burau 2004). This reading suggests that the government's introduction of Medisave and hospital fees, together with the use of the rhetoric of self-help and personal responsibility, was an attempt to both meet and restrict rising middle-class expectations by replacing government regulation with the archetypal middle-class mechanisms of financial constraint and self-regulation. If it worked, then managed self-regulation would provide a sustainable basis for curtailing health costs into the long term.

HOSPITALS

The most expensive part of any modern health care system is always hospitals, so it should not be surprising that the core of the 1984 reforms is found in this sector. The reforms were foreshadowed as early as the May 1981 announcement that the government intended to reduce 'subsidies' to hospitals and polyclinics.[5] This initiative was followed by overt government efforts to encourage the establishment of private hospitals[6] and across-the-board increases in hospital fees.[7] The expansion of expensive private hospitals at the expense of subsidized public hospital wards seems to have been an attempt to take advantage of the perception that Singaporeans had turned a socio-economic corner, and had become a bourgeois-cum-wealthy society; though the advent of parallel 'privatization' moves in the school sector in the pursuit of 'excellence' in the late 1980s suggests that the 'privatization' of health was merely one aspect of a much broader ideological push that wilfully saw generic benefits in the private sphere.

Regardless of motivation, these moves reached their logical conclusion when the government announced, in May 1984, that government hospitals would move towards privatization, not in the sense that ownership would change, but they would be run as private enterprises: collecting fees for services, relying less on government 'subsidies', competing for business and balancing their budgets. The trailblazer in this new enterprise was to be the National University Hospital (NUH), which was restructured in 1987, followed by the National Skin Centre in 1988 and Singapore General Hospital in 1989 (Toh Mun Heng and Low 1991). American consultants were duly engaged and the 'privatization'/'restructuring' programme continued into the 1990s, although it stopped a long way short of including all government hospitals. The National University Hospital provided the model for the 'restructured' hospitals. It was broken down into 50 cost centres that had to pay their own way. A seemingly benevolent interpretation of National University Hospital's experience was provided by Toh Mun Heng and Linda Low in 1991: 'The "privatization" exercise at NUH is said to have provided new and more personalised services, promoted staff motivation, deployed nurses more effectively, and enabled greater financial accountability, among other advantages. ... Doctors are made more circumspect when requesting certain tests which indirectly keeps the cost to patients under control, too' (p. 32). Yet even this rosy view was balanced by some fairly damning criticisms that questioned the value of the entire enterprise: 'On the other hand, charges in the NUH have increased ... Government subsidies have not remained at the same level over the years ... There is no concerted effort to contain costs with measures aimed at the supply side, such as physicians' earnings and mode of practice. The benefits of "privatization" of the NUH are difficult to prove or refute given the paucity of information and financial data [released by the government and NUH]' (Toh Mun Heng and Low 1991: 32). One could add that, in terms of public accountability, nothing much has changed since this assessment and there is still no reliable basis for judging the strengths and weaknesses of the overall 'privatization' programme.

An integral part of the package of hospital reform was the deliberate increase of differentiation within the hospital sector. Not only was there to be a fundamental distinction between luxurious private hospitals for the wealthy (of Asia, not just Singapore) and government hospitals, but highly expensive tertiary care and specialized clinical facilities were concentrated in a small number of major hospitals (originally just the National University Hospital and Singapore General Hospital). Meanwhile, most hospitals were designated as 'community hospitals', offering only primary and secondary care and a limited range of specialist services, distributed sensibly among the community hospitals. Over the years, gaps in the system were sometimes filled by specialist 'centres' and 'institutes' (such as the National Cancer Centre, founded at the end of 2001) that are not hospitals *per se*, but together with established hospitals provide tertiary services in designated niches. Since 1999, coordination in the distribution of specialist services has reached a new level of sophistication with the creation of two public health care 'clusters', the National Healthcare Group and Singapore Health Services. Each of these comprises several hospitals, including one of the two 'flagship' tertiary hospitals, a number of the specialist 'centres' and 'institutes', and a collection of government polyclinics. These clusters are designed to maximize efficiency, service and quality, and minimize duplication and waste. They also operate cooperatively to ensure that the use of day surgery is maximized to minimize costs and overheads. There is really no way of knowing whether they achieve these goals, but it is difficult not to be impressed by the professionalism of the system.

MEDICAL SAVINGS ACCOUNTS

Beyond the hospitals, the Singapore scheme today has three core institutional components, including a medical savings account called Medisave and a top-up 'catastrophe insurance' scheme called MediShield. A third core component, Medifund, operates as a national endowment fund to assist the very poor. These components form an integrated system that is almost officially called the '3Ms'. Medisave and MediShield operate within a broader government-regulated compulsory savings scheme called the Central Provident Fund. Unlike the recent American experiments in medical savings accounts, which are voluntary, employer-sponsored and managed by insurance companies, the Singapore system is universal, compulsory and micro-managed by the government. The institutions composing the Singapore health system are depicted in Figure 7.1.

Medisave[8]

The feature of the Singapore health system that has attracted the most international attention is the compulsory savings scheme, Medisave. Since its inception in 1984, Medisave has operated on the principle that every person in the paid workforce contributes into a personal, but government-managed 'Medisave' account, which builds up a nest-egg to cover the patient's share of hospitalization costs. This is necessary because every ward of every hospital in Singapore charges fees representing at least 19 per cent of total costs, with the government meeting the balance from general revenue. Private hospitals charge the patient 100 per cent of costs.

The rates of contribution to Medisave range from 6 per cent of monthly income for those below 35 years to 8.5 per cent for those over 60, except that the self-employed over 60 pay only 8 per cent. A cap on monthly contributions protects high-income earners from having to contribute unreasonable amounts to the scheme, and those people who reach a set maximum balance in their Medisave accounts have their contributions diverted to other government-regulated savings mechanisms within the structure of the Central Provident Fund. This threshold is currently S$30,000 (Ministry of Health 2004a), which is 77.8 per cent of the average annual income for a wage or salary earner (Ministry of Manpower 2004). This represents a huge increase in the threshold over just a few years. In 1999, the threshold was S$17,000 (Ministry of Health 2000a), which represented 47 per cent of the average annual income for wage and salary earners (Ministry of Manpower 2000).

Contributions are tax-free, earn interest and form part of one's estate upon death. To protect one's Medisave account from being run down, the member does not have complete freedom to pay all hospital costs from Medisave. A strict schedule of payments operates, and Medisave will not pay beyond those limits. If a person chooses a hospital or a ward that charges more than the standard rates, then the cost must be met privately or from MediShield. MediShield also sets itemized limits on payments, and the remainder must be paid out-of-pocket by patients. It is the responsibility of the patient and the family to choose affordable options. Financial counselling is available upon booking and admission. Patients who have insufficient funds in Medisave to cover their costs may commit their

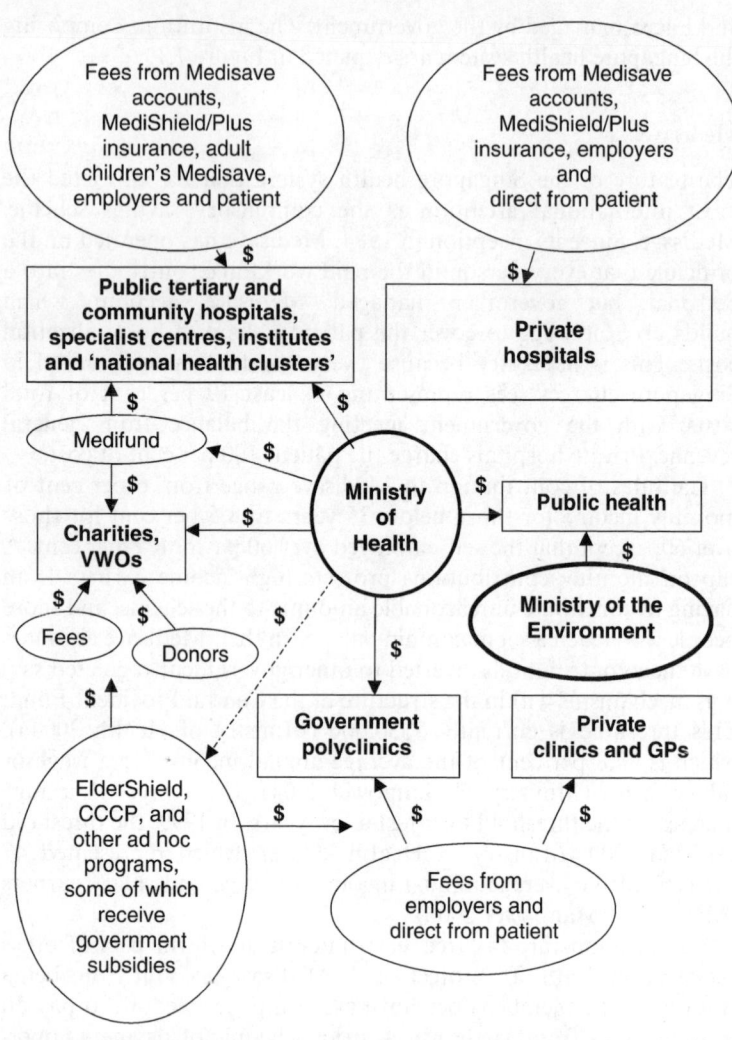

Figure 7.1 The institutions comprising the Singapore health system.

future Medisave contributions towards the bill, except for bills related to assisted conception procedures, outpatient renal dialysis, radiotherapy, chemotherapy and AZT treatment. Without a sufficient Medisave balance, people requiring these treatments must meet their bills another way, or go without treatment.

As well as hospitalization costs, Medisave will meet a small number of outpatient services such as day surgery, radiotherapy, *in vitro* fertilization and hepatitis B vaccination. Otherwise, Medisave does not interact with either outpatient or non-hospital medical services. (Private medical practitioners operate without any special financial ties to the state or the 3Ms, and government clinics and hospital outpatient services rely upon direct government subsidies.)

MediShield/MediShield Plus

MediShield is a basic, low-cost, catastrophic illness insurance scheme to help Medisave members meet hospital expenses resulting from a major or prolonged illness. While Medisave is compulsory for all workers, MediShield is a voluntary 'opt-out' scheme introduced in 1990. Premiums can be paid from Medisave accounts.

MediShield pays benefits when a hospital bill exceeds a high 'deductible' amount that cannot be claimed. MediShield will then pay 80 per cent of the amount above the deductible. The remainder can be paid from Medisave, except in particular, prescribed circumstances. There is, however, no deductible (and therefore no MediShield co-payment) for a handful of long-term, expensive procedures, including outpatient kidney dialysis, chemotherapy and radiotherapy. MediShield has a daily claim limit designed to allow a patient to attend the bottom two classes of ward (open wards with an 81 per cent government subsidy or wards with up to 10 beds per room and a 65 per cent government subsidy).

MediShield Plus is a more expensive version of MediShield targeted at high-income earners. It has very high deductibles, and provides sufficient coverage to enable a patient to attend a private hospital or one of the top two classes of ward in the public hospitals (private wards and wards with fewer than five beds per room).

Medifund

Even with the security of Medisave, there are still people who are unable to meet any costs. Rather than waiving the fees for such people, the government has established an endowment fund to offer charity-style relief. The capital from this fund is left untouched, and interest is distributed to public sector hospitals and charity organizations that consider applications for assistance and allocate the funds. Medifund was established in 1993 with an initial capitalization of S$200 million. The capitalization has been increased by S$100 million a year and now stands at its target of S$1 billion (Ministry of Finance 2004).

ElderShield

ElderShield is the latest incremental change in the system of the 3Ms. Introduced in 2002, this is an opt-out severe disability insurance scheme for all Medisave account holders over the age of 40. When premiums cease at age 65, the member will be covered under ElderShield for life, but benefits are restricted to S$300 per month and are only designed to help defray the costs of home nursing or home care.

PRIMARY HEALTH CARE

Whereas the government provides 80 per cent of the hospital care for Singaporeans and the private sector provides just 20 per cent, in primary health care the situation is reversed, with 80 per cent of the primary care services provided by private practitioners and government polyclinics providing the remaining 20 per cent. Government polyclinics receive a substantial government subsidy, which, in 1996, amounted to 54 per cent of total operating costs (Ramesh and Holliday 2001). On the other hand, the private sector receives no government subsidies except for the newly launched Primary Care Partnership Scheme, whereby a number of selected private clinics receive direct subsidies that enable them to charge polyclinic rates to the elderly for specific common ailments (Ministry of Health 2004a).

VOLUNTARY WELFARE ORGANIZATIONS

Another element of the Singapore system is government aid and Medifund-based financing to charity organizations that care for the poor who require long-term institutionalized care. This reliance upon voluntary welfare organizations is not usually considered to be part of the health system, but without it many poor people would be destitute and completely deprived of care.

PUBLIC HEALTH

Public health is monitored by the Epidemiology and Disease Control Division of the Ministry of Health, but control measures concerning vector-borne and food/hygiene-related diseases are managed by the Ministry of the Environment (Ministry of the Environment 2004).

The Ministry of the Environment is justly proud of its many achievements in these fields. The Centre for Communicable Disease in the Tan Tock Seng Hospital is the only centre for the treatment and control of communicable diseases. Until 2003, the Centre was primarily concerned with HIV/AIDS, but today SARS is its main concern.

PRELIMINARY RESERVATIONS ABOUT THE SINGAPORE 'SUCCESS'

A large measure of the international interest in the post-1984 Singapore health system lies in the perception that it has beaten the modern dilemma of burgeoning health expenditure. Singapore runs a modern, effective health system that absorbs 3.63 per cent of GDP (Ministry of Manpower 2004) and 7.4 per cent of government expenditure (Ministry of Finance 2004). The government and many others attribute its success primarily to the 3Ms. As the Minister for Health said modestly in his budget speech in March 2004, 'Our 3M framework is far from perfect, but it is probably the best healthcare financing model in the world today' (Ministry of Health 2004b)

I argue here and elsewhere[9] that medical savings accounts have been only a minor element in the Singapore system, and that the explanations for Singapore's success – in so far as it is a success – lie elsewhere. Regardless of the tendency of Singapore's medical savings accounts to encourage personal responsibility in health matters, there is no evidence that they have been effective in restraining health costs. Singapore's record of successfully keeping its health costs low is attributable primarily to heavy-handed government cost control of both inputs and outputs, rationing based on wealth, and to social and demographic features peculiar to Singapore. Unfortunately, the negative features of government control and rationing are intrinsic features of what is otherwise a laudable achievement: the building of a modern low-cost health system that works satisfactorily for most people, most of the time.

The levels of government expenditure on the health sector are certainly low by Western standards – but even on this point two serious qualifications need to be introduced. First, the Singapore government does not follow OECD standards in measuring health expenditure. This makes international comparisons extremely difficult, and adds to the risks of using Singapore as a model for other countries. Furthermore, the government is highly secretive about the detailed operation of its system, and has made neither the data source nor method of its calculations available to anyone outside those in the Civil Service and government who need to know: not to the public, not to academic researchers. So although we can safely say that expenditure is low by Western standards, it is probably higher than the government's published figures suggest.

Second, the contrast between Singapore's level of health expenditure appears less stark when compared with other developed East Asian countries rather than to the USA, Europe and Australia. The Hong Kong and Taiwan governments each spend around 5 per cent of GDP on health: a figure higher than Singapore's 3–4 per cent, but not drastically so. In itself this does not diminish the Singapore achievement, but should mitigate any tendency to idolize it.

PERSONAL RESPONSIBILITY

As was originally envisioned in the early 1980s, the key component of the Singapore system was to be the fostering of personal responsibility for one's own health and that of one's family. From the start 'responsibility' – and its sibling, 'choice' – have always been key concepts; hence, there are virtually no bureaucratic or legal restrictions (as opposed to financial restrictions) limiting one's choice of doctor, clinic or hospital; but financial counselling is a routine part of the admission procedure when being admitted to hospital. Although this chapter argues that the importance of responsibility and choice has diminished in the 1990s, they still remain the central elements of the rhetoric. The promotion of 'personal responsibility' extends to media campaigns promoting health and fitness, and employer-sponsored rewards for workers who take no sick leave (Goh Chok Tong 1982b). The institutional linchpin of this attitude is Medisave, which ensures that everyone who can possibly afford to pay anything is paying something for his or her own health care.

In the process of ushering in this new regime, the government introduced a paradigm shift on the way Singaporeans think about health care – a shift that brought the government's rhetoric and actions on health into alignment with its approach to other aspects of social and economic life. The very language of health care dialogue ensures that no-one slips into a state-dependent mode of thinking. Hence, when the government put in place a mechanism to assist the very poor, it refrained from making this expenditure part of the ordinary health budget, but instead established an endowment fund that operates like a charity. It should also be noted that no-one in Singapore speaks of 'government expenditure' on health. The term used in Singapore is 'government subsidies' (see Ministry of Health 2004b).

MORAL HAZARD

As a simple matter of principle, most people will regard the encouragement of personal responsibility as a positive step in any aspect of life, but the operation of the principle in this case can be stated more explicitly. Medisave and MediShield are designed to avoid the 'moral hazard' associated with government-supplied health cover, and even with most private health insurance. Moral hazard was defined, thus, by Toh Mun Heng and Linda Low (1991): 'A moral hazard problem is encountered when payment of medical expenses is borne by a third party, either an insurance company or the government, affecting the individual's own behaviour. It may lead the individual to overconsume medical services and his doctor to overtreat. It has nothing to do with morality but represents a misallocation of resources by a particular method of finance. Since the third party, be it the government or the insurance company pays the full cost, the individual bears no financial burden or faces a zero price for medical care. Consequently, consumption is greater following the law of demand' (p. 9).

It may have been thought that a degree of increased use of health services, particularly by the poor, was part of the purpose of a benevolent health-funding scheme, but to the Singapore government it is a trap to be avoided. Nevertheless, it was found that although the introduction of Medisave reduced the moral hazard considerably, it did not reduce or even contain health expenditure. In fact, immediately following the introduction of Medisave in 1984, the rate of increase of health expenditure per capita jumped from 11 to 13 per cent per annum (Hsiao 1995). The share of GDP absorbed by health expenditure also increased in the immediate post-Medisave period, due largely to a sudden increase in expenditure on doctors' fees and the purchase of new technology as hospitals competed with each other for business and reputation in the new fee-paying environment (Toh Mun Heng and Low 1991).

GOVERNMENT CONTROL

Eventually, the government realized that merely avoiding moral hazard and encouraging personal responsibility was insufficient to restrain increases in health costs. In 1993, direct government control of costs replaced personal responsibility as a central plank in the government's health policy, though not in its promotional material. The Ministerial Committee on Health Policy put it as follows in its 1993 White Paper: 'Market forces alone will not suffice to hold down medical costs to the minimum. The health care system is an example of market failure [to produce the result desired by the government]. The government has to intervene directly to structure and regulate the health system' (p. 3).

The Ministry of Health uses the same words to justify its funding philosophy today, and over the years since the 1993 White Paper it has introduced a substantial number of initiatives to enforce control and rein in costs. Working towards the stated end of 'prevent[ing] over-supply of medical services and dampen[ing] demand' (Ministry of Health 1999), the Ministry of Health has:

- controlled the introduction of technology and specialist disciplines in government hospitals (Ministry of Health 1999);
- introduced price caps on all medical services delivered in government hospitals (Low 1998);
- introduced a predetermined rate of subsidy for government hospitals (leaving the responsibility on the hospitals to break even) (Ministry of Health 1999);
- restricted the number of government hospital beds (Massaro and Wong 1995) and periodically released new land for the development of private hospitals (Ministry of Health 1999);
- tightened its control on the supply of doctors in the country (Massaro and Wong 1995), ensuring at the same time that specialists make up no more than 40 per cent of the medical profession (Ministry of Health 1999).

A further comment is warranted on these measures. The last measure is seen to be critical, since the Ministry of Health is convinced that 'to a significant extent health services are supply driven', and that 'countries with more doctors tend to spend more on health care' (Ministry of Health 1999). Apart from controlling the number of medical graduates produced by local universities, in 1993 the government reduced from 176 to 28 the number of overseas medical schools whose degrees were recognized locally

(Massaro and Wong 1995), a clamp that was loosened only in 2003 when the number was revised up to 71 (Ministry of Health 2004a).

On the question of price caps, it should be noted that costs are kept genuinely low in government hospitals, even though they are increasing and can often seem expensive to patients. Singapore General Hospital, together with the National University Hospital, is the flagship of the government hospitals, and offers high-quality tertiary care, general surgery and a wide range of specialist facilities. The daily fee for Standard Ward Class C (9-bed, no air-conditioning, most heavily subsidized) is S$25 (US$15 as of May 2004). With an 81 per cent subsidy, this means that the real full cost is S$131 (US$77). Even for those staying in single-bed rooms (with an 8 per cent subsidy), the real full costs of a single-bed room with air conditioning, toilet, television, and so on is only S$272 (US$160). The real cost of surgery is capped at S$1842 (US$1081) per operation for the most heavily subsidized patients. Of this, the patient pays up to S$350, which in a best case scenario should be mostly covered by Medisave and MediShield. For patients in single-bed rooms, the real cost of an operation is capped at S$8954 (US$5255) (Singapore General Hospital 2004). These figures include anaesthetic, surgeon's fees, and so on. The rates of Singapore General Hospital are comparable to those of other public hospitals (Ministry of Health 2004a), though since it is a deliberate part of the Singapore health philosophy to maximize efficiency by minimizing duplication of services, Singapore General cannot provide a precise point of comparison with any other hospital. These caps, however, do not bind private hospitals. Gleneagles Hospital, for instance, charges S$3509 (US$2060) a day for its most luxurious suite (Gleneagles Hospital 2004).

It is also important to note that even though Medisave accounts are the personal accounts of individual members, the government determines on what procedures they can be spent, where they can be spent and at what rate. The government's high level of control is not usually mediated even by private or employer-sponsored health insurance schemes, since although such schemes exist and are growing in Singapore, they have failed to become dominant players in the health industry (Ramesh 1992; Tan Teck Meng and Chew Soon Beng 1997; Low 1998). The main exceptions to this rule are those civil servants and retired civil servants who still enjoy free, unlimited employer-sponsored health benefits under a scheme that was closed to new business during the 1990s.

Direct government controls are thus a central feature of Singapore's health funding regime, but even in tiny, not-very-democratic Singapore, this technique has its limits. The government found the ceiling of its political will when, throughout the 1980s, it gradually reduced the proportion of C Class beds – those used by the poorest sections of the community. In the end, pressure from government backbenchers forced the Ministry of Health to replenish the C Class bed supply (Toh Mun Heng and Low 1991).

RATIONING

Implicit in government control of inputs is the principle of rationing health services based on wealth. The 1993 White Paper on Health stated this without voicing the criteria of wealth: 'We cannot avoid rationing medical care, implicitly or explicitly. Funding for health care will always be finite. There will always be competing demands for resources, whether the resources come from the State or the individual citizens. Using the latest in medical technology is expensive. Trade-offs among different areas of medical treatments, equipment, training and research are unavoidable' (Ministerial Committee on Health Policies 1993: 17).

Although the government is committed to ensuring the provision of 'basic health care' for the population, it is not embarrassed about excluding particular procedures from that definition. For instance, Medisave cannot be used to cover labour ward and associated costs beyond a third child, or long-term hospital care (Tan Teck Meng and Chew Soon Beng 1997). MediShield does not cover a wide range of conditions including congenital abnormalities, cosmetic surgery, maternity charges, abortion, dental work, infertility and contraceptive procedures, sex change operations, mental illness and personality disorders, AIDS, drug addiction or alcoholism, treatment of injuries arising from direct participation in civil commotion or strikes, and self-inflicted injuries. MediShield is also protected from a considerable amount of liability because, even though the government runs it, it operates on insurance underwriting principles, and so it excludes some illnesses if the patient was already receiving treatment before joining MediShield. These illnesses include blood disorder, cancer, stroke, chronic liver cirrhosis, chronic obstructive lung disease, chronic renal disease (including failure), coronary artery disease, degenerative disease, ischaemic heart disease, rheumatic heart disease and systematic lupus erythematosus (Ministry of

Health 1999; Central Provident Fund 2004). For the very poor, and for lower and middle-income earners with insufficient Medisave funds, obtaining treatment for these conditions has been problematic in Singapore; Medifund will be able to help some people, but there can be no assumptions that one will be treated.

The significance of this list of exclusions can be appreciated by the similarity between the list of Medisave exclusions (both complete and conditional) and the list of National Health Priority Areas (NHPA) in Australia. The NHPA is an initiative of Australia's nine Commonwealth, state and territory governments, and focuses on 'diseases and other conditions that contribute most significantly to Australia's burden of illness and for which there is potential for the burden to be significantly reduced' (Australian Institute of Health and Welfare 1999: 93). The NHPA list accounted for 40 per cent of total hospital patient days in Australia in 1998–1999. Two of the three most prevalent conditions on the list also appear on the list of MediShield exclusions: cardiovascular disease and control of cancer. Care involving dialysis, and care related to the treatment of HIV, mental health and diabetes, also appear on the NHPA list of prevalence and on the MediShield list of exclusions (Australian Institute of Health and Welfare 1999). The only items on the NHPA list that do not appear on the MediShield list of exclusions are asthma and personal injury. It should also be noted that except for assisted conception procedures, all the procedures for which a patient is precluded from committing *future* Medisave funds also appear on the NHPA list: outpatient renal dialysis, radiotherapy, chemotherapy and AZT treatment. Clearly, rationing has been an important element in the control of Singapore's health costs.

LESSONS

Learning 'the lessons' of the 3Ms is no easy task. The first difficulty is in establishing whether the 3Ms has 'worked', which is not made easier by the Singapore government's reticence about providing figures on which to base detailed analysis, or by the fact that hospital restructuring was introduced in conjunction with Medisave. Regardless of these qualifications, Hsaio (1995) leaves no room to doubt that Medisave failed to curtail costs. This is a sensitive point for advocates of medical savings accounts. Massaro and Wong (1995) were so defensive on this point that they argued Medisave was not intended to contain costs, but 'to ensure that when Singaporeans enter the medical marketplace, they are able to pay the costs of their own care without relying on the charity of others or subsidies from the state' (p. 278). Although it is true that this was the stated focus of the reforms, it is disingenuous to argue that the government was not trying to contain costs.

Despite this heavy qualification, we cannot ignore the fact that Singapore spends a lot less on health care than most, if not all, developed countries, and yet still ends up with a system that provides a modern, efficient and technically universal service. This success still begs an explanation. The heart of the success is unquestionably the strict regime of controls and rationing, but some incidental features of Singapore society have also helped. The most important such factor is that Singapore has yet to face the costs of an ageing population, which is one of the major factors straining health systems in other developed countries.[10] In 1991, 6.2 per cent of Singapore's population was aged 65 or over, as opposed to proportions between 10.9 per cent and 15.4 per cent for the USA, Canada, UK, Australia, New Zealand and West Germany (Ministerial Committee on Health Policies 1993: Appendix B). In 1988, the Ministry of Health estimated that by 2030, 52 per cent of the population will be 60 years or older, though later figures suggest that this trend may have slowed a little (Toh Mun Heng and Low 1991; Low 1998). This is a serious concern for the government when it is realized that, in 1996, the aged of Singapore (65 and over) were admitted to hospital at 2.8 times the frequency of their younger counterparts, and stayed in hospital an average of 1.66 times as long. They were also higher consumers of the two most heavily subsidized classes of ward (Prescott 1998). Thus, an increase in the proportion of aged will inevitably increase demand for health services. The Ministry of Health is, therefore, resigned to further increases in both national and government health expenditure and is continually reviewing the health system to deal with actual and anticipated problems. It expects the rate of Medisave contributions to approach 10 per cent of each person's monthly income in due course (Ministry of Health 1999) and it has recently foreshadowed the creation of a US$600 million fund to subsidize nursing homes to be run by voluntary welfare organizations (i.e. charities) for the elderly poor.[11] This latest development – with its systemic extension of the 'charity' principle – suggests that parsimony and paternalism, rather than personal responsibility, provide the real conceptual framework of Singapore's health-funding system.

Let us also not ignore the benefits derived from Singapore's ubiquitous systems of social and institutional pressures that encourage and pressure people to keep fit and healthy. The most powerful of these is National Service. Since the early 1970s, all male Singaporeans have been notionally[12] called up for National Service, after which they are expected to stay fit and ready for annual call-ups throughout most of their working life. The Singapore Armed Forces faced a regular problem with unfit reservists[13] and even unfit raw recruits from school throughout the 1970s and 1980s, and in the process of trying to address this problem it incidentally inducted half the Singaporean population into consciousness of the need for exercise and healthy eating. The first systemic attempts to tackle this dilemma began only in 1987[14] and, therefore, cannot have affected fitness levels before that time, but the incentive to remain fit and healthy was present and strong among Singaporean men from the late-1960s. This National Service driven fitness regime is probably only partially effective, but it must nevertheless make some contribution to national health standards.

The role of National Service is greater when one considers the flow-on effect in the workplace. Employers – especially large corporations and government-linked companies – are encouraged to provide exercise space and equipment for their employees and to promote 'healthy living'. Although only men have a National Service driven incentive to keep fit, the equipment and the campaigns are not gender specific, and no doubt contribute to the growing culture of fitness and healthy living among middle-class Singaporean women. Exercise facilities at white-collar workplaces are regarded as commonplace. Even out in the earthier environment of hawker stalls and food courts in Singapore's 'heartland', one cannot escape the signs encouraging one to 'ask for less sugar' and 'ask for more vegetables', or the anti-smoking campaigns.

A further factor contributing to the low expenditure on health is the anomaly of traditional Chinese medicine. All the ethnic groups, but particularly the majority ethnic Chinese population, contain significant minorities that rely on a mixture of Western and traditional medicines, or even turn to Western medicine as only a last resort (Somjee 1995). The Ministry of Health (1995) estimates that about 12 per cent of daily outpatient users also visit traditional Chinese medicine practitioners. The significance of this figure is that, despite the fact that the government has regulated the practice of traditional Chinese medicine since November 2000, it operates outside the government's health-funding regime, and is excluded from its national health expenditure figures, thus artificially depressing expenditure figures.

SYSTEMIC FAULTS

Even with the advantages provided by Singapore's peculiar demographics and society, the 3Ms have still failed substantial sections of the population. Most obviously, the chronically sick are extremely vulnerable, as the Minister for Health freely admits: poor people (and many not so poor) requiring long-term institutionalized care must currently rely upon charity organizations, which in turn receive some support from the government (Prescott 1998). In recognition of this weakness, the government has initiated the Comprehensive Chronic Care Programme, which piggy-backs on the government polyclinics and provides subsidized long-term health care to those suffering from three specific chronic conditions: diabetes, high blood pressure and high cholesterol (Ministry of Health 2000b).

The poor – including the working poor and most of the aged – are also seriously disadvantaged, even if they are not chronically sick. Old women who, even in Singapore, are more likely to have been housewives – whether as wives, widows or divorcees – for most of their lives are particularly vulnerable (Low 1998). Medisave helps such women only if their husbands left money in their own account or voluntarily funded a Medisave account for them.

An alternative solution is to call upon adult children to help. Currently more than 65 per cent of private funding for acute care for those 65 and over derives from the Medisave accounts of adult children (Prescott 1998). But if one's children are low-income earners, this may not be an option, and in any case would be merely shifting the burden of poverty within the pool of the poor. This highlights a serious problem with the family-based self-help concept: it can, and does, result in calling on one disadvantaged group to subsidize another. Malays are especially vulnerable to this trap because they have been, and continue to be, an economically disadvantaged group in Singapore due to systemic discrimination (Lee 1998; Rahim 1998) and, therefore, are more likely to have the crippling combination of poorly paid jobs, poor aged parents, small Medisave accounts and no MediShield cover.

Even middle-class groups have more exposure than one might expect. For instance, the moves in 2004 to stop high- and middle-income earners from using C Class wards (the most heavily subsidized) have brought to public scrutiny the fact that surgery and serious illness can be financially crippling for the relatively well off, even with Medisave and MediShield providing a lot of coverage.[15]

The children of middle-income earners have also been left relatively exposed, because they are covered by MediShield only if they are included on their parents' plans and the parents pay an extra premium. In 1999, a small campaign was launched to encourage parents to cover this gap (Central Provident Fund 1999). The existence of this group shows how easy it is to fall through the cracks of the rather *ad hoc* Singapore system, which is why the government is continually conducting reviews and amending the system to change its character and increase its scope.

Pauly and Goodman (1995), in their 1995 defence of the 3Ms, accused William Hsiao of using 'an out-of-context quote from a government White Paper' to give the impression that Singapore is ready 'to replace the current system with government regulation and controls' (p. 278). They reiterated their confidence that 'Singapore is firmly committed to individual choice and free markets'. Alas, this is only true for those with a capacity to write a cheque for medical services or who enjoy generous employer-sponsored medical benefits. For these exclusive groups, Singapore offers world-class private hospitals and open access to top specialists – but for the poor and even for the lower middle class, the government has increased its controls over the health market since 1993.

For most of the population, the cost of moving outside the parameters set by the 3Ms (for instance, by having a fourth baby) is prohibitive. Far from allowing an open market, the government even regulates the number of doctors and specialists with the stated purpose of dampening demand for health care. The level of government control and the level of rationing of health services to the poor are so stringent that it would require great political will and bureaucratic efficiency to introduce them into a larger polity. This control and rationing, and the concomitant manipulation of demand by controlling supply, tarnishes Singapore's considerable achievement of building a modern health system that works satisfactorily for most people, most of the time. Medical savings accounts provide the core of the institutional framework of the Singapore system, but the practical and spiritual heart of the system lies in control and parsimony.

HEALTH CARE VERSUS EFFICIENCY

By March 2003, the government was smugly pleased with the health system it had created. It was clear that the government was open to infinite incremental improvement in the health system, but the fundamentals were taken for granted. Then came SARS (severe acute respiratory syndrome). The Singapore government eventually responded to this epidemic with exemplary vigour, throwing the resources of not just the Ministry of Health, but also that of the Army, police and the networks of government-linked 'grassroots organizations', into the task of tracking down suspected carriers, enforcing rigid quarantines, and maintaining supplies of food to unfortunates who were being quarantined in their own homes.

Yet as one who was resident in Singapore during the whole of the SARS threat in 2002, I can say that the government's response was painfully slow in coming. For the first 5 weeks of the SARS outbreak (13 March to 20 April 2003), it was clear that there were no protocols or contingency plans to deal with an epidemic, and the responses were *ad hoc* and reactive. The public marker of the ending of this rudderless period was the effective removal of the SARS response from the hands of the Minister for Health, Lim Hng Kiang (as a preliminary to removing him from the portfolio), and the creation of two ministerial committees ('combat teams' in the government's parlance) to handle the crisis.[16] It even took 5 weeks before the government began supplying free ambulances to take suspected SARS cases to hospital (13 March to 17 April).[17] Until then, SARS suspects generally made their way to hospital by taxi or public transport, as was recommended by official bodies such as the Office of Student Affairs at the National University of Singapore.[18]

Even when the government ramped up its handling of SARS, the response contained many stage-managed displays designed purely for international and domestic audiences rather than to combat SARS. I became highly conscious of the scale of this when I read in *The Straits Times* on 24 April 2002 that thermal imaging units (to detect fever) had been introduced at Changi Airport and at the Woodlands and Tuas checkpoints (leading into Malaysia) the previous day. This was a surprise to me because I passed through Woodlands Checkpoint twice on that day and there were no thermal imaging units in sight. A colleague passed through Changi Airport on the same day and also reported the absence of thermal imaging units.

Responding to SARS required a dramatic switch in health care philosophy from a focus on efficiency, cost savings and personal choice, to a focus on universal health protection as a matter of urgency. The great strength of the Singapore health system is that it delivers satisfactory outcomes at low cost to most of the population most of the time. In an epidemic, this was not good enough.

It is clear the Singapore government learnt a lot from SARS and has realized the seriousness of the threat of epidemics, but there should be no illusions: the government was singularly unprepared to deal with an epidemic and had to learn on the run. The upside is that it did learn quickly and is likely to handle the next threatened epidemic much better. As a result of this experience, Singapore now has stringent quarantine laws and protocols, enforceable by large fines and public humiliation. The uniquely Singaporean system of social monitoring and pressures has now been expanded to facilitate routine temperature-taking and monitoring of high fevers at short notice. The military, police and a myriad of other social instruments are now geared in an emergency to track the movements of suspected carriers, and those with whom they might have come into contact. The Communicable Disease Centre has been upgraded from being a rundown, low-tech collection of communal blocks designed to cope with HIV/AIDS, and now includes a state-of-the-art series of isolation wards, ready for the next epidemic.

Yet in his Budget Speech on 17 March 2004, Health Minister Khaw Boon Wan made it clear that the focus on efficiency and cost savings still provides the core of the Singaporean health care philosophy. He stated explicitly that he considers less consumption of public health services to be a positive outcome in its own right, and conclusive proof that the Singapore health philosophy of personal responsibility and self-help is among the world's best practice (Ministry of Health 2004b).[19] Singapore's ratio of hospital beds to population currently stands at 1 : 348 (Ministry of Health 2004a). A glance at the opening paragraphs of this chapter will confirm that in 1960 (one year out from full colonial rule) the ratio of hospital beds to population was 1 : 229, a deterioration of 52 per cent in 44 years. In Singapore, the government regards this as an achievement.

NOTES

1 Figures on class and poverty are not precise, because the categories are extremely subjective, and also because the government is not very forthcoming about providing data. Those wishing to pursue such statistics can turn to the government's statistics website at http://

www.singstat.gov.sg/, or turn to official publications such as Leow Bee Geok (2001).
2 There was also a 2 year interlude when Singapore was a state of Malaysia.
3 It should, however, be noted that the decline in the supply of hospital beds by the mid-1980s may not have been solely or even primarily due to demographic pressures. As early as 1981 the government was already foreshadowing a reduction in the number of beds (*The Straits Times*, 11 May 1981).
4 *The Straits Times*, 11 April 1969.
5 *The Straits Times*, 11 May 1981.
6 *The Straits Times*, 10 April 1982, 24 December 1982.
7 *The Straits Times*, 17 December 1982.
8 The descriptions of Medisave, MediShield and Medifund are based on information provided by the Central Provident Fund and Singapore Ministry of Health. See Central Provident Fund (2004) and Ministry of Health (2004a).
9 This chapter draws heavily on an earlier work by the author (Barr 2001).
10 In 1996, industrialized countries' per capita health care expenditure on the aged was up to five times that of the expenditure on the under-65s (Japan) and rarely less than twice the figure. The Netherlands, the USA, Australia, Switzerland, Finland, the UK and New Zealand all spent approximately four times the amount on the aged than they did on the younger section of the population (Prescott 1998: 13).
11 *International Market Insight Reports*, 13 April 2000.
12 In fact for many years most young Malay males were not called up for National Service. This discriminatory practice ceased by the early 1980s.
13 *The Straits Times*, 21 April 1986, 'Unfit reservists get another try: Mindef [Ministry of Defence] gives three chances to pass fitness test'.
14 *The Straits Times*, 10 January 1987, 'Gearing up students for rigours of military life: Defence and Education ministries form fitness panel'; 1 July 1987, 'Mindef goes to schools to get boys into shape'; 'Keeping fighting fit is a national commitment'.
15 In the end the government decided to allow the wealthy to use the lower standard wards, but changed the rules so that they will not receive the full subsidy (*The Straits Times*, 1 March 2004).
16 *The Sunday Times*, 20 April 2004.
17 Ministry of Health Press Release, 17 April 2003 (Ministry of Health 2004a).
18 An official notice issued by the NUS Office of Student Affairs, dated 1 April 2003, recommended that people with SARS-like symptoms 'go immediately to the Accident and Emergency Dept at TTSH [Tan Tock Seng Hospital] by taxi or public transport'.
19 Khaw Boon Wan said: 'Last week, my Ministry published a paper comparing the utilization of medical services in Singapore with several

developed countries. Singapore has done well. We have lower hospital admissions per capita. Our patients generally do not overstay' (Ministry of Health 2004b).

REFERENCES

Australian Institute of Health and Welfare (1999) *Australian Hospital Statistics 1998–99* (available at: http://www.aihw.gov.au/publications/health/ahs98-9.html/; cited on 10 August 2000).

Barr, M.D. (2001) Medical savings accounts in Singapore: a critical inquiry, *Journal of Health Politics, Policy and Law*, 26(3): 707–24.

Blank, R.H. and Burau, V. (2004) *Comparative Health Policy*. Houndmills: Palgrave.

Central Provident Fund (1999) *MediShield/MediShield Plus Handbook* (available at: http://www.cpf.gov.sg/publication/medisave.asp/; cited on 30 July 1999).

Central Provident Fund (2004) *MediShield/MediShield Plus Handbook* (available at: http://www.cpf.gov.sg/; cited on 30 April 2004).

Gleneagles Hospital (2004) Website (available at: http://gleneagles.com.sg accessed on 7 May 2004).

Goh Chok Tong (1982a) Singapore Government Press Release. Speech by Mr Goh Chok Tong, Minister for Health and Second Minister for Defence, at the Singapore General Hospital (SGH), 6 March 1982 (available at: National Archives of Singapore, http://www.museum.org.sg/NAS/nas.shtml/ accessed on 10 May 2004).

Goh Chok Tong (1982b) Stay well for health, in S. Jayakumar (ed.) *Our Heritage and Beyond: A Collection of Essays on Singapore, Its Present and Future*. Singapore: Singapore National Trades Union Congress.

Hsiao, W.C. (1995) Medical savings accounts: lessons from Singapore, *Health Affairs*, 14: 260–7.

Lee Kuan Yew (1981) Full steam ahead – each citizen its own home, *Petir*, 11: 4–15.

Lee, W.K.M. (1998) Income protection and the elderly: an examination of social security policy in Singapore, *Journal of Cross-Cultural Gerontology*, 13: 291–307.

Leow Bee Geok (2001) *Census of Population 2000: Households and Housing*. Statistical Release #5. Singapore: Singapore Department of Statistics.

Lim, L.Y.C. (1989) Social welfare, in Kernial Singh Sandhu and P. Wheatley (eds.) *Management of Success: The Moulding of Modern Singapore*. Singapore: Institute of Southeast Asian Studies.

Low, L. (1998) Health care in the context of social security in Singapore, *SOJOURN: Journal of Social Issues in Southeast Asia*, 13: 139–65.

Massaro, T.A. and Wong, Y.-N. (1995) Positive experience with medical savings accounts in Singapore, *Health Affairs*, 14: 267–9.

Ministerial Committee on Health Policies (1993) *Affordable Health Care: A White Paper*. Singapore: Ministry of Health.

Ministry of the Environment (2004) Website (available at: http://www.env.gov.sg/ accessed on 6 May 2004).

Ministry of Finance (2004) Budget Speech 2004 (available at: http://www.mof.gov.sg/ accessed on 30 April 2004).

Ministry of Health (1995) *Traditional Chinese Medicine: The Report by the Committee on Traditional Chinese Medicine (October 1995)* (available at: http://www.gov.sg/moh/ accessed on 9 August 2000).

Ministry of Health (1999) *Report of the Cost Review Committee – Response of the Ministry of Health* (available at: http://www.gov.sg/moh/mohiss/review.html/ accessed on 4 August 1999).

Ministry of Health (2000a) Various Ministry of Health hospital websites (available at: http://www.gov.sg/mohhiss/hospsvcs/; cited on 10 August 2000).

Ministry of Health (2000b) New Primary Healthcare Initiatives (available at: http://www.gov.sg/moh/releases/; cited on 21 August 2000).

Ministry of Health (2004a) Ministry of Health website (available at: http://www.moh.gov.sg; cited on 30 April 2004).

Ministry of Health (2004b) Ministry of Health Budget Speech, Wednesday 17 March 2004 by Mr Khaw Boon Wan, Acting Minister for Health (available at: http://www.moh.gov.sg/; cited on 30 April 2004).

Ministry of Manpower (2000) *Labour Market, First Quarter 2000*. Singapore: Ministry of Manpower.

Ministry of Manpower (2004) Website (available at: http://www.mom.gov.sg; cited on 4 May 2004).

Pauly, M.V. and Goodman, J.C. (1995) Medical savings accounts: the authors respond, *Health Affairs*, 14: 277–9.

Prescott, N. (ed.) (1998) *Choices in Financing Health Care and Old Age Security*. Proceedings of a Conference Sponsored by the Institute of Policy Studies, Singapore, and the World Bank, 8 November 1997. Washington, DC: International Bank for Reconstruction and Development.

Rahim, L.Z. (1998) *The Singapore Dilemma: The Political and Economic Marginality of the Malay Community*. Kuala Lumpur: Oxford University Press.

Ramesh, M. (1992) Social security in Singapore, *Asian Survey*, 32: 1093–108.

Ramesh, M. and Holliday, I. (2001) The health care miracle in East and Southeast Asia: activist state provision in Hong Kong, Malaysia and Singapore, *Journal of Social Policy*, 30(4): 637–51.

Saw Swee-Hock (1991) Population growth and control, in E.C.T. Chew and E. Lee (eds) *A History of Singapore*. Singapore: Oxford University Press.

Singapore General Hospital (2004) Website (available at: http://www.sgh.com.sg; accessed 5 May 2004).

Singapore Infomap (2004) Website (available at: http://www.sg/; cited on 30 April 2004).

Somjee, G. (1995) Public health policy and personnel in two Asian countries, *Journal of Asian and African Studies*, 30: 90–105.
Tan, N. (1991) Health and welfare, in E.C.T. Chew and E. Lee (eds) *A History of Singapore*. Singapore: Oxford University Press.
Tan Teck Meng and Chew Soon Beng (eds) (1997) *Affordable Health Care: Issues and Prospects*. Singapore: Prentice-Hall.
Toh Mun Heng and Low, L. (1991) *Health Care Economics, Policies and Issues in Singapore*. Singapore: Times Academic Press for the Centre for Advanced Studies, National University of Singapore.

8

HONG KONG
Derek Gould

Population 2003	6.8 million
Ethnic composition 2003	Chinese (95%), others (5%)
Capital city	Victoria
Live births per woman 2002	0.96
Infant mortality rate per 1000 live births 2002	2.3
Life expectancy at birth 2002 (male/female)	78.6/84.5 years
Total health expenditure as a percentage of GDP 2002	5.1%
Government health expenditure as a percentage of total health expenditure 2002	51.9%
Total health expenditure per capita 2001 (US$ PPP)	n/a
Practising physicians per 1000 population 2003	1.4
Health system	Health, Welfare and Food Bureau (policy maker and public sector resources allocator); Hospital Authority and Department of Health (public sector providers); Food and Environmental Hygiene Department (service provider and licensing authority); out-of-pocket and insurance-funded private sector providing Western and traditional Chinese medicine.

Political system	Executive-led, non-party government with appointed policy secretaries. Single-chamber legislature with geographical and functional constituencies.

Sources: Census and Statistics Department (2004), Health, Welfare and Food Bureau (2004), Hong Kong SAR Government (2003a,b,c)

INTRODUCTION

The Hong Kong Special Administrative Region of the People's Republic of China is a developed, post-industrial economy with a population of nearly 7 million people. A geographical area of only 1072 square kilometres, combined with a mountainous topography, has made land for housing a precious commodity. Acccordingly, population growth has resulted in increasing urbanization, with most people now living in high-density, high-rise residential developments in the city and in nine new towns.

Despite overcrowding, Hong Kong has attained admirable health indices in terms of longevity, low infant mortality and the incidence of once-common infectious and communicable diseases. However, until recently, performance in these areas has led to complacency and a false sense of security about the quality of the health care system as a whole.

While Hong Kong's health care services and facilities have moved in tune with a rising standard of living and other social changes, and are now as advanced as those in any developed country, the system itself has remained largely static. The method of financing and delivery is little different now than it was when the government first promulgated its service policy in 1964. Indeed, the public–private dichotomy that arose in the nineteenth century continues to be a dominant feature in the twenty-first century. While other advanced economies have moved towards integrated systems led by primary care practitioners, health care in Hong Kong remains compartmentalized and heavily reliant on medical specialization delivered in public hospitals. Funding continues to be fragmented, rather than all services being paid for from pooled resources As a result, the system has been variously criticized as being under-planned and under-regulated (Yuen 1992), seriously outdated (Harvard Team 1999) and 'a huge castle [built] on sand' (*South China Morning Post*, 10 September 2003). The system's shortcomings became obvious when the 1997 Asian currency crisis and consequent economic downturn, combined with outbreaks of H5N1 avian flu and SARS, pushed it close to breaking point.

A BRIEF HISTORY OF HEALTH POLICY

The following overview draws generally on Choa (1985, 2000), Collins (1952), Eitel (1983), Endacott (1964, 1973), Endacott and Hinton (1962) and Sayer (1975). A more comprehensive description can be found in Gauld and Gould (2002).

The 1840s saw the start of Hong Kong as a base for British and other European trade with China. It was not a healthy location to conduct business and tropical fevers were rife. At that time, governments generally did not see the provision of personal health care services as being their responsibility and limited their activities to matters of public health (Beaglehole and Bonita 1997). The Hong Kong government's early efforts were thus restricted to draining swampy ground and ensuring basic sanitation to try to curb seasonal outbreaks of malaria and cholera.

While civil servants, the police, prisoners and accident victims had access to the Colonial Surgeon and the Civil Hospital, others had to fend for themselves. This vacuum in demand was quickly filled by private practitioners and missionary bodies that opened clinics and hospitals for European patients, while traditional Chinese medicine practitioners met the needs of the local population who shunned Western medicine. Under the guise of a policy of *laissez-faire*, the government allowed private providers to operate with virtually no regulation.

Following expansion in 1859, the Civil Hospital opened its doors to fee-paying patients, plus vagrants who were treated for free. This marked a shift in the government's service policy and the beginning of an incremental commitment to provide ever-increasing facilities for the general public.

The need for a hospital to provide free traditional Chinese medicine services for Chinese residents on an inpatient basis was met in 1870 with the opening of the Tung Wah Hospital. Managed and run by a local charitable organization, construction was funded jointly by the government and from charitable donations. The government also made a small contribution towards the hospital's operating costs and had powers of inspection (Collins 1952; Tung Wah Group 1970; Sinn 1989). Tung Wah was the financing and delivery model for the many subvented hospitals that were to follow and became the third leg of Hong Kong's tripartite hospital system, which included: (1) government hospitals funded by the public purse; (2) subvented hospitals managed by charitable bodies with some government financial assistance; and (3) private hospitals funded by patients' fees and/or charitable donations.

As population and demand increased, so too did the number of health care providers. This prompted British-registered doctors to petition the government to protect their interests. The result, in 1884, was an ordinance limiting the practice of Western medicine to holders whose qualifications were recognized by the General Medical Council of the United Kingdom. Reflecting the principle of professional autonomy and self-regulation, the legislation also made doctors accountable to their peers, rather than to the government. Few controls were imposed over the growing number of private hospitals. Instead, it was expected that the medical superintendent – being a registered doctor – would exercise professional responsibility to ensure that proper standards were met.

Population growth throughout the latter half of the nineteenth century led to overcrowded and insanitary living conditions. Although the government was compelled to take action by repeated outbreaks of cholera and other diseases, vested interests thwarted its attempts to impose 'British standards' on a Chinese community. Landlords feared that better accommodation and drainage would increase their costs and reduce their profits, while tenants were worried about having to pay higher rents. Consequently, the Building and Nuisances Ordinance of 1856, the appointment of a Sanitary Committee in 1862 and the Public Health Ordinance of 1887 all achieved little effect.

The substandard level of public health and hygiene became manifestly evident in 1894 when bubonic plague broke out and spread rapidly through the densely populated Chinese sections of the city. The government sought to contain the disease by inspecting and de-infesting private residences. This was criticized by the community as being unnecessarily intrusive. Outbreaks continued intermittently for the next 30 years, with the average mortality rate exceeding 90 per cent. Trapped between public demands to solve problems and community objection to the proposed solutions, the government responded by introducing a series of sanitation measures that were largely cosmetic. Reflecting the contemporary view that a doctor's role was curative, not preventive, these measures had little medical or public health input.

It was not until 1929 that various health and hygiene-related functions were consolidated under a newly created post of Director of Medical and Sanitary Services, whose incumbent was an expert in public health (Wellington 1930). His recommendations led, in 1936, to a more logical reorganization of responsibilities – a Medical Department (which operated government hospitals and dispensaries, and inspected subvented hospitals) and a Sanitation Department (which looked after environmental hygiene). The latter department was placed under the control of an Urban Council, which had the Director of Medical and Sanitary Services as its vice-president and official adviser (Wellington 1935; Mills 1942; Ho 1946; Miners, 1987).

While the government struggled to impose a public health administration, it left personal health services to develop on their own. Although the population continued to grow steadily, new government hospitals and dispensaries were only opened on an *ad-hoc* basis. The shortfall in demand was partially met by Tung Wah opening two more subvented hospitals, while private and charitable hospitals stepped in to cater for fee-paying and poor patients, respectively. Primary care continued to be delivered largely by private practitioners of Western and traditional medicine.

The Second World War left the health care system in a shambles, with facilities destroyed, damaged or looted and trained medical personnel in short supply. While Britain took the opportunity to introduce a National Health Service, the government in Hong Kong sought only a return to the pre-war system. Its efforts to achieve even this modest level of service were frustrated by a swelling population, consisting not only of returning former residents but also refugees fleeing the civil war raging across the border on the Chinese Mainland. To accommodate the new arrivals, wood-and-tinsheet squatter villages sprang up on hillsides. Overcrowded and without running water or proper sanitation, these substandard dwellings were an ideal breeding ground for communicable diseases such as tuberculosis (Endacott 1973), which placed a heavy burden on medical services.

Despite the construction of several new facilities, the 1950s saw public hospitals continuing to be severely overcrowded: patients were accommodated on canvas camp beds and overflowed from wards into the corridors, while non-urgent cases joined ever-lengthening waiting lists. A shortage of nurses often left patients' needs unattended (see Hong Kong *Hansard* 1964: 63–4). Conditions were so unpleasant that no-one who could beg or borrow enough to afford a private hospital would choose to use a public one. To relieve the pressure, the government opened outpatient clinics to provide not only treatment, but also patient education and disease screening.

Taking stock of the situation in the 1960s, the government decided its policy should be 'to provide, directly or indirectly [i.e. through the subvented sector], low cost or free medical and personal health services to that large section of the community which is unable to seek medical attention from other sources' (MacKenzie 1962: 44; Hong Kong Government 1963). It was conservatively estimated 'that 50 per cent of the population are unable to afford unsubsidised outpatient medical care and that 80 per cent are unable to afford unsubsidised inpatient treatment' (Hong Kong Government 1964: 11). On the basis of this, in 1964 the government published its first-ever medical White Paper aimed over the following 10 years 'to provide, within the limitations imposed by the Colony's financial and economic circumstances, augmented clinic and hospital services designed to meet the most urgent medical and health needs' (p. 11). Its target was to increase the bed-to-population ratio to 'a minimal ratio of provision' of 4.25 per thousand by building additional government hospitals and expanding the subvented sector. With more local residents choosing Western treatment over traditional Chinese medicine for primary health care, the government also aimed to establish one general outpatient clinic for every 100,000 population.

Thanks to a healthy economy and a population that had not increased as fast as forecast, a review 10 years later found that the 1964 targets had generally been met. Another White Paper was published, this time aiming for a bed-to-population ratio of 5.5 per thousand and an improvement in the quality of hospital facilities and accommodation – particularly the eradication of camp beds (Hong Kong Government 1974). The government also took the opportunity to reinterpret and expand its 1964 policy as a commitment to ensure the provision of medical services to all and not just to the poor, although it would on future occasions tend to 'forget' that it had made such a promise.

Growth in the Medical and Health Department through the 1970s and into the 1980s was not matched by a willingness to update its style of management. Decision making remained highly centralized, creating inflexibility and inefficiency at the operational level. After years of public dissatisfaction and growing concern expressed by members of the Legislative Council, the Secretary for Health and Welfare acknowledged shortcomings in medical administration and service delivery, although he defended the health care system as a whole. He proposed a review of 'the management system of our medical services, with particular reference to hospitals, their organization and their management' (Hong Kong *Hansard*, 9 November 1983: 185).

The outcome of the review by overseas consultants was the 'Scott Report'. This recommended, *inter alia*, the establishment of a statutory Hospital Authority responsible for overall management of all government and subvented hospitals. These would then become 'public hospitals' with a common fee structure, but otherwise operating with a high degree of devolved authority. While continuing to be funded largely by the government, the Hospital Authority would be independent of the Civil Service and thus able to practice private sector management and financial methods. The Scott Report also made recommendations to alleviate overcrowding and improve the working environment, and proposed that responsibility for public health be taken over by a separate government body (Scott Report 1985).

In October 1988, the government appointed a Provisional Hospital Authority, consisting of a 26-member committee serviced by a secretariat of civil servants on loan. The Medical and Health Department was disbanded on 1 April 1989, with its staff being split between an interim Hospital Services Department (responsible for public hospitals and specialist clinics) and a Department of Health (responsible for general outpatient clinics and public health). Following preparatory work and the production of a 'how to do it' report by the Provisional Hospital Authority (1989), the Hospital Authority was inaugurated on 1 December 1990 and finally took over the management of all public hospitals from the Hospital Services Department a year later.

Although primarily an organizational reform, the creation of the Hospital Authority did have a side-effect on government policy. Incorporated into the Hospital Authority Ordinance (and curiously out of place among all the legislative provisions) was an undertaking that no-one should be prevented, through lack of means, from obtaining adequate medical treatment (Hospital Authority Ordinance, section 4(d)). Although legally applying only to the Hospital Authority, the government subsequently adopted this as a statement of its overall health care policy.

In parallel with these developments, the government undertook an in-house review of primary care. While ostensibly an examination of the whole sector, most of the 102 recommendations made in the resultant Report of the Working Party on Primary Health Care (1990) were in fact concerned with improving the management and operation of the Department of Health and little attention was given to the role of, or relationship with, private practitioners.

While the establishment of the Hospital Authority and the review of primary health care led to improvements in public sector facilities during the course of the 1990s, each exercise was tackled in the government's typically piecemeal fashion. The opportunity was not taken to examine the operation of the system as a whole or tackle important questions of health care financing and the public–private interface. This omission was to have severe consequences in the future as service demands on the public sector increased.

Even more neglected by the government was the entire traditional Chinese medicine sector. In the 1842 Treaty of Nanking (Nanjing), by which China ceded Hong Kong to Britain, the latter undertook not to interfere in the customs and practices of the Chinese community in Hong Kong. This was used as a pretext for non-intervention into traditional Chinese medicine for the next 150 years. It was not until after Britain had agreed to return Hong Kong to Chinese sovereignty, and a provision in the 1990 Basic Law that required the government 'to formulate policies to develop Western and traditional Chinese medicine' (Basic Law, Article 138), that things slowly began to move forward. Following the appointment of a Working Party on Chinese Medicine in 1989, and the presentation of its report in 1994, the government finally enacted a Chinese Medicine Ordinance in 1999, although several more years would pass before all of its provisions were brought into effect.

THE MAKING OF HEALTH POLICY

Health policy is the responsibility of the Health, Welfare and Food Bureau, which oversees the work of the Hospital Authority, the Department of Health and (following a reorganization in 2002) the Food and Environmental Hygiene Department. The key health system structures are outlined in Figure 8.1.

As with other governments, Hong Kong's has two types of health policy – service policy defines the respective roles of the public and private sectors in the provision and funding of services, while regulatory policy determines the operating environment for health care providers and users. As shown in the preceding section, in Hong Kong both types of policy making have been characterized by their minimalism and introduction in a piecemeal fashion only in reaction to crisis or public outcry. The government has not formulated a role for the

182 Comparative health policy in the Asia-Pacific

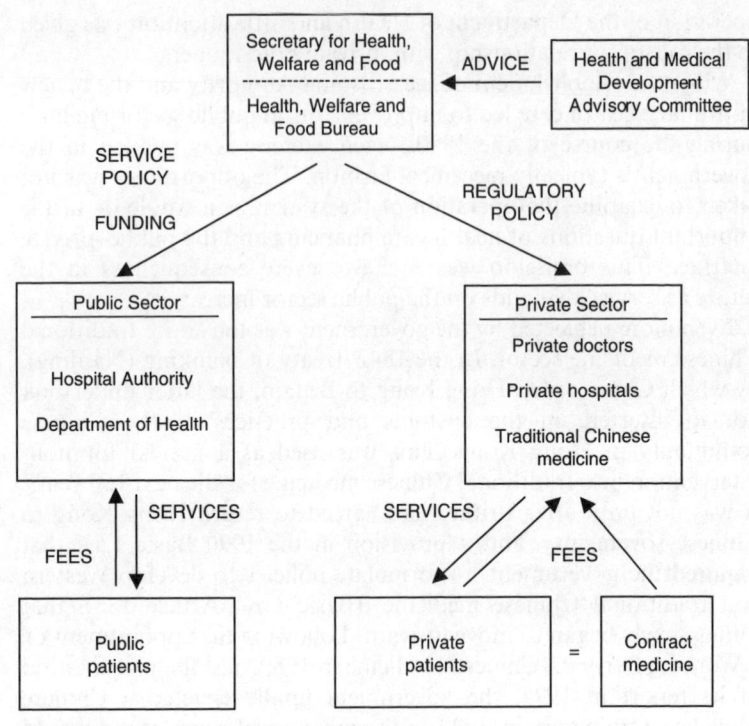

Figure 8.1 The Hong Kong health system.

private sector and has also been demonstrably reluctant to regulate private providers. The legislation which purports to impose controls over them generally allows them to operate in the way they wish to. This is largely due to the way the government makes policy and also to the amount of influence wielded by the medical profession.

In the process of policy making (especially regulatory policy for the medical profession and health care providers), the government relies extensively on the appointment of working parties, comprising leading academics and practitioners in the relevant field, to consider the issues and advise on the way ahead. Two reasons may be ascertained for this. First, the government's various policy bureaux (equivalent to ministries in most countries) are staffed by generalist administrators who lack the expertise to formulate proposals on professional matters. Secondly, given the tendency of most senior professionals to be both protective and parochial, the recommendations that emerge from working parties consisting of 'insiders' often reflect aspirations among members of the profession which are only incrementally different from current practice, rather than being radical in nature. Such proposals are thus less likely to be rejected than if they had been made by government 'outsiders'.

Reports of working parties are generally published for public consultation. Most attract relatively few responses, with views from affected parties tending to outnumber those from members of the public. This feedback provides the government with a sword that it can use to cut two ways. Negative comments can be exaggerated to block or change proposals which the government opposes, or be downplayed as numerically insignificant if there is a policy the government wishes to implement. However, such is the political influence of the medical profession (and deference given by the government) that any proposal which is strongly opposed by them is unlikely to succeed, no matter how widespread the public support.

The translation of policy proposals into legislation is frequently assigned to a government-appointed preparatory committee, again consisting of leading figures in the field, together with a sprinkling of community figures to represent the general public. When their task has been completed, members of the preparatory committee can expect to find themselves appointed to the statutory body which their legislation has created to regulate the providers. With this in mind, members tend to devise procedures that they would not find onerous to implement or that would not be objectionable to their professional colleagues. The outcome of much regulatory policy is, therefore, to make statutory those procedures which providers are already practising voluntarily, or give statutory protection to privileges being enjoyed by established providers.

For the government, such policy making by proxy is politically expedient. It avoids the administration becoming embroiled in factional disputes, while reserving the right to make changes to proposals or legislation in response to political pressure without appearing weak or contradictory. What the process lacks most is democracy. Preparatory committees and working parties tend to consist of middle-class professionals who are not representative of the majority of health care consumers.

THE HEALTH-CARE SYSTEM AND SERVICES

The distinguishing feature of the Hong Kong health care system is that it comprises a collection of independent providers, each working in their own market niche (see Figure 8.1). Allowed to operate in a free market, various providers have emerged to take advantage of whatever opportunities exist, while the government has by default (and at times with certain reluctance) taken up needs that remain unmet. The result of this 'policy of benign neglect' is a system that is 'highly compartmentalized', with a lack of coordination between primary and secondary/tertiary levels and between public and private sectors (Harvard Team 1999: 6).

As at 31 December 2002, Hong Kong had 10,731 doctors, of whom 9627 were on the 'local list' and 1104 were on the 'overseas list' (Medical Council of Hong Kong 2003). The latter comprises doctors registered to practise in Hong Kong but residing overseas. Excluding them gives Hong Kong a ratio of 1.4 doctors per 1000 population. This is low compared with developed countries, but similar to countries such as China and Taiwan, where traditional Chinese medicine contributes to a substantial proportion of health care consultations.

Around half of the doctors work in the private sector, while 4299 are employed by the Hospital Authority and 539 by the Department of Health (Census and Statistics Department 2003). The continuing debate on whether there is a shortage or surplus of doctors – as indicated by long waiting times in the public sector, compared with low patient volumes in the private sector – suggests that the distribution of doctors between the two sectors is imbalanced. The situation is exacerbated by current economic conditions, a result of which is the public sector being chosen by patients seeking cheaper treatment and by medical graduates seeking income security.

The Medical Council's specialist register includes the names of 3015 doctors who have completed a 6 year course of postgraduate education and training recognized by the Hong Kong Academy of Medicine, which entitles them to advertise themselves as specialists (Medical Council of Hong Kong 2003). However, the profession asserts that the purpose of the specialist register is indicative and not limiting – that is, any doctor can *work* as a specialist, providing he does not *claim* to be one (*HKMA News*, August 1998). Conversely, many specialists in obstetrics and gynaecology and paediatrics are the point of first contact for women and children patients, rather than relying on referral from a general practitioner.

There are 7707 traditional Chinese medicine practitioners (Hong Kong SAR Government 2003b). Except for a small number employed by the Tung Wah Group of Hospitals, and in traditional

Chinese medicine clinics run by the universities for teaching purposes, most work in the private sector.

The public sector has always been dominated by hospital services and this is reflected in the relative size and budgets of the Hospital Authority and Department of Health. The former has 49,800 staff and is allocated HK$30 billion a year in public funds by the Health, Welfare and Food Bureau (Hong Kong Hospital Authority 2004), compared with 6268 staff and HK$3 billion a year for the latter (Department of Health 2002).

The Department of Health is the government's public health and regulatory authority, having responsibility for health education, disease surveillance/prevention and the registration of hospitals and health professionals. It also operates specialized clinics that screen and treat communicable diseases, and provides a limited amount of other primary care. In 2003, the Department of Health was further downsized by the transfer of its general outpatient clinics to the Hospital Authority. This reflects a gradual realignment of functional responsibilities, with the Department concentrating on community health services while the Authority provides individual health services.

The Hospital Authority operates 43 public hospitals and 47 associated specialist clinics that screen and book patients for hospital admission, as well as providing outpatient and follow-up services. Specialist clinics charge HK$100 for the first attendance and HK$60 subsequently, with drugs supplied at HK$10 per prescription item (or HK$20 per item if a supply for more than 16 weeks is dispensed). General outpatient clinics charge HK$45 per consultation, which includes a few days' supply of medicines. The fee for a stay in a general acute bed in a public hospital is HK$100 per day, including food, accommodation, tests and all treatment/surgery, plus an admission fee of HK$50. Convalescent, rehabilitation, infirmary and psychiatric beds are charged at HK$68 per day. Most patients are accommodated in wards nominally containing six to eight beds, but which often have additional 'temporary' beds added. A small number of second- and first-class private rooms are available at HK$2600 and $3900 per day for acute hospitals and $2200/$3300 for other hospitals, with additional charges for consultation and surgery (Hong Kong Hospital Authority 2004).

In terms of market share, the Hospital Authority dominates the inpatient sector with 29,505 beds, compared with a total of 2853 beds provided by Hong Kong's twelve private hospitals (Hong Kong SAR Government 2003c). The latter also operate at a lower occupancy ratio; thus calculated in terms of annual inpatient bed-days, the Hospital Authority accounts for 94 per cent of the total provision (Health and Welfare Bureau 2000).

The situation is reversed with regard to primary care, with the private sector dominating. Private practitioners provide 54.8 per cent of consultations, public doctors 20.4 per cent and traditional Chinese medicine practitioners 22.7 per cent (Census and Statistics Department 2000). In contrast to a century ago, most Chinese now feel comfortable consulting a Western doctor. Only 4.3 per cent use traditional Chinese medicine exclusively, while 23.6 per cent use a combination of Western and traditional medicine (*South China Morning Post*, 2 March 2001). Preference is often determined by the type of ailment and it is not uncommon for people to take Western drugs and traditional herbal remedies simultaneously in the belief that 'more is better'.

The majority of doctors in the private sector, particularly those with only a basic qualification, work as solo practitioners. Their clinics, located in residential areas (commonly in public or private housing estates), cater mainly to residents of the neighbourhood. The average fee for a brief consultation and 2–3 days' supply of medicines is HK$150. More established doctors, specialists and partnerships have suites in the commercial district and command higher fees in the region of HK$400. Although economic pressures forced one-fifth of specialists and one-quarter of general practitioners to reduce their fees by an average of 10 per cent between mid-2001 and mid-2002, the Patients' Rights Association believes that doctors are still charging too much (*South China Morning Post*, 7 March 2003).

Surplus medical personnel, combined with prohibition of doctors' advertising and soliciting for patients, have led to the development of 'contract medicine'. This refers to arrangements in which a profit-making agent gathers together a group or 'panel' of doctors and negotiates the fees to be charged to patients the agent refers. The agent (who can be an independent broker, an insurance company or a business that owns one or more doctors' practices) then finds patients, typically by packaging and selling staff medical benefits schemes to employers.

While most patients pay for each consultation on an out-of-pocket basis, medical insurance and contract medicine have been increasing in popularity and now account for 30 per cent of general outpatient financing (Harvard Team 1999). The effects have been mixed. Enrolees are restricted in choice to their employer's panel doctors, but have their medical costs subsidized. By joining a panel, solo practitioners are able to provide better integration of primary and specialist care. They gain access to more patients, but must give agents substantial rebates. The Medical Council has had to warn doctors to ensure that their resultant income 'is not so low as to compromise the quality of care' (*South China Morning Post*, 5 January 2001). Meanwhile, doctors who do not belong to any panel may be marginalized and lose patients. Insurers have access to a large patient base on which to perform data analysis, but this has yet to translate into population-based management, better preventive care or more efficient use of medical facilities.

As with other professions, the government has allowed doctors to regulate themselves and be responsible for their own discipline. This is left in the hands of the Medical Council, whose members (except for token laypeople) are all doctors. In the public sector, dissatisfied patients can complain to the Hospital Authority or Department of Health as the doctor's employer. For private practitioners, the patients' only recourse is to the Medical Council. Complaints are mainly about the failure to make a proper or timely diagnosis or to give proper advice (29 per cent), and unsatisfactory results of surgery (25 per cent). As the arbiter of what constitutes malpractice or disregard of professional responsibility to patients, the Council only requires doctors to meet the standards of their peers and not the standards demanded by the community. In 2002, the Medical Council received a total of 287 complaints but reached a guilty finding in only seven cases, with 80 per cent having been dismissed at the preliminary stage without a full hearing by the Council (Medical Council of Hong Kong 2003). The absence of a requirement for continuing medical education among general practitioners, and the lack of peer review for solo practitioners, combined with self-regulation and insufficient external oversight has led to Hong Kong being criticized for having a highly variable quality of health care (Harvard Team 1999).

The typical traditional Chinese medicine dispensary will share half a shop premises with a Western medicine store, which sells non-prescription drugs, toiletries and household cleansers. Many traditional Chinese medicine dispensaries have a resident or visiting practitioner who provides consultations on the premises. Diagnosis is based on consideration of the symptoms and patient's history, physical examination and careful pulse-taking from both wrists. The patient is then given a prescription which details the quantities of various herbs to be boiled together and drunk as an infusion. The exact composition will depend on both the patient's illness and the stage of recovery. Traditional Chinese medicine consultation fees are in the range of HK$30, with each dose of herbs costing HK$35–40. A course of treatment for upper respiratory tract infection usually requires two or three consultations and prescriptions.

Previously subject to no control whatsoever, resulting in occasional incidents of mistaken dispensing and poisoning, traditional Chinese medicine has in the past few years been progressively brought into line with the regulatory structure of Western medicine. A Chinese Medicine Ordinance was passed in July 1999 to regulate the practice of traditional Chinese medicine practitioners and the use, manufacture and trading of Chinese medicines. This combines the function of the Medical Registration Ordinance, the Pharmacy and Poisons Ordinance and the Antibiotics Ordinance, which regulate Western doctors and medicines. A Chinese Medicine Council of Hong Kong (equivalent to the Medical Council for doctors) was established under the Ordinance in September 1999 (Department of Health 2004). As a result of the legislation, traditional Chinese medicine practitioners and dispensers are now required to hold recognized qualifications and/or training, and only recognized herbs are permitted to be dispensed.

The freedom with which patients can move among various providers on the basis of their own choice and affordability, rather than by referral, creates inefficiency in the system. The provider chosen may not be the appropriate one for the treatment needed. Records and tests may be duplicated, with each provider holding an incomplete medical history. Providers' inability to see 'the big picture' means that most treatment tends to be episodic and lacking in coherence. Apart from childhood immunizations, little preventive care is practised. As a result, increased resources have to be spent on treatment of otherwise avoidable illnesses. One example of this is the growing problem of childhood obesity. Viewed from the perspective of a long history of rural poverty and malnutrition, the traditional Chinese belief that plump children are healthy is only gradually giving way to an understanding of increased risk of diabetes, high blood pressure and heart trouble in adulthood. Despite this, little preventive work is being done to encourage a healthy diet and lifestyle among the younger generation.

CURRENT HEALTH SYSTEM AND POLICY CHALLENGES

Although the Scott Report (1985), the Provisional Hospital Authority (1989) and the Working Party on Primary Health Care (1990) all thought that there was need to go beyond making structural reforms and to address the larger issue of health care financing and delivery for the system as a whole, the government on each occasion failed to follow up. Public services have undergone successive improvements and expansions without any re-examination of the fee structure. As a result, patients have come to expect access to more and better services for the same nominal charges.

A major obstacle to reform is the compartmentalized way in which the health care system operates and is funded. Private doctors cannot admit and treat patients in public hospitals and Hospital Authority/Department of Health doctors cannot work in private hospitals. Public funds are not used to buy services from private sector providers, only to meet the operating costs of the Authority and the Department. The private sector is funded by patients' out-of-pocket payments and by private medical insurance schemes. The only private money entering the public sector is in the form of patients' fees, which in the case of the Hospital Authority represents only 2.5 per cent of its recurrent operating expenses (Health and Welfare Bureau 2000). All providers seem content to maintain the *status quo* and preserve (if not expand) their existing market share. They have shown little interest in working together, as evidenced by the lack of support for any reforms aimed to develop an integrated health system. Failure to communicate across sector boundaries was all too evident during the 2003 outbreak of SARS (see below), when private doctors were unable to access their SARS patients' Hospital Authority records and when the government failed to disseminate information and guidelines about SARS to private practitioners, pharmacists and traditional Chinese medicine practitioners in a timely fashion, hampering the coordination of disease prevention efforts (SARS Expert Committee 2003).

Related to compartmentalization is the government's failure to define its financial responsibility as regards citizens' eligibility for subsidized health care. The government's policy is that no-one should be denied adequate medical treatment through lack of means (Hong Kong Government 1993). As a statement of eligibility and entitlement, this is woefully inadequate. While it provides some vague assurance of a medical safety net, the government manipulates the meaning by implicitly defining the key terms. Accordingly, 'adequate' is measured against the level and type of services provided in the public sector, including waiting time. 'Lack of means' is not based on financial criteria or the ability to afford a private provider. It defaults to include anyone who is prepared to queue for public treatment. Heavy reliance is placed on patients' self-selection to regulate demand. This worked in the past when the choice was between an inferior but cheap public sector and a superior but expensive private sector. However, once Hospital Authority and Department of Health facilities improved in quality, while retaining their low fee structure, it ceased to be an effective mechanism.

The government does not subsidize its citizens' medical expenses. Rather, it subsidizes public providers to deliver services to eligible patients at nominal fees. The distinction is not merely one of semantics. For someone to receive subsidized treatment, they must be able to gain access to a public facility. In the case of Department of Health (not Hospital Authority) general outpatient clinics, the issue is one of capacity. The clinics can only meet 11 per cent of the demand for primary care consultations (Census and Statistics Department 2000). For Hospital Authority clinics, there are discouragingly long waiting times for specialist consultation and non-urgent hospital admissions. Statistics on this are not made public. Although patients who use the private sector are saving the government money, they receive no financial subsidy or reimbursement from the government. While public and private funding, if pooled together, are sufficient to meet the costs of public and private providers, the government alone cannot afford to cover the costs of all health care that is delivered in Hong Kong.

Following the establishment of the Hospital Authority, operating costs for public hospitals increased as salaries in the former subvented hospitals were raised to be in line with salaries in the former government hospitals. Improved standards of accommodation and service also attracted more patients to the public sector. However, it was not until 1993 that the government began to consider whether the increased costs would be sustainable in the longer term. In 1993, the Health and Welfare Bureau published a public consultation document entitled 'Towards Better Health'. This raised concerns that the ageing population, increasing medical costs and rising community expectations would exacerbate the overloading of public facilities and put financial pressure on the government. There was also a lack of interface between the public and private sectors, which resulted in overcrowding in the former and spare capacity in the latter. The document offered two collections of ideas for fee charging and fee waiving, two forms of insurance for funding health services and a scheme of rationing to allocate medical resources. Some of the proposals were left over from recommendations in the Scott Report but never implemented, while others were gleaned from health systems in other countries. While indicating a preference for a system of differential subsidies according to the type of service and affordability to patients, the government did not try to 'sell' any of the approaches as concrete policy proposals (Hong Kong Government 1993).

When the document was published, the proposals met with little understanding from the medical profession, the media or the public. In the midst of a robust economy, with the government recording budget surpluses, few could grasp the concept of a future when the public sector would be unable to make ends meet under the present financing system. The proposals were widely misunderstood and criticized as a ploy by government to shirk its responsibilities by passing the funding burden onto poor patients. Opposition was widespread (*Hong Kong Standard*, 27 and 31 August 1993). Of the various approaches proposed, only two component parts were acceptable to the community – semi-private beds and voluntary insurance.

Semi-private beds were introduced on a trial basis in 1994, offering public hospital patients a better standard of accommodation in return for a higher daily fee of HK$600–800. However, while popular with patients, the idea had several drawbacks as far as the Hospital Authority was concerned. First, instead of just diverting patients from general ward beds, their relative cheapness actually attracted more patients away from the private sector, adding to public sector demand. Second, they took up more space, thus reducing hospital bed capacity. Third, although costing more to run, a peculiarity in the government's inflexible funding mechanism meant that they attracted less subvention, for which even higher patient fees were unable to compensate. These drawbacks provided the Hospital Authority with no incentive to upgrade its accommodation, despite public demand.

In early 1995, discussions were held between the Health and Welfare Bureau and the medical insurance industry over implementation of a voluntary insurance scheme tailored to financing semi-private beds. However, when the trial semi-private bed scheme failed to develop into full operation, the insurance proposal was quietly shelved (Liu and Yue 1998).

In 1997, the government made a second reform attempt when the Health and Welfare Bureau invited consultants from the Harvard School of Public Health to examine the existing financing system and recommend options that would 'better integrate the public/ private sectors and primary/secondary/tertiary health care services' (Information Services Department 1998).

The consultants' report, published in 1999, was scathing in its criticism of the government's 'policy of benign neglect', under which it only reacted in response to crises and with piecemeal solutions. Its *laissez-faire* attitude had led to four serious defects in the health care system: a highly variable quality of care; questionable financial sustainability; compartmentalization; and dominance by public hospitals at the expense of primary care and community medicine (Harvard Team 1999: 4–9). The findings were a slap in the face for the government and the medical profession alike.

Apart from recommending that the government take steps to improve its competency in health policy making generally, the consultants offered five options to address the system's specific problems. Three were 'throwaways' designed to show that popularly advocated solutions – doing nothing, capping the government's health budget and raising patient fees – did not address the problems (Harvard Team 1999: 11–12). Borrowing from experience in Japan, New Zealand, Singapore, Sweden and the UK, the remaining two options were parts of a two-stage scheme that would completely revolutionize the way health care was financed and delivered.

For the first stage, it was proposed to introduce a Health Security Plan and a savings account for long-term care (Medisage), each financed by mandatory employer/employee contributions of 2.5–3 per cent of the employee's salary. Contributions to the Health Security Plan would be used to purchase insurance from a quasi-government Health Security Fund. Patients could seek treatment for catastrophic and chronic illnesses from either the public or private sector, for which the Health Security Fund would make payment at standard rates. The Hospital Authority and Department of Health would cease to receive government subvention and would instead compete with the private sector by charging for services at cost. Medisage contributions would go into a personal savings account to be commuted upon retirement or permanent disability to purchase a single-premium long-term care insurance policy (Harvard Team 1999: 12–16). The second stage would break the Hospital Authority down into 12–18 regional health integrated systems, competing with each other and with the private sector to provide enrolees with a defined package of preventive, primary, outpatient and hospital care, in return for a prepaid monthly or annual fee (Harvard Team 1999: 16–17).

The proposals were technically sophisticated but politically naïve, offending practically all vested interest groups. While the public generally agreed that there was need to reform the health care financing and delivery system, there was little support for the Harvard Team's ideas of how reform should be achieved (Health and Welfare Bureau 2000). Employers and employees baulked at having to make mandatory contributions when the economy had entered into recession and their livelihoods were affected. The Hospital Authority did not relish the idea of losing subvention and its position of monopoly by being broken up into small units having to compete for income with the private sector. Private providers found the idea of standard payment rates and prepaid contracts anathema to their established way of charging for services. Chronic patients feared a decline in services and worried that Medisage would be insufficient to meet their long-term needs. Above all, even though the government would continue its existing levels of funding, via the Health Security Fund, the proposals were seen as a relinquishment of its responsibility for health care.

As with the 1993 consultation document, the public failed to see the big picture because the problems and conceptual solutions were too removed from the reality of the present system and fee structure to be appreciated. Even policy makers were not convinced that such radical steps were necessary. They found comfort in the view of one economist who asserted that health care costs would not rise as fast as the Harvard Team had calculated (*South China Morning Post*, 15 April 1999), that population ageing was so slow as not to be a problem (*Hong Kong Standard*, 21 April 1999) and that with a modest 2 per cent growth in the economy, the government would have sufficient funds to meet public sector expenses (Yuen 1999). However, what no one foresaw was that the current recession would be a prolonged one, heralding a change in Hong Kong's economic fundamentals under which even 2 per cent GDP growth would be unattainable. Pursuing what the Legislative Council's medical functional constituency representative called a 'less decisions, less mistakes' approach (Leong 1999), the government took the widespread criticism as a sign that the public needed to know more before it could take any decision on the way ahead. The Harvard Team's recommendations were accordingly shelved.

The government made a third review attempt in 2000. Ostensibly, a follow-on to the Harvard Team's consultancy study (Health and Welfare Bureau 2000), this contained little in common with its predecessor. While agreeing in general with the system's previously identified shortcomings (although not their severity), the 2000 consultation document proposed a totally different set of solutions. The delivery system, quality assurance and financing were treated as discrete subject areas, each with its own challenges to be addressed on a piecemeal basis. Grand in vision and philosophy, the document was liberal in its use of synonymous verbs like 'strengthen', 'reorganize' 'develop', 'facilitate', 'promote', 'enhance', 'improve' and 'revamp' with regard to existing services, facilities and arrangements, rather than proposing any radical changes. It was also notably short on detail as to how its aims would be achieved and provided almost no statistics to support its proposals (*South China Morning Post*, 13 December 2000).

Despite economic conditions which caused the Hospital Authority to experience its first-ever budget deficit and lengthening queues for public treatment, the Secretary for Health and Welfare explained that the government had recalculated the Harvard Team's projections and found that health care financing was not as unsustainable as it had been made out to be. Future funding needs could therefore 'be addressed through less radical changes' (*South China Morning Post*, 26 January 2001). These included public-sector supply-side cost containment, additional user charges, prioritization of services and longer-term proposals for a watered-down medical savings scheme (Health and Welfare Bureau 2000) – all devices that would help the Health Authority balance its accounts, rather than provide financing solutions for citizens or the health care sector as a whole.

The seriousness of the Harvard Team's concerns about highly variable quality of care, compartmentalization and dominance by public hospitals were similarly downplayed. The former two problems were left to be solved by modest and incremental changes (such as continuing medical education, adoption of common protocols and improved communication), many of which were already in hand or whose voluntary adoption by the private sector had been the subject of prior consultations. The latter would be addressed by the Hospital Authority boosting its community-based services and taking over the Department of Health's general outpatient clinics. If the Harvard Team's recommendations were flawed by being technically sophisticated but politically naïve, then the government's low-key and piecemeal solutions were exactly the opposite, with effectiveness being sacrificed for acceptability.

Although the government did not consider that there were serious defects in primary and preventive care, the Harvard Team's findings in this area were somewhat vindicated by the outbreak of H5N1 avian flu in 1997, which killed 6 of the 18 people it infected. Although having its origins in farms where poultry, pigs and humans lived side-by-side, the virus was introduced into the local population by poor environmental hygiene in the markets where live birds were sold, and by lack of health awareness on the part of staff and customers handling the birds.

After a period of not knowing how to respond to this new situation, the government reacted with creditable decisiveness in ordering the culling of 1.6 million birds and the introduction of a monthly 'rest day' during which markets were cleaned and disinfected. Widely criticized at the time, the slaughter has since come to praised for having saved the world from a possible pandemic had the virus spread among the population and mutated into a form that was transmissible from human to human (*South China Morning Post*, 29 January 2001). Although falling short of a total solution (which could have been achieved by the unpopular step of prohibiting the sale of live birds completely), culling has become the government's standard response whenever the virus has been found through routine testing.

While experience has honed the government's ability to cope with the H5N1 virus, it has not led to any system-wide improvement in disease control. Hong Kong was, therefore, again caught unprepared when SARS broke out in March 2003. Due to poor infection control, it spread rapidly among staff and patients of the hospital where the index patient had been admitted. A second large outbreak occurred when the virus was spread throughout a residential building by a defective drainage system, killing 42 residents. With insufficient surge capacity to cope with infectious diseases, patients had to be turned away and facilities closed down as public hospitals struggled to accommodate all suspected SARS cases. As with the plague epidemic of 1894, the population watched in fear as the then unidentified SARS virus spread, seemingly unstoppable and untreatable by the medicine of the day. The economy, already weak, suffered further as tourism ceased and residents stayed at home. By the time SARS had been brought under control nearly 3 months later, it had infected 1755 people, killed 300 and caused massive financial losses.

In its report, published in October 2003, a government-appointed SARS Expert Committee was highly critical of the organizational and systemic defects which had impeded the government's handling of the outbreak. These included the absence of disease control contingency plans; poor command structure, coordination, definition of responsibilities and communication within and among the Health and Welfare Bureau and its departments; poor communications between the public sector and private doctors and hospitals; shortfalls in disease surveillance and epidemiology; lack of expertise in infection control; and substantial weaknesses in hospital design and environment, including overcrowded wards and outdated facilities (SARS Expert Committee 2003).

The Committee made 46 recommendations based around a proposed Centre for Health Protection that would have 'responsibility, authority and accountability for the prevention and control of communicable disease' (SARS Expert Committee 2003: 29). If implemented, the recommendations would be more than just another *ad-hoc* or piecemeal solution. Instead, they would put in place integrated arrangements to boost the government's ability to deal with not just another SARS outbreak, but any infectious disease.

The government responded with surprising alacrity. Within 6 months of the Expert Committee's recommendations, it had restructured the Department of Health to redirect HK$1 billion of its annual budget and 1300 of its staff to a new Centre for Health Protection. This was launched on 1 April 2004 (*South China Morning Post*, 2 April 2004), just in time to respond to a new SARS outbreak across the border in Mainland China.

CONCLUSIONS

The history of health care in Hong Kong has been characterized by a policy of governmental *laissez-faire* and professional self-regulation, interrupted by piecemeal reactions to crises. As a result, service delivery is highly compartmentalized and there is no integrated funding mechanism that embraces all providers and users. Quality of care is highly variable and doubts have been cast on the system's financial sustainability as the population ages.

Reviews over the years have led to organizational reforms within the public sector, while leaving the basic system untouched. The latest review of health care financing and delivery, in 2000, proposed a number of discrete and incremental measures. How effective these will be in remedying the system's shortcomings remains to be seen. However, with a stated lead of time of up to 20 years for some of these measures to be introduced, the community is assured of a long wait. A more immediate and pressing concern for most people is the government's weakness in disease prevention and control, as revealed by the H5N1 avian flu and SARS outbreaks. The community waits anxiously to see whether the new Centre for Health Protection will be able to protect their lives and livelihoods.

REFERENCES

Beaglehole, R. and Bonita, R. (1997) *Public Health at the Crossroads; Achievements and Prospects*. Cambridge: Cambridge University Press.
Census and Statistics Department (2000) *Thematic Household Survey Report No. 3*. Hong Kong: Government Printer.
Census and Statistics Department (2003) *Hong Kong Annual Digest of Statistics 2003 Edition*. Hong Kong: Government Logistics Department.
Census and Statistics Department (2004) *Selected Measures of Fertility, 1981–2002*. Unpublished document.
Choa, G.H. (1985) A history of medicine in Hong Kong, in *Medical Directory of Hong Kong*. Hong Kong: The Federation of Medical Societies of Hong Kong.
Choa, G.H. (2000) *The Life and Times of Sir Kai Ho Kai*, 2nd edn. Hong Kong: Chinese University Press.
Collins, C. (1952) *Public Administration in Hong Kong*. London: Royal Institute of International Affairs.
Department of Health (2002) *Annual Report 2001/2002*. Hong Kong: Government Logistics Department.
Department of Health (2004) Website (available at: http://www.info.gov.hk/dh/main_ser/index.htm).
Eitel, E.J. ([1895] 1983) *Europe in China*. Hong Kong: Oxford University Press.
Endacott, G.B. (1964) *Government and People in Hong Kong, 1841–1962*. Hong Kong: Hong Kong University Press.
Endacott, G.B. (1973) *A History of Hong Kong*, 2nd edn. Hong Kong: Oxford University Press.
Endacott, G.B. and Hinton, A. (1962) *Fragrant Harbour: A Short History of Hong Kong*. Hong Kong: Oxford University Press.
Gauld, R. and Gould, D. (2002) *The Hong Kong Health Sector: Development and Change*. Dunedin/Hong Kong: University of Otago Press/Chinese University Press.
Harvard Team, The (1999) *Improving Hong Kong's Health Care System: Why and For Whom?* Hong Kong: Printing Department, HKSAR Government.
Health and Welfare Bureau (2000) *Lifelong Investment in Health*. Consultation Document on Health Care Reform. Hong Kong: Printing Department, HKSAR Government.
Health, Welfare and Food Bureau (2004) Personal communication.
Ho, S. (1946) A hundred years of Hong Kong. Unpublished PhD thesis, Princeton University, Princeton, NJ.

Hong Kong Government (1963) *Hong Kong 1962*. Hong Kong: Government Printer.
Hong Kong Government (1964) *Development of Medical Services in Hong Kong*. Hong Kong: Government Printer.
Hong Kong Government (1974) *The Further Development of Medical and Health Services in Hong Kong*. Hong Kong: Government Printer.
Hong Kong Government (1993) *Towards Better Health*. Hong Kong: Government Printer.
Hong Kong Hospital Authority (2004) Website (available at: http://www.ha.org.hk).
Hong Kong SAR Government (2003a) *Hong Kong: The Facts – Population*. Hong Kong: Information Services Department.
Hong Kong SAR Government (2003b) *Hong Kong: The Facts – Public Health*. Hong Kong: Information Services Department.
Hong Kong SAR Government (2003c) *Hong Kong 2003*. Hong Kong: Information Services Department.
Information Services Department (1998) *Hong Kong Information Note: Review of the Healthcare System*. Hong Kong: Information Services Department.
Leong, C.H. (1999) *Health Care Reform – A Better Alternative*. Unpublished document.
Liu, E. and Yue, S.Y. (1998) *Health Care Expenditure and Financing in Hong Kong*. Hong Kong: Provisional Legislative Council Secretariat.
MacKenzie, D.J.M. (1962) Medical and Health Department, in Hong Kong Government (ed.) *The Government and Its People*. Hong Kong: Government Printer.
Medical Council of Hong Kong (2003) *Annual Report 2002* (available at: http://www.mchk.org.hk/annual/eng/2002/table.pdf).
Mills, L.A. (1942) *British Rule in East Asia: A Study of Contemporary Government and Economic Development in British Malaya and Hong Kong*. London: Oxford University Press.
Miners, N. (1987) *Hong Kong Under Imperial Rule, 1912–1941*. Hong Kong: Oxford University Press.
Provisional Hospital Authority (1989) *Report of the Provisional Hospital Authority*. Hong Kong: Government Printer.
SARS Expert Committee (2003) *SARS in Hong Kong: From Experience to Action. A Summary Report of the SARS Expert Committee*. Hong Kong: Government Logistics Department, HKSAR Government.
Sayer, G.R. (1975) *Hong Kong 1862–1919: Years of Discretion*. Hong Kong: Hong Kong University Press.
Scott, W.D. and Co. (1985) *The Delivery of Medical Services in Hospitals: A Report for the Hong Kong Government*. Hong Kong: Government Printer.
Sinn, E. (1989) *Power and Charity: The Early History of the Tung Wah Hospital. Hong Kong*. Hong Kong: Oxford University Press.
Tung Wah Group of Hospitals Board of Directors (eds) (1970) *One*

Hundred Years of the Tung Wah Group of Hospitals, 1970–1970, Volumes 1 and 2. Hong Kong: TWGH.

Wellington, A.R. (1930) *Public Health in Hong Kong*. Report to the Hong Kong Government, CO 129/531. Hong Kong: Government Printer.

Wellington, A.R. (1935) *Medical and Sanitary Report for the Year 1935*. Hong Kong: Government Printer.

Working Party on Primary Health Care (1990) *Health for All: The Way Ahead*. Report of the Working Party on Primary Health Care. Hong Kong: Government Printer.

Yuen, P.P. (1992) Medical and health, in J.Y.S. Cheng and P.C.K. Kwong (eds) *The Other Hong Kong Report 1992*. Hong Kong: Chinese University Press.

Yuen, P.P. (1999) The sustainability of Hong Kong's health care system: a population based projection, *Policy Bulletin*, 11 (May–June): 5–9.

9

NEW ZEALAND
Robin Gauld

Population 2003	4 million
Ethnic composition 2003	European (80%), Maori (14.7%), Pacific peoples (6.5%), Chinese (2.9%), Indian (1.7%)
Capital city	Wellington
Live births per woman 2003	1.92
Infant mortality rate per 1000 live births 2000	5.8
Life expectancy at birth 2000 (male/female)	76.0/80.9 years
Total health expenditure as a percentage of GDP 2002	8.2%
Government health expenditure as a percentage of total health expenditure 2002	77.9%
Total health expenditure per capita 2002 (US$ PPP)	1835
Practising physicians per 1000 population 2000	2.2
Health system	Tax-funded, Ministry of Health (central policy maker/funder), 21 district health boards (local planners/service purchasers), state-dominated hospital sector, private-dominated primary care sector.

| Political system | Single-chamber, Cabinet-dominated parliamentary democracy. |

Sources: OECD (2003), Statistics New Zealand (2003)

INTRODUCTION

The developed island-state of New Zealand is home to some 4 million people divided across two islands: three-quarters live in the North Island, the remainder in the South Island. Eighty-five per cent reside in urban areas, with around a third of the population in the Auckland metropolitan area.

When it comes to health policy, New Zealand has had a tumultuous ride in recent years. Governments from across the political spectrum have experimented with a range of policy approaches and initiatives and, in keeping with this, various health system structures. Since 1989, New Zealand has had four completely different systems for the delivery of publicly funded health care, giving it the dubious title of 'most restructured' in the developed world. The structures include an area health board system (1989–91), a competitive internal market system (1993–96), a central planning and purchasing system (1997–2000) and the present district health board system (2000–). Through the restructuring period, when key changes corresponded with general elections and a change of government, planning and purchasing responsibilities have been decentralized, marketized, centralized, then decentralized again, while service providers have been required to compete and then collaborate with one another. Furthermore, there has been a shift in thinking about health policy: through most of the 1990s, the key focus of policy and services was on individuals and on contractual and financial accountability; since 2000, the emphasis has been on populations, participation and health improvement.

The restructuring, however, has had little impact on historically determined institutions. There remain tensions and a lack of integration between primary and secondary care, public and personal health, and the private and public components of the health sector. Similarly, policy makers continue to grapple with socioeconomic and geographical inequities that affect service access, while, until very recently, there have been few changes to the ways in which services have been funded. Added to this, New Zealand's health policy makers, planners and providers today face problems confronting most advanced countries: an ever-expanding budget and service demand; the question of how to prioritize and ration services; how best to configure the health care system; how to improve health service governance and quality; and how to better promote preventive medicine and public health.

This chapter overviews the history of New Zealand health policy and system development, then describes the present arrangements before, finally, considering key challenges.

A BRIEF HISTORY OF NEW ZEALAND HEALTH POLICY AND THE HEALTH-CARE SYSTEM

Detailed histories of New Zealand health policy and service development are available elsewhere (e.g. Davis 1981; Hay 1989; Dow 1995; Gauld 2001). The following is an overview.

The institutions underlying New Zealand's contemporary health care system and policy machinery have their roots in the Social Security Act 1938. Before 1938, there had been limited central government commitment to health care and no systematic organization of it: health was often seen as a local government and individual responsibility, although central government did, on occasion, attempt regulation and service provision. The result was a confusing mix of central and local governing boards, public, private and voluntary services, with considerable regional variations in terms of funding and access. With the Social Security Act 1938 came the world's first attempt to create a national health service offering free and universal access to general practitioner and hospital services. However, in a significant policy compromise, the Labour government then in power allowed general practitioners to retain their private business status and independence from the public sector; instead of becoming state-salaried employees, a notion they objected to, they received government subsidies and reimbursable patient co-payments for each consultation. Individual hospital doctors did agree to state employment, laying foundations for a state monopoly in hospital services and private domination of general practice. Nonetheless, hospital specialists retained the right to practise privately alongside their public sector employment. The government contribution to health expenditure (previously 39 per cent) almost doubled following the 1938 legislation (Davis 1981: 7).

The 'national' system was far from perfect and many of today's policy difficulties stem from it. These include a lack of integration between primary and secondary care and the public and private sectors; an uncomfortable tension between central and local sources of finance and control; problems accessing general practice due to high patient part-charges as subsidies failed to keep up with inflation; expanding hospital waiting lists and hospital underfunding; inadequate preventive medicine and health promotion strategies; and inequities fuelled by expanding medical insurance and the 'dual' health system, with the insured guaranteed access to private facilities, that this created (Hay 1989).

Despite periodic reviews, the system remained largely untouched until the 1980s when the system of area health boards was introduced. Developed over several years from 1981 under both a National (centre-right) and then a Labour (centre-left) government, 14 area health boards were finally pulled into place in 1989. These were regionally based semi-elected bodies charged with planning, providing and integrating publicly funded health services for their populations. Coinciding with New Zealand's state-sector reforms of the late–1980s, area health boards were given a series of financial and public health goals and targets that they were required by contract with the government to focus on (Beaglehole and Davis 1992).

By 1990, the area health boards appeared to be performing reasonably well, although there were considerable regional variations (Treasury 1990). There had been reductions in average length of hospital stay, health care expenditure remained stable and below the OECD average, boards were engaging in strategic planning and needs assessments, they were developing integrated care programmes around selected services, and the system was simple with low transaction costs (Ashton *et al.* 1991). The area health boards were also developing strong local presence and public support. On the downside, general practice costs and pharmaceutical subsidies continued to rise at around 6 per cent per annum, there were problems within boards of 'dual accountabilities' to both the government and local electors, and there remained a divide between public and private medicine.

In 1990, a National government concerned with reducing public spending and creating social service markets (Boston and Dalziel 1992) was elected and subsequently announced a radical health system redesign (Upton 1991). Known as the 'health reforms', new structures to be implemented by mid-1993 included:

- Four government-funded independent regional health authorities designed to plan and purchase services for their geographical

population bases from 'the market' (e.g. public and private providers). Competing with the regional health authorities were to be alternative health care plans. Members of the public would be free to invest their per capita potion of government health care money with a purchaser of choice. Despite interest in the concept, the government never allowed alternative plans to emerge.
- Transforming existing public hospitals into 23 Crown health enterprises. Each Crown health enterprise was governed by a board of directors expected to return a profit to government on its investment. These enterprises were to compete in an open tender system – against one another and others – for service delivery contracts offered by regional health authorities.
- An independent Public Health Commission to advise on and purchase population health services. The Commission was disestablished in 1994 as its advice often contradicted the government's market-oriented policy in areas such as housing. Moreover, crucial interests, such as the food, alcohol and tobacco industries, had pressured the government about the Commission's unfavourable advice on the health impacts of their products.
- A Core Services Committee to establish a public consultation process aimed at defining and limiting publicly funded health services and patients, thereby creating certainty for purchasers and providers about their responsibilities. The Committee swiftly recognized the impossibility of its task and, by 1992, moved to developing guidelines for clinical practice and patient prioritization (see below).
- Redeveloping the Department of Health into a policy-oriented Ministry of Health.

The attempt to create a health planning and purchasing market spawned numerous problems. An enormous amount of time and money was spent negotiating funding contracts. Many of the required new managers recruited predominantly from private business to regional health authorities and Crown health enterprises found the health arena difficult, and high staff turnover reflected this. In turn, this complicated contracting and relationship-building processes. While the health reforms did elicit information on the range, volumes and costs of services, information sharing ceased in the competitive environment for reasons of 'commercial sensitivity'. Despite claims that competition would produce efficiency gains, the opposite happened: Crown health enterprises required additional debt funding of around 12 per cent per annum, while hospital waiting lists grew rapidly.[1] There is evidence that the austerity drive associated with the reforms undermined patient safety (Stent 1998). Local populations felt increasingly alienated from the business-oriented Crown health enterprises who, unlike the former area health boards, worked covertly and held all meetings in private. The public's only source of input into health decision making was via the regional health authorities, which had minimal local presence, influence over, or even interest in, the daily decisions of providers.

The health reforms produced some positives. These included the emergence of independent practitioner associations, which are general practitioner organizations initially formed for ensuring effective contract negotiations with the regional health authorities. The independent practitioner associations have since become an established feature of health care delivery in New Zealand, with over 70 per cent of general practitioners affiliated, and many of the associations moving into capitated budgets for laboratory services and pharmaceutical prescribing (Malcolm *et al.* 1999). The independent practitioner associations are presently leading the development of the government's favoured Primary Health Organizations (see below). There were gains for indigenous Maori health through regional health authority funding dedicated 'by Maori, for Maori' services (Barrett 1997). These continue to flourish and today there are around 400 such services. The regional health authorities were responsible for creating Pharmac, a subsidiary company to manage the publicly funded pharmaceutical purchasing schedule. Pharmac remains in existence and claims to have kept pharmaceutical costs under firm control using various techniques such as reference pricing and open tendering (Gauld 2001).

Following the formation of a new coalition government at the 1996 election, and the difficulties with the health reforms, further changes were enacted. These included creating a national purchaser, the Health Funding Authority, through combining the regional health authorities. The Crown health enterprises were renamed hospital and health services to reflect a new focus on 'public service', although there remained an expectation that hospitals would be business-like. The Health Funding Authority was to focus on national consistency and equity in its purchasing strategies, and it moved towards 'benchmarking' its contracts to ensure both safe funding levels and comparability between regions and services. Nonetheless, the inequities perpetuated by consigning planning and purchasing to the market proved difficult to rectify, and many policies inherited by the Authority had been implemented through the competitive era. For example, each Crown health enterprise had developed different scoring systems for prioritizing elective surgery patients, meaning it was impossible to compare between funding levels or thresholds for access in different parts of the country. Service purchasing prices also differed markedly between regions and Crown health enterprises due to contract bargaining processes.

By the end of the Health Funding Authority reign, the health sector had clear direction. Following government policy, a population-based funding formula, sensitive to local circumstance, was under development, and the Authority was engaging in strategic planning, negotiating long-term contracts and focusing on health determinants and reducing inequalities (Creech 1999). A particularly popular coalition policy was implementing free general practitioner visits for those under the age of 6. However, the Health Funding Authority model was criticized for lacking closeness to local populations and not understanding their needs. Service contracting and open tendering, which remained at the heart of the Authority's operations, were also denounced for perpetuating competition.

'DISTRICT HEALTH BOARDS' AND THE PRESENT HEALTH-CARE SYSTEM

The 1999 election produced a new coalition government, this time led by a reinvigorated Labour Party, with similarities to Britain's New Labour, interested in social democracy and rebuilding civil society and institutions. In pre-election campaigning, Labour announced its preference for health system structure (Labour Party 1999), arguing that public confidence in the health system, which was considered to be low (Donelan *et al.* 1999), needed to be restored, that there was a need for a health sector 'vision', that the Health Funding Authority promoted unhealthy competition, and that the community lacked input into health care decision making. Labour actioned its plans immediately after the election and enabling legislation, the New Zealand Public Health and Disability Act 2000, was subsequently enacted.

Central to the new system, which both in structure and aims closely resembles the earlier system of area health boards, are 21 district health boards. The key structures of the system are shown in Figure 9.1. Essentially, the district health board structures represented the government's desire to:

- recentralize control over the health care system, through shifting many of the Health Funding Authority's funding functions to the Ministry of Health, which is directly responsible to the Minister of Health and Cabinet;
- focus the health sector on population-based public health strategies and health status improvement;
- strengthen primary care;
- increase coordination between different parts of the health care system;
- facilitate local control and community participation in decisions over health care needs assessment, planning, funding and management.

The district health boards were constructed out of the existing hospital and health services (hence, the rationale for 21 district health boards), with a crucial difference: the hospital and health services were hospitals, whereas the district health boards have a much broader ambit with responsibility to provide health care for, and improve the health status of, their regional population. In keeping with this, each district health board must conduct a local health care needs assessment and, based on this, plan and purchase an appropriate range and mix of services from providers within their districts. The district health boards are also expected to focus on reducing inequalities in health care access and outcomes among different population and disease groups, increasing service access particularly at the primary care level, and prioritizing services within allocated funding. The district health boards are to be funded using a weighted population-based formula (more on this below). Community consultation is central to all work of the boards.

The government chose to give the Ministry of Health overall responsibility for the health sector. The Ministry, therefore, has a range of roles as chief policy adviser (political), sector analyst (technical) and funder. These roles often do not sit comfortably with one another as ministry officials find themselves having to defend government directives, which frustrates service providers, while attempting to forge good relationships with the sector and produce practicable policy solutions. In keeping with the government's decentralization policy, much policy work is, of course, conducted by the district health boards and other agencies such as Pharmac. This often leads to clashes, played out in the media, between local and central actors. Pharmac, for instance, may restrict a certain drug; public outcry will follow, along with the Minister of Health's

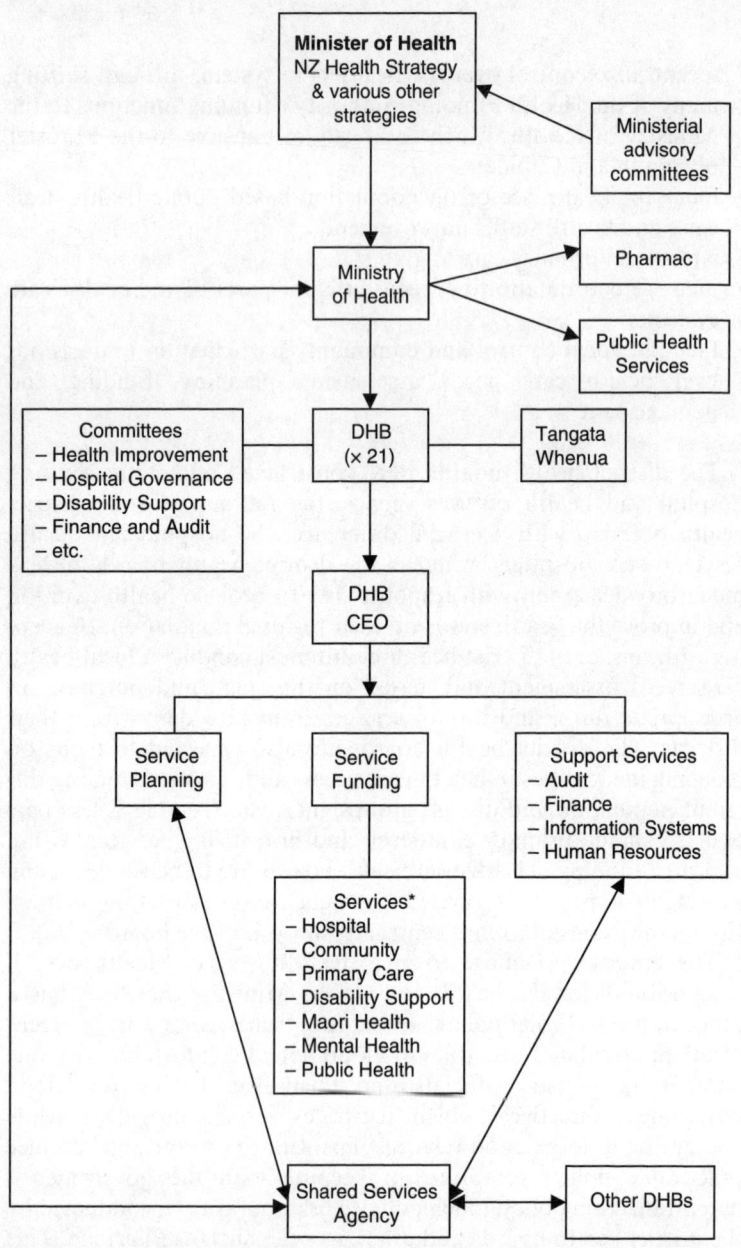

Figure 9.1 The district health board (DHB) system. *Services are funded variously by district health boards, the Ministry of Health and private funding sources.

involvement. Similarly, poor district health board performance or unpopular decisions swiftly come to national attention and political involvement. As discussed below, decentralization is also promoting inter-district inconsistencies that are of concern to policy makers and affected areas.

The 'vision' for the health sector is provided by the New Zealand Health Strategy (King 2000) and accompanying strategies that contain key health priority areas, goals and targets to guide strategic and operational planning for the district health boards and the activities of the multitude of community agencies under contract to provide services to the boards. The performance of the district health boards is assessed against these goals and targets, although many planners and providers have voiced concern about the difficulty of responding to the wide range of different strategies and goals and turning these into practical service initiatives.[2] The government has responded by issuing 'tool kits' that provide 'evidence and "best practice" for achieving health gains for different population groups; evidence on action that can be taken by different health providers and also agencies outside the health sector; [and] indicators by which performance may be measured' (King 2000: 31). While the tool kits are strong on evidence, the district health boards and providers need to translate best practice information into practicable initiatives.

Each district health board consists of a governing board served by a chief executive and staff of planners and managers. Of the eleven members composing the governing board, seven are elected, with the Minister of Health appointing four members (including the posts of chair and deputy chair) to ensure balanced expertise and representation. Legislation makes it clear that the district health boards are to serve the Minister, placing members hoping to represent constituents or speak out about government policy in a difficult position.

The first district health board elections occurred in conjunction with the 2001 local government elections. Whether elected members emerged from an informed voting process is debatable, given that 1050 candidates contested 146 seats. In most electorates, voters had lengthy candidate lists from which to choose; the largest had 80 contesting two seats. Turnout at the elections was around 40 per cent (Gauld 2002). In keeping with government commitment to honour the Treaty of Waitangi, New Zealand's founding document, two members must be of indigenous Maori ethnicity.

Each district health board has been required by law to establish two sub-committees, one responsible for community health, another for hospital services management. The boards must produce, in consultation with the community, a five-year strategic plan, as well as an annual plan outlining services to be funded. Each board is also required to establish formal relationships with local Maori tribes. For most district health boards, this means the development and maintenance of multiple tribal relationships; there is a similar situation for many tribes who span two or three district health board regions. For economies of scale, the boards have themselves created five inter-district 'shared services' agencies. Similar in some ways to the former regional health authorities, these provide services for their parent district health boards such as information and contract management, needs assessments, and legal, financial and human resources. The boards and chief executives also collaborate through a national forum established for this purpose, District Health Boards New Zealand.

The district health board system, while offering many positives, has at least in the interim added complexity to health care policy making and service delivery. First, there has been an entire reconfiguring of health planning and funding mechanisms. With the shifting structures, relationships between funders and providers have had to be reconstituted and, as with the preceding restructurings, considerable cultural change has been required. Second, there are now 21 separate organizations, as well as the Ministry of Health, performing the functions of the previous single Health Funding Authority, meaning considerable repetition across districts, a complex administrative web of vertical and horizontal relationships and contracts, and stretching of resources. There is speculation that mergers of district health boards can be expected, requiring further restructuring. About 10–14 district health boards may be more appropriate, as for the earlier area health boards. Fourth, funding for some services (e.g. disability support and public health) has been retained within the Ministry of Health, meaning that the district health boards are only responsible for planning these and that service providers must form a service delivery relationship with relevant boards and a funding relationship with the Ministry of Health.

Fifth, the government continues to promote new policy developments, such as 'primary health organizations', which impact on district health boards and service organization. Primary health organizations are formal groups of primary care providers (general practitioners, physiotherapists, practice nurses, etc.) established on a non-profit basis and required to engage the community in their planning and governance processes. These organizations are required to 'manage' patient care using population-based strategies and preventive measures, and are funded on a capitated basis in accordance with the number and projected health care needs of enrolled patients (Ministry of Health 2002c). The government intended that the primary health organizations would be established in all parts of New Zealand by around the middle of 2004, although in practice many areas remain uncovered due to provider resistance as compliance, governance and administration costs exceed establishment funding.

In keeping with increasing 'budget-holding' for various services (to begin with, largely pharmaceuticals and laboratory tests, but inevitably budgets for secondary and other care), their expanding management function and building of closer relationships with the hospital sector, the primary health organizations may naturally inherit various planning and purchasing functions of the district health boards. In turn, the need for district health boards could diminish. This raises the issue of whether a careful analysis of the government's policy proposals was conducted prior to implementation. For instance, if district health boards are ultimately unnecessary, restructuring strain could have been minimized if the Health Funding Authority had been retained and primary health organizations developed instead of district health boards. Maori health providers and the many small rural health trusts established to govern services in remote areas have also expressed concern about the potential loss of autonomy that membership of a primary health organization poses. Similarly, concerns have been raised about likely medical dominance of the primary health organizations.

Many institutional arrangements have remained largely unaffected by the shift to district health boards. Hospitals, while now owned by district health boards, continue to deliver their services although they are coming under increasing pressure to reduce costs and service coverage (see below). Independent practitioner associations remain the dominant organizing framework for general practice, although, as noted, primary health organizations promise to replace them. The impact on the numerous community providers of disability support, mental health and other health care services has largely been in terms of them having to forge new contractual relationships – a not insignificant process – with a new set of planning and funding institutions. That said, the goals of the government's various health strategies have served as a broad focal point for the sector, albeit a complicated one given the range of strategies and goals. For patients, the changes have gone largely unnoticed with services continuing to be provided. Hospital waiting lists for non-urgent services persist, as do problems of service integration, and inter-regional access and equity.

CURRENT HEALTH SYSTEM AND POLICY CHALLENGES

Health care financing, demand and rationing

In 2001–2002, New Zealand spent $NZ10.68 billion on health and disability services: 22.1 per cent of this (NZ$2.36 billion) was from private sources, 16.1 per cent of which came from personal payments, 5.7 per cent from health insurers and 0.3 per cent from non-government organizations. The remaining 77.9 per cent ($NZ8.319 billion) was government funded; 7.5 per cent of this came via the Accident Compensation Corporation.[3] Of public funding, 76.1 per cent was allocated to personal health (via district health boards, general practitioners, pharmaceutical subsidies and other providers), 18.5 per cent to disability support services and 1.9 per cent to public health (Ministry of Health 2004).

Health expenditure in New Zealand, as elsewhere, has been growing, despite increasing attempts to make service delivery more efficient and to control access. Between 1980 and 1989, government expenditure on health increased 23 per cent. In 1989, total GDP health spending was 6.6 per cent (compared to the OECD average of 7.6 per cent). Between 1990 and 1999, public spending increased by 36 per cent. By 2001, health accounted for 8.2 per cent of GDP (OECD average 8.4 per cent). Between 1990 and 2001, real annual per capita health spending grew at 3 per cent, outpacing New Zealand's 2.5 per cent GDP growth. In 1989–90, health care consumed 12.6 per cent of total government expenditure; in 2000–2001, this had expanded to 18.3 per cent.

Since 1996, there has been considerable pressure to increase health expenditure in recognition that between 1988–1989 and 1992–1993 'real per capita funding fell by 16 per cent' (Ministry of Health 1996), as the government tightened the health budget through the era of area health boards and lead-in to the competitive system. In 2002, the district health boards carried a combined deficit (representing services delivered that were unfunded) of $NZ303 million. In response to pressure for increased health spending, the government announced a funding injection of around $NZ2.4 billion to be released through 2002–2005. Much of this is to cover inflation costs and the establishment of primary health organizations, while those eligible for the new funding must demonstrate a 0.5 per cent efficiency gain (Ministry of Health 2002a).

In tandem with expenditure, service demand and throughput have also increased markedly over recent years. In the decade to 1999–2000, raw medical and surgical hospital discharges increased by 3.4 and 3.7 per cent per annum, respectively, with a more rapid increase in the last 3 years of the decade. In 1999–2000, there were approximately 410,000 discharges, of which around 300,000 were for urgent treatments and 110,000 for non-urgent treatments. Demand for certain high-volume specialties has been driving the increases. For instance, internal medicine discharges rose 6.6 per cent per annum in the 3 years to 1999–2000, while orthopaedics increased at 6.8 per cent per annum. Reflecting the trend towards greater use of day-stay surgery and community care, the average length of stay in hospital has fallen by over 50 per cent, from 6.6 days in 1988–89 to 3.2 days in 1999–2000 (Ministry of Health 2001).

Despite the increasing public expenditure and service efficiency, there remain significant gaps between health care demand and capacity to provide services. The pressure is expected to intensify in accordance with demographic change. Current projections show that the population aged over 65, which places particular demands on the health system, will have increased from 11.9 per cent in 2003 to 25.3 per cent by 2050, with a nine-fold increase in those aged over 90 (Statistics New Zealand 2003). Meanwhile, the tax base to pay for services is proportionately declining. At 1.92 births per woman, the population is not replacing itself, making the government reliant on immigration and economic growth.

The question of how to close the funding-demand gaps is ever-present. Some district health boards are under pressure due to the introduction from 2003 of a new population-based funding formula, which will see them losing funding as this is more evenly distributed. The formula calculates district funding based on demographics, disease profiles, ethnic composition and health service utilization rates. Other district health boards, particularly those with high Maori, Pacific Island and low socioeconomic populations that suffer from poorer health status, stand to gain from the population-based funding formula. These regions, however, tend to have been previously under-funded.

Hospitals are forbidden from raising extra money by charging patients directly, although at least one district health board has explored doing so for certain services. The government is keen to see hospital funding, which consumes around 59 per cent of the personal health budget (the OECD average is approximately 40 per cent), reduced in favour of improved primary care. Hospitals, which remain free-of-charge and universally accessible, have pursued various measures to stem demand. These include allowing general practitioners to operate observation rooms on hospital premises, thus keeping patients out of more expensive hospital beds, giving patients vouchers to visit private after-hours services, hospital-in-the-home schemes, and integrated care and community initiatives targeted at particular patients and conditions that prove costly when not closely managed in primary care settings. It has also been difficult to restrict general practice and pharmaceutical funding, given the traditional fee-for-service subsidy arrangement.

Potentially, the most radical funding change will be seen with the implementation of primary health organizations, which will be funded on a capitation basis in accordance with the numbers of enrolled patients. In theory, this will cap primary care costs, while providing an incentive to keep patients healthy and closely manage their health care. Primary health organizations in areas with considerable health inequalities and deprivation are also receiving additional funding to reduce patient charges and boost accessibility. This has been a source of discontent, as anecdotal evidence suggests that general practitioners not eligible for deprivation funding (e.g. those in wealthy communities) have been losing patients choosing to travel for care to subsidized practices. Areas without primary health organization coverage remain funded on the traditional fee-for-service basis.

Pharmac, meanwhile, continues to pursue new cost-containment measures such as focusing on curtailing drug demand. Techniques include issuing guidelines to general practitioners to promote appropriate prescribing, as well as patient education programmes. The agency has been particularly concerned with reducing antibiotic use and reliance on pharmaceuticals for treatment of lifestyle and natural conditions such as sexual dysfunction and baldness (Pharmac 2002).

Inevitably, the district health boards (and the health sector *per se*) are looking at ways of limiting their commitments as they are under firm government instructions to reduce their 'deficit' levels. The two key methods for doing so are 'prioritization', required by legislation of district health boards in their strategic planning processes, and application of the hospital 'booking system' for non-urgent treatments.

Prioritization first emerged under the auspices of the former

Health Funding Authority and was a rekindling of the Core Services Committee's earlier efforts to develop a list of publicly funded services. The key difference was that where the Core Services Committee sought public consensus on which to base rationing schemes, the Health Funding Authority pursued managerially controlled approaches using quality-adjusted life years and cost-utility analysis so that services could be ranked in accordance with individual treatment benefits and cost effectiveness. The district health boards have tended to use a mix of public consultation and managerial control in their prioritization exercises. Due to the decentralized nature of the district health boards, local preference and needs assessments, each board has developed a unique prioritization scheme (see Hefford and de Boer 2003). In some cases, scoring systems, developed by board officials in limited consultation with the interested public, have been used to rank services in terms of factors such as cost effectiveness, capacity to benefit, cost per patient, and contribution to reducing health inequalities and promoting good health. The resulting scores have facilitated rankings that have largely applied to demands for new services due to limited scope for cutting existing services.

The Core Services Committee was renamed the National Health Committee in 1995, with a much broader role in advising on a range of health policy issues. The National Health Committee has facilitated the work of a variety of clinical guidelines groups, the recommendations of which are published on a website designed for professional use (www.nzgg.org.nz). The National Health Committee has also been involved in developing systematic processes for identifying and evaluating new technologies and treatments as 'one of the foremost prioritization challenges in health systems today is deciding which new technologies to publicly fund' (National Health Committee 2002: 5). New technology assessment intersects with, but is separate from, the prioritization work of the district health boards.

Perhaps the most enduring and controversial rationing work to emerge from the Core Services Committee/National Health Committee is the 'booking system' designed to replace waiting lists for non-urgent hospital treatments. The booking system sees patients being 'scored' against clinical priority assessment criteria covering the level of severity or disability and capacity to benefit from treatment. If enough points on the assessment scale are obtained, the patient is then 'booked' for surgery. Those with insufficient points are referred back to their general practitioner for further treatment, or can pay for an operation in the private sector. The booking system has been plagued with problems.

First, due to implementation through the competitive market era, individual hospitals developed unique clinical priority assessment criteria in isolation from one another meaning that, until recent efforts at standardization, it has been impossible to compare scores at a national level or work out whether service access between hospitals is equitable. Second, it quickly became clear that funding levels were insufficient to treat all patients whose scores deemed them clinically eligible for treatment. This created a new waiting list of patients falling between the 'clinical' and 'financial' treatment thresholds. The district health boards are presently using clinical priority assessment criteria as a key rationing tool, routinely raising the level of points required for surgery as they attempt to reduce funding deficits. Again, this is leading to considerable regional access inequities, depending on the financial condition of the district health board, and suffering among patients experiencing deterioration until they have enough points to qualify. There have been numerous reports of patients dying while awaiting heart surgery, young children suffering while waiting for ear grommets, and elderly housebound by cataract and joint problems that could be easily rectified by surgery. The insured and those able to afford it, of course, can be swiftly treated in the private practices of the very same surgeons holding joint appointments in public hospitals. They can also circumvent long waiting times for specialist assessment by visiting a private specialist in the first instance who can refer directly to the public sector for treatment.

Public health

The organization and delivery of population-based public health services has remained largely unchanged through the restructuring period. Presently, there are 12 public health districts and corresponding offices, making for an uneasy fit with the 21 district health boards Moreover, public health is largely funded directly by the Ministry of Health. Public health offices provide a range of services, including health promotion, protection and infectious disease control, while some public health services such as cancer screening and immunization programmes are provided by district health boards and primary care providers.

The demands on public health services are increasing, in keeping with the government's emphasis on health determinants. Public health services today are attempting to work more closely with one another, district health boards and other agencies and sectors that influence health status. The threat of SARS saw considerable interagency collaboration. In the future, there is likely to be a closer working relationship with primary health organizations, with their focus on population health. It is possible that development of the primary health organizations, and the likelihood that they will assume functions traditionally in the realm of public health services, will further challenge the minute public health funding allocation.

Public health services in Auckland face challenges associated with migration from Asia and the Pacific, increasingly mobile populations and poverty – in particular, a rise in disease outbreaks. These place great strain on the public health workforce and, as with the district health boards, services then have to be prioritized, meaning that 'non-urgent' yet important health promotion activities receive less attention (Bullen and Simmons 2003).

Cancer screening programmes present a considerable challenge for New Zealand policy makers. Cervical and breast screening programmes were established through the competitive and subsequent restructuring era and, as a result, have suffered from a number of problems. These include a lack of central attention and leadership, a failure among central government policy makers to recognize the differences between population-based programmes (which require central oversight) and personal health services (which may be adequately provided in a climate of decentralization and competition), inadequate information systems and quality control processes, and inattention to workforce development (Coppell and Brown 2003). Presently, screening services are provided by regional agencies and there remain flaws in the population register – a key element of a sound programme – from which invitations for screening are made, and a lack of laboratory quality control. A recent independent review of the troubled cervical screening service noted that, despite the establishment of a National Cervical Screening Unit, the Ministry of Health was yet to act on important recommendations from an earlier inquiry into screening failures (McGoohan 2003).

In common with other countries, government and health sector concern is growing over the increasing incidence of costly 'lifestyle diseases' including heart disease, diabetes, cancers and respiratory problems. A 2003 Ministry of Health commissioned report suggested the introduction of a 'fat tax' on particular foods and beverages. While this was quickly downplayed by the Minister of Health, the problem is unlikely to disappear and remains a topic of hot debate. Health insurers have also indicated interest in setting higher premiums for those at risk of lifestyle diseases.

A final public health issue confronting the government and health care providers is the disparity of health outcomes between ethnic groups. Data show that life expectancy for Maori and Pacific Island people has remained static since 1980, but improved for other New Zealanders. The reasons for the growing differences are complex and multifaceted. Suggestions include the impact on lower socioeconomic groups, in which Maori and Pacific Island people are over-represented, of market-oriented public policies introduced throughout the 1980s that affected access to health services, housing, income and education (Ajwani *et al.* 2003). This adds weight to the need for culturally appropriate health services designed for disadvantaged groups, particularly Maori and Pacific Island people. It also underscores the importance of the government's health inequalities reduction and social development policies (Ministry of Social Development 2001; Ministry of Health 2002b), and of cross-sector strategies and service coordination required of district health boards and government social policy agencies.

Health system and service delivery issues

Since the mid-1990s, service integration has been a key, albeit varied, concern of New Zealand's health policy makers and planners. An initial wave of interest in the concept was in response to anti-collaborative behaviour stimulated by the competitive health reforms, and the 'gaps' between providers this perpetuated. In the late-1990s, the Health Funding Authority emphasized integration and funded a series of pilot projects. Presently, it is assumed that integration will keep costs down as well as provide for a 'seamless' patient experience. As noted, the district health boards are expected to develop integrated services, as are primary health organizations and other providers. The Health Funding Authority pilots, however, demonstrated that integration is a complicated issue dependent on a number of factors. These include developing trust and cooperation between service providers, flexible financial and organizational arrangements so that money follows patients and systems can be tailored to circumstance, and strong leadership and provider commitment to integration (Russell *et al.* 2003). In many respects, New Zealand's continually changing health system works against integration, as does restricted development capacity resulting from under-funding.

The restructuring era has been detrimental to the development of coherent health information systems and technology. Throughout the 1990s, central government took a 'hands-off' approach to information management and technology. Meanwhile, the contractual nature of health care funding, and information demanded by this, meant providers rapidly developed their own information systems in the absence of central coordination or of clearly identifiable information management and technology policy. The result is multiple co-existing information systems with differing purposes (e.g. contracting and financial transactions, clinical information, management information) that do not easily interconnect, and a host of other problems related to inadequate data collection, transfer, information system architecture, security and privacy policies (Gauld 2004). The state of information management and technology is taxing in the present environment where collaboration is expected and a government goal is for electronic information to flow freely among services, in turn facilitating integration. An information strategy released in 2001 listed 79 wide-ranging recommendations for the way forward (WAVE Advisory Board 2001). A range of central government units and initiatives has since been launched, but implementing the recommendations will take several years.

In common with other countries, the issue of quality has come to prominence in health policy and service delivery. Driving concerns have been rising patient demands, evidence of medical misadventure, and concerns about system stress and fragmentation resulting from ongoing restructuring. A recent study found that around 12.9 per cent of New Zealand hospital patients experienced some sort of medical or systemic error (Davis *et al.* 2002). There are essentially two approaches to ensuring clinical and service quality. *Continuous quality improvement*, seen as a supportive approach, emphasizes developing working environments in which continuous learning is valued and attention to quality is part of everyday life. *Quality assurance* is focused on establishing a static set of minimum standards that providers are judged against, which highlight and discipline sub-standard performances. The Ministry of Health has been working on various quality mechanisms since at least 2000. Its approach is effectively one of quality assurance (Seddon 2003). The result is growing concern about individual hospital and clinical performance data disclosure and increasing resort to 'defensive' medicine (Roberts 2003).

Since 2000, the health workforce has become an issue of considerable concern. Throughout the 1980s and especially the 1990s, the predominant view was that workforce planning should be a market responsibility. This has had significant impacts on the training opportunites for, support and coordination of health professionals. Other factors have also contributed to increasing stress and declining health workforce morale, including: the lack of trust in health professionals characteristic of the market era and an emphasis on increasing efficiency and accountability as opposed to clinical quality and patient care (Hornblow 1997); ballooning indebtedness of new graduates in the health professions due to 'user pays' education policies introduced throughout the 1990s (O'Grady and Fitzjohn 2001); and the attractiveness of overseas work environments. Although data are poor, due to lack of central collection, there is considerable anecdotal evidence of staff shortages in nursing and many medical and allied specialties. Shortages in radiotherapy have been particularly acute: district health boards have even had to fly cancer patients to private Australian clinics for treatment unable to be locally provided. Owing to waiting lists, the district health boards also have been experiencing difficulty providing radiotherapy within internationally recommended time-frames. Staff shortages have also impacted on surgical waiting lists, the viability of a range of professional services in different parts of the country, the provision of care in rural areas and stress among the workforce.

In 2000, in response, the government established the Health Workforce Advisory Committee to advise on the way forward. The Committee subsequently issued two reports: a 'stocktake' and a framework to underpin future workforce development (Health Workforce Advisory Committee 2002a,b). While the introduction of the Committee has been welcomed, its ability to drive workforce improvements and development has been questioned. Its small budget means it has limited capacity for inquiry or influence. Moreover, and perhaps because of this, it operates in tandem with a number of other workforce-focused initiatives: the Ministry of Health has its own workforce development team, while the district health boards, both individually and collectively, have initiated workforce projects (Adam 2003; New Zealand Medical Association 2003).

CONCLUSIONS

It is too early to judge how well New Zealand's present health care system is performing and, by implication, whether the policy mix is appropriate. The government has suggested that the system of district health boards is aimed at the long term and will be producing results – better population health, better participation and reduced inequalities – by 2010. That said, as discussed in this chapter, New Zealand faces a range of complicated health policy and system challenges. These include:

- maintaining a balance between central and local control over the system and managing the tensions intrinsic in the decentralized and democratized structure;
- developing mechanisms that ensure inter-regional equity of funding and service access;
- dealing with increasing pressure to restrict health expenditure, to do so fairly or somehow increase funding (the government has not ruled out consideration of a dedicated health tax at some future point);
- promoting a robust and adequate health workforce committed to a culture of learning and quality improvement;
- enhancing coordination across the system with appropriate integration initiatives and information technology.

As this chapter has noted, change in the health system structure is ongoing due to the development of primary health organizations and probable district health board mergers, as is the emergence of new health policy issues – the challenge of obesity, for example. Research suggests that the New Zealand health sector is weary from change and that this diverts energy from pressing tasks (Gauld 2003). Accordingly, so long as change is a focus of the sector, and the sector is in a consistently inchoate state, endeavours to forge prudent solutions to problems are likely to be piecemeal, occurring at differing points of the health sector, and beset with problems of coordination, implementation and appropriateness.

NOTES

1 In 1973, when numbers were first collated, there were 33,000 people awaiting public hospital treatments. By 1992, there were 64,000 on waiting lists. In 1995, those waiting numbered 85,574, or 24 per thousand of the total population (Ministry of Health 1997). Numbers peaked in 1998–1999 at around 95,000.
2 Individual strategies, each containing goals and targets, have been issued for: primary care, Maori health, Pacific health, mental health, child health, disability support, older people, quality improvement and public health.
3 The Accident Compensation Corporation is a statutory insurance corporation that provides compulsory, comprehensive, accident insurance to

all New Zealanders. Its funding is from a mix of employer, employee and other subscriptions. Injury or accident patients have their costs, including loss of income, paid for by the Corporation; by contrast, those who are unwell must fund such costs themselves.

REFERENCES

Adam, B. (2003) The challenges of running a District Health Board, in R. Gauld (ed.) *Continuity amid Chaos: Health Care Management and Delivery in New Zealand*. Dunedin: University of Otago Press.

Ajwani, S., Blakely, T., Robson, B., Tobias, M. and Bonne, M. (2003) *Decades of Disparity: Ethnic Mortality Trends in New Zealand 1980–1999*. Wellington: Ministry of Health and University of Otago.

Ashton, T., Beasley, D., Alley, P. and Taylor, G. (1991) *Reforming the New Zealand Health System: Lessons from Other Countries*. Report of the Study Group to the Health Boards of New Zealand Council.

Barrett, M. (1997) Maori health purchasing: some current issues, *Social Policy Journal of New Zealand*, 9: 124–30.

Beaglehole, R. and Davis, P. (1992) Setting national health goals and targets in the context of a fiscal crisis: the politics of social choice in New Zealand, *International Journal of Health Services*, 22(3): 417–28.

Boston, J. and Dalziel, P. (eds) (1992) *The Decent Society: Essays in Response to National's Economic and Social Policies*. Auckland: Oxford University Press.

Bullen, C. and Simmons, G. (2003) Tackling the rise of infectious diseases in Auckland: a regional public health service's response, in R. Gauld (ed.) *Continuity amid Chaos: Health Care Management and Delivery in New Zealand*. Dunedin: University of Otago Press.

Coppell, K. and Brown, T. (2003) Organising national cancer screening programmes in New Zealand, in R. Gauld (ed.) *Continuity amid Chaos: Health Care Management and Delivery in New Zealand*. Dunedin: University of Otago Press.

Creech, W. (1999) *The Government's Medium-Term Strategy for Health and Disability Support Services 1999*. Wellington: Ministry of Health.

Davis, P. (1981) *Health and Health Care in New Zealand*. Auckland. Longman Paul.

Davis, P., Lay-Yee, R., Briant, R. *et al.* (2002) Adverse events in New Zealand public hospitals: occurrence and impact, *New Zealand Medical Journal* (available at http://www.nzma.org.nz/journal/115-1167/271/ accessed on 13 September 2004).

Donelan, K., Blendon, R.J., Schoen, C., Davis, K. and Binns, K. (1999) The cost of health system change: public discontent in five nations, *Health Affairs*, 18(3): 206–16.

Dow, D. (1995) *Safeguarding the Public Health: A History of the New Zealand Department of Health*. Wellington: Victoria University Press.
Gauld, R. (2001) *Revolving Doors: New Zealand's Health Reforms*. Wellington: Institute of Policy Studies.
Gauld, R. (2002) Democratising health care governance? New Zealand's inaugural District Health Board elections, 2001, *Australian Health Review*, 25(4): 142–8.
Gauld, R. (2003) The impact on officials of public sector restructuring: the case of the New Zealand Health Funding Authority, *International Journal of Public Sector Management*, 16(4): 303–19.
Gauld, R. (2004) One step forward, one step back: restructuring, evolving policy and information technology and management in the New Zealand health sector, *Government Information Quarterly*, 21(2): 125–42.
Hay, I. (1989) *The Caring Commodity: The Provision of Health Care in New Zealand*. Auckland: Oxford University Press.
Health Workforce Advisory Committee (2002) *The New Zealand Health Workforce: A Stocktake of Issues and Capacity*. Wellington: HWAC.
Health Workforce Advisory Committee (2002a) *The New Zealand Health Workforce: Framing Future Directions*. Wellington: HWAC.
Hefford, M. and de Boer, M. (2003) Service planning and prioritisation in a District Health Board, in R. Gauld (ed.) *Continuity amid Chaos: Health Care Management and Delivery in New Zealand*. Dunedin: University of Otago Press.
Hornblow, A. (1997) New Zealand's health reforms: a clash of cultures, *British Medical Journal*, 314: 1892–4.
King, A. (2000) *The New Zealand Health Strategy*. Wellington: Ministry of Health.
Labour Party (1999) *Labour on Health: Policy – September 1999*. Wellington: New Zealand Labour Party.
Malcolm, L., Wright, L. and Barnett, P. (1999) *The Development of Primary Care Organisations in New Zealand: A Review Undertaken for Treasury and the Ministry of Health*. Wellington: Ministry of Health.
McGoohan, E. (2003) National cervical screening programme and progress towards implementation of the Gisborne Inquiry recommendations, June (available at: www.csi.org.nz/other_reports/CSIMcGooganFINAL REPORT.pdf accessed 14 August 2003).
Ministry of Health (1996) *Sustainable Funding Package for the Health and Disability Sector*. Wellington: Ministry of Health.
Ministry of Health (1997) *Purchasing for Your Health 1995/96*. Wellington: Ministry of Health.
Ministry of Health (2001) *The Health and Independence Report*. Wellington: Ministry of Health.
Ministry of Health (2002a) *Doing Better for New Zealanders: Better Health, Better Participation, Reduced Inequalities*. Wellington: Ministry of Health.

Ministry of Health (2002b) *Reducing Inequalities in Health*. Wellington: Ministry of Health.

Ministry of Health (2002c) *A Guide for Establishing Primary Health Organisations*. Wellington: Ministry of Health.

Ministry of Health (2004) *Health Expenditure Trends in New Zealand 1990–2002*. Wellington: Ministry of Health.

Ministry of Social Development (2001) *The Social Development Approach*. Wellington: Ministry of Social Development.

National Health Committee (2002) *New Technology Assessment in New Zealand: Discussion Document*. Wellington: NHC.

New Zealand Medical Association (2003) Crisis in the medical workforce. Paper prepared for the Health Workforce Summit, March.

OECD (2003) *OECD Health Data 2003*. Paris: Organization for Economic Cooperation and Development.

O'Grady, G. and Fitzjohn, J. (2001) Debt on graduation: expected place of practice and career aspirations of Auckland medical students, *New Zealand Medical Journal*, 114(1142): 468–70.

Pharmac (2002) *Post-Election Briefing to the Minister of Health*. Wellington: Pharmaceutical Management Agency.

Roberts, P. (2003) *Snakes and Ladders: The Pursuit of a Safety Culture in New Zealand Public Hospitals*. Wellington: Institute of Policy Studies.

Russell, M., Cumming, J., Slack, A., Peterson, D. and Gilbert, A. (2003) Integrated care: reflections from research, in R. Gauld (ed.) *Continuity amid Chaos: Health Care Management and Delivery in New Zealand*. Dunedin: University of Otago Press.

Seddon, M. (2003) Aiming for a quality health service: quality improvement in the New Zealand health sector, in R. Gauld (ed.) *Continuity amid Chaos: Health Care Management and Delivery in New Zealand*. Dunedin: University of Otago Press.

Statistics New Zealand (2003) *Future Population: Summary of Latest Trends* (available at: www.statistics.govt.nz; accessed 8 August 2003).

Stent, R. (1998) *Canterbury Health Limited: A Report by the Health and Disability Commissioner April 1998*. Auckland: Health and Disability Commissioner.

Treasury (1990) *Performance of the Health System*. Wellington: The Treasury.

Upton, S. (1991) *Your Health and the Public Health: A Statement of Government Health Policy*. Wellington: Government Printer.

WAVE Advisory Board (2001) *From Strategy to Reality: The WAVE Project: Health Information and Management Technology Plan*. Wellington: Ministry of Health.

10
CONCLUSION
Robin Gauld

Each of the eight case study chapters in this book provides a detailed overview of health policy and service delivery in its respective territory. This chapter places material from the preceding chapters in a comparative context. First, it discusses some prominent themes. Next, it compares and contrasts the eight systems across key issues introduced in Chapter 1: historical development and its impact, health system organization, public health, and rationing and demand management. Third, the chapter looks at whether it makes sense to think of an Asia-Pacific model of health policy and systems. The concluding section considers the benefits and shortcomings of the comparative approach, and areas for future research.

SOME KEY THEMES

Several themes are evident across the eight health systems under examination. First, despite the fact that all of the territories (except China) face a similar range of health policy problems, including how to curtail costs, stem demand, protect and promote public health, and provide accessible, efficient and high-quality services, each has a unique set of responses and health system. Although this complicates comparisons, there are similarities between elements of the various health systems, as discussed in this chapter.

Second, in all cases there is considerable government commitment in the health care arena. Yet, in each, there is also substantial private sector involvement. Government commitment appears to be increasing over time, in common with OECD member-countries (OECD 2003), with ever-more-sophisticated solutions required for increasingly complex issues. The expanding commitment is partly a result of the pressures outlined in Chapter 1, driving governments towards more involvement in regulation and funding arrangements.

For example, in both Korea and Taiwan, social insurance funds have been combined in an effort to obtain greater control and more effective organization. In Japan, the state is deeply involved in the process of setting fees to be paid by social insurers to providers. In the early 1990s, the Hong Kong government established a new agency, the Hospital Authority, to improve the efficiency of public hospital management. This has been a source of increasing government involvement in health care financing and delivery. Commitments at all levels of the Chinese health system are increasing, although the pressures for this differ from the other health systems covered in this book: growing affluence and the need to couple this with social development, particularly in deprived rural areas; the breakdown of former health care arrangements linked to communist employment and societal structures and a requirement for substitutes; and the demand for improved regulatory and disease control systems. The Singapore government is deeply involved in health system regulation and subsidization. It remains concerned about the implications of population ageing and recently introduced a new ElderShield insurance scheme designed to subsidize home care costs for the elderly. Both the Australian and New Zealand governments are involved in all elements of health care amid increasingly complicated and politicized structures that require ever-more state intervention.

Following the above, experiences suggest a demand for state involvement in health care, at the very least as a coordinator of the health system and of policy implementation, particularly where there are various funding sources and delivery arrangements.

Third, discussions throughout this volume confirm that health policy is shaped by politics, as argued elsewhere (Walt 1994; Barker 1996; Blank and Burau 2004; Roberts *et al.* 2004). Governments in each of the eight territories have emphasized different health policies and made explicit choices and concessions over policy direction. As noted below, policies and service arrangements have been influenced by history. Influence has also come from a range of political factors, including international experience, perceived public preferences and interest group pressure, the political ramifications of retaining the *status quo* or pursuing change, government's broader public policy strategy, and issues in relation to the implementation process that serve to distort policy design (Hill and Hupe 2002).

There is clear evidence that the medical profession and other interests remain a considerable political force and influence on health policy in Japan, Hong Kong, Korea and Taiwan. Attaining a balance between various interests is an established trait of Japan's health policy processes. Resistance by the medical profession to pharmaceutical policy reform in Korea created a need for the government to engage in a funding trade-off. In Taiwan, public opinion led to compromises over insurance premium rises. In Hong Kong, institutional elites are customarily involved in policy making in a highly consultative and exhaustive process that usually results in confirmation of the *status quo*. By contrast, in New Zealand, government determination throughout the 1980s and 1990s eroded the once considerable power and involvement of the medical lobby and other interest groups in the policy process, opening the way for implementation of a succession of radical reforms. The Singapore government's anti-welfare, self-help message is consistently expressed in all health policy.

Fourth, each of the territories has a 'safety net' of some sort to ensure health care access for the less well-off. There are pockets of commitment in China to extending service access and funding to the poor, notably through creation of a fund to which patients can make reimbursement claims, but much work remains in developing this. The Chinese scheme bears a likeness to Singapore's Medifund scheme. Korea's government-funded Medicaid covers a small percentage of the population unable to pay social insurance premiums, while both Japan's and Taiwan's social insurance cover the entire population. With their British colonial origins, Australia, Hong Kong and New Zealand each ensure universal health care access through state-funded services.

Fifth, it is apparent that none of the eight systems is ideal or straightforward. Each features both positive and negative elements that are a function of entrenched institutional arrangements, policy design and the need for policy compromises. For example, for the most part, Singapore's low-cost funding and delivery structures serve the population well. However, rationing remains a fact of life for many, while public health structures were initially inadequate to cope with SARS. Hong Kong's advanced public hospitals are among the world's best, yet the system lacks effective means to control access and there is no integration between the public and private sectors. The imperfections in the various systems suggest caution is required when seeking to emulate 'successful' policies, as noted elsewhere (Rose 1993), while the extent to which it is possible to transfer policy from one unique context to another remains questionable. It is unlikely, for instance, that Singapore's funding and rationing regime could be transferred to Australia, Hong Kong or Taiwan, where existing systems differ substantially, service access remains relatively open and government does not necessarily have Singapore's capacity for control.

HEALTH SYSTEMS IN COMPARISON

The introductory chapter of this book listed a series of topics to be covered across the different functions and 'levels' of each health system under study. These included:

- the history of health policy and service development;
- health system financing and organization;
- the role of public health; and
- rationing and demand management.

The following paragraphs revisit these issues in a comparative perspective.

The influence of history

Clearly, each of the eight territories has a unique health sector history and developmental path. If patterns can be found, these tend to be at a conceptual level. A key issue in the study of policy is 'path dependency', the notion that historical developments are a significant determinant of existing policy arrangements and capacity for change (Putnam 1993; Wilsford 1994). This occurs as the institutions and structures surrounding health policy and the health system, such as bureaucracies, policies and regulations, public perceptions and interest groups, become entrenched.

Path dependency is certainly evident in most of the eight cases, although care needs to be taken with generalizations. Australia's experience shows a strong attachment to and building upon existing systems, with the main changes in recent years occurring at the sub-sector level in areas such as pharmaceutical budget management, insurance market regulations and quality improvement. In China, path dependency is partly a consequence of government commitment to stability and carefully managed transition. A fundamental challenge is moving the health system away from historical administrative and financing practices to developing new institutional arrangements that foster trust and accountability. In its 150 years of health system development, Hong Kong has had one attempt to break from history, with the creation in the 1990s of the Hospital Authority and Department of Health. This occurred only after consistently voiced concerns and development of a consensus that the health system required reform. Nonetheless, existing behavioural traits persisted in the new organizational environment and policy making continues to be a laboured process. In Japan, the origins of many arrangements can be traced back to the founding of modern medicine and the way in which the health system subsequently developed. Because of entrenched institutions, the Japanese health system has been remarkably resilient to change in the post-war period.

Korea and Taiwan have more recent health policy and system histories, and they have both achieved large-scale policy change. However, their health systems now appear well established and accepted, and achieving further change will be less straightforward. The New Zealand case is an interesting outlier in that, through the 1990s, three fundamental health policy changes were implemented. That said, underlying institutions, including funding mechanisms, divides between the public and private sectors and between primary and secondary care, remained relatively unaffected. Finally, while fundamental change was enacted in Singapore in the 1980s, with the establishment of medical savings accounts and hospital corporatization, developments since then seem to confirm that existing arrangements will persist through any future attempts at reform. In addition, the personalized nature of savings accounts has meant Singapore's funding system is probably among the most entrenched of the eight studied in this book.

Health system organization

The systems covered in this book are comprehensive, albeit in the case of China highly variable in terms of service scope and population coverage. However, they vary considerably in terms of basic organization. This section discusses the regulation, funding and provision of health care in the eight study territories.

Regulation

In all cases, government has a fundamental role as health system regulator, although again China is something of an exception as regulatory functions and capacity are often underdeveloped. In each case, the regulatory role is significant across the public and private sectors. For example, in Korea, Japan and Taiwan, where the private sector dominates service provision, the government plays a key role in setting and monitoring professional and facility standards. In each of the eight study regions, a central government agency, such as a Department or Ministry of Health, has ultimate responsibility for implementing health policy and monitoring regulations, although in the case of Australia and China the existence of central and state governments means responsibilities are divided between different institutional levels. As a testament to the complex world of health -care organization, in each of the territories other bodies are also required. Some regulatory bodies can be seen as part of central government. Examples include the separate central agencies in New Zealand and Australia dedicated to controlling the purchase of government-subsidized pharmaceuticals, the Hong Kong Hospital Authority, which manages public hospitals on behalf of the government, and its new Centre for Health Protection charged with disease control.

A step away from central government are medical and nursing councils and quality control agencies responsible for upholding or promoting standards of professional practice. Added to these are bodies such as Hong Kong's new Traditional Chinese Medicine Council, which registers and regulates traditional medicine practitioners. Some regulatory bodies, such as the social insuring agencies in Korea, Japan, Taiwan and Singapore, exist in statute; others, such as New Zealand's 'shared service agencies' and 'independent practitioner associations' are not required by law but nonetheless fulfil significant regulatory functions in that they receive government funding and interpret, implement and work with a range of government regulations and regulatory bodies.

Funding

The organization of funding varies widely between the eight case study jurisdictions. In some cases, this reflects elements of path dependency; in others, it reflects political choices, attempts to streamline arrangements, and perceived public preferences about funding options. In a number of the 'Asian' cases, insurance-based funding dominates, while in Hong Kong, Australia and New Zealand, the general tax pool remains the primary funding source, particularly for advanced care. In none of the eight territories could it be said that funding arrangements or resources are adequate (more on the latter below and later in the chapter), or that they are free from controversy. The arrangements confirm suggestions elsewhere that there are many options for how best to fund health services (Mossialos *et al.* 2002; Hussey and Anderson 2003).

In five of the study areas, despite strong government presence in the health sector, total health care expenditure remains low. Expenditure as a percentage of GDP in each of China, Hong Kong, Korea, Singapore and Taiwan compares very favourably against the 2001 OECD average of 8.4 per cent of GDP (OECD 2003). At the same time, with the exception of China, the health system in each of these territories performs very well indeed. Patients can generally expect a high standard of care across the spectrum of service delivery, and there is virtually universal service access. That said, service co-payments in Korea, Taiwan and Singapore pose potential barriers to access for many, raising questions about the adequacy of their health-funding arrangements. Under pressure to extend service coverage, and to do so in a precarious economic environment, the era of low-cost, high-performing health systems of the Asian 'tiger' economies appears to be under threat. Whether these territories will accept expenditure levels that match Australia, New Zealand and other developed world countries remains to be seen. In the other three study regions, Australia, Japan and New Zealand, expenditure is nearer the OECD average. Notably, each has a higher proportion of public expenditure than the five 'lower' expenditure territories where, with the exception of Taiwan, private funding sources figure strongly.

There is considerable commitment across the case study areas to insurance as a government-mandated health funding source. The exclusions to this are China, Hong Kong and New Zealand. In the last two cases, insurance is largely a private good available to those who choose to purchase it. Health care in China is funded in a myriad of different ways, with variations between different regions and levels of its health system. These include some private insurance, central and local level government funding and compulsory Singapore-style employer-based insurance schemes in urban areas. Patient fees and charges for pharmaceuticals and medical technology are a sizeable source of funding. Hong Kong remains committed to the traditional tax-based funding that developed through its history as a British colony, although only around half of all funding is from government. Similarly, New Zealand's funding is predominantly from the central government tax pool. In the remaining five territories, government-mandated insurance is the norm, albeit with a range of variations.

A notable characteristic of the insurance arrangements in Japan, Korea, Singapore and Taiwan is the fact that there is no insurer competition, combined with a single government-managed fee schedule. This contrasts with the situation in the USA of multiple competing insurers and fee structures (Scott 2001; Kovner and Jonas 2002). The social insurance schemes of Korea and Taiwan bear similarities to one another in that, in each, there is a government-run single national insurer, funded by a mix of employer and employee contributions and government supplements. Korea previously had separate social insurers for different population groups, with the aim of total population coverage. Inequities between the financing methods of the different insurers and financial problems led to the creation, in 2000, of a single insurer. Taiwan's national insurance scheme was established only in the mid-1990s following increasing pressure to extend insurance to the entire population and remove financial barriers to health care. However, the Korean and Taiwanese insurance systems are far from trouble-free. Korea faces difficulties with fee structures and insurance coverage, while there is recognition in Taiwan that its system contains a number of perverse incentives, such as promoting the growth of large and expensive hospitals, and could require reform.

The health insurance system in Singapore is also run by government, but contrasts with the Korea and Taiwan models in that funds are not risk-pooled, but are the property of individual medical savings account holders. The Singaporean system is complex and tightly controlled, with strict regulation over how funds can be used. The core scheme, Medisave, largely funds secondary care. Additional insurance can be obtained through the MediShield scheme, while for those without insurance the government-funded Medifund functions like a charity, granting money for eligible recipients. The Japanese insurance system is closest to the Singaporean one, if only for the fact that there are a range of schemes. That said, Japan's insurers are employment-based, as was the case in Korea before its merger; Singapore's three schemes are aimed at people of different financial status. The Australian Medicare scheme, funded largely from general taxes, is a key financing mechanism aimed at reducing financial barriers to access. Its existence has been attributed to a decline in uptake of private insurance, an issue of concern to Australian policy makers.

In each of the eight cases, funding mechanisms are complex and under constant review. This is particularly so where different mixes of funding sources exist. Cases in point are Australia and Singapore, where government makes regular funding policy adjustments. Japan's multiple social insurers paint a particularly complex picture. However, some simple rules regarding benefit coverage and cross-subsidization between insurance funds have ensured an egalitarian system. Japan's fee-setting process, which requires consultation and 'balancing' between the interests of the government and different providers, is also an involved undertaking. New Zealand, with its comparatively straightforward system of direct central government funding and subsidies, is constantly adjusting funding arrangements. In the early 1990s, in pursuit of efficiency, it established dedicated purchasing agencies to buy services for the public on behalf of the government from 'competing' providers. The purchaser–provider split remains in place today. The New Zealand government is presently concerned with equitable funding between regions and providers. The introduction, with the health reforms of 2000, of a new and allegedly fairer population-based funding formula is proving contentious as funding levels, which historically favoured some regions, are redistributed to previously under-funded regions.

Budgetary pressure is a feature in most of the eight case studies, spawning a variety of responses. Hong Kong and New Zealand have had debates about alternative sources of funding. In the early 1990s, New Zealand introduced short-lived and highly politicized hospital part-charges at great expense to providers, who had to develop and enforce billing systems. Recently, the New Zealand government mooted the possibility of introducing a dedicated health tax. In Hong Kong, there is government commitment to establishing Singapore-style insurance funds. However, this policy has not been well received and there has been political reluctance to move away from the *status quo*. Singapore continues to add new insurance schemes to cover emerging at-risk groups such as the elderly; it has also raised account thresholds and premium rates, as has Taiwan. In Korea, there are problems of funding inequities as well as growing pressure to raise premiums or develop new funding sources to reduce often prohibitive patient co-payments. Similar pressures are evident in China, where patient charges account for over 58 per cent of health expenditure and millions of people have neither health insurance coverage nor guaranteed access to health care. Japan, meanwhile, faces particular pressures related to a stagnant economy and to funding long-term care for an expanding ageing population. Its response has been to raise social insurance premiums, adjust insurance regulations and create a long-term aged care insurance.

One of the more interesting features of the various systems is the way in which public funding is used in different parts of the health sector for different purposes and with different ramifications. In Australia, the public Medicare insurance is largely aimed at hospital care, with more emphasis on private expenditure at the point of service at the primary care level. In China, inadequate funding combined with poor regulation provides incentives for a myriad of uncontrolled service charges. The considerable funding inequities between urban and rural areas pose a particular policy challenge. In Hong Kong and New Zealand, public funding is largely consumed by hospitals, with very little being channelled into primary care. However, in New Zealand present policy initiatives are increasing public funding of primary care, although this is aimed at disadvantaged populations. In Japan, Korea and Taiwan, public funding is used largely to support social insurance. The Singapore government uses funding in a very calculated manner to control service costs and subsidize various forms of care, in turn limiting the growth in expenditure from medical savings accounts and providing incentives for private providers to keep costs down.

Provision

Variations in provision are also evident across the eight territories. A common theme is private sector dominance in primary-level medical care. However, in most cases, government is also involved in some form, while patient co-payments for medical services and pharmaceuticals are a significant component of health care expenditure. In Australia and New Zealand, government provides subsidies to private general practitioners, particular patients and for pharmaceuticals. There are elements of organized primary care group practices in each of Australia, New Zealand and Hong Kong and, to a lesser degree, in Japan, Korea and Taiwan. In New Zealand, in the 1990s, more than 70 per cent of primary care doctors joined group practices; government has worked closely with these to develop more effective methods of service funding and organization. In Hong Kong, Singapore, Korea and Japan, in parallel with the private system, government provides only limited and basic primary medical care facilities for low-income people. In China, various state-funded primary care arrangements exist. In many remote and poverty-stricken rural areas, only basic primary care is offered and often by practitioners without formal training.

Traditional oriental medicine is widely practised and utilized in all the case-study areas except for Australia and New Zealand. In most cases, its delivery and underlying philosophy is completely separate from mainstream Western medicine. Korea, Japan and Taiwan each allow for social insurance to pay for some traditional practices. China, of course, has a long history of traditional medicine and both Chinese and Western medicine are routinely available in hospitals and primary care settings. Possibly the greatest recognition of traditional medicine outside of China occurred in Hong Kong, in 1999, with the creation of its Traditional Chinese Medicine Council.

At the secondary and tertiary levels, there are notable differences in organization. Government dominates hospital services in Australia, Hong Kong, New Zealand and Singapore. In Australia, private hospitals are a significant player, with around a 35 per cent market share, yet the public sector remains the key provider of advanced treatments. In Hong Kong, the advancing quality of highly subsidized open-access public hospitals and their attractiveness to patients is the source of creeping public expenditure, as well as a concern to private hospital providers, whose market share is diminishing. New Zealand attempted, with its market reforms of the early 1990s, to contract out publicly funded hospital work to private providers. However, few competitors emerged and transaction costs were high. The present government views public hospitals as preferred providers. The Singapore government is heavily involved in public hospital ownership. Korea, Japan and Taiwan can be grouped together as systems where hospital services are almost entirely provided in the private sector. In Japan, the most revered hospitals, which account for only a small proportion of total hospitals and beds, are attached to university medical schools.

There are few examples across the study territories of integration between different service providers and levels of health care. The New Zealand case illustrates the difficulties in attempting to create robust working relationships between primary and secondary care and public and private providers. Its efforts commenced in the late 1990s and have been expressed in government policy, various funding incentives and pilot programmes. Despite this, integrated care success stories are difficult to find. Australia also facilitated a series of 'coordinated care trials' in the 1990s, with similar results to New Zealand. Singapore has made some attempt at integration with its two regional health clusters; although being required to 'compete' with one another (Holliday 2003), these clusters may be closer to North America's managed-care organizations. The Hong Kong government has issued various policy statements in recent years outlining its desire for integration. However, practical initiatives are yet to surface. Integration does not presently feature in the policy dialogue or systems of China, Korea, Japan or Taiwan.

Quality of care, including professional practices, patient safety and service organization, rose up the international health policy agenda in the 1990s, and is an issue of concern in all eight regions. China, of course, remains in a state of developing basic service infrastructure; while quality is highly questionable, this is but one of a series of problems that needs to be tackled. The other study locations provide varying responses to quality. Australia has established a quality control council with a range of functions including to provide leadership, develop plans for quality improvement and facilitate appropriate provider responses. Its approach is to promote a culture of learning from mistakes and of continual improvement. New Zealand has issued high-level policy responses and implemented a credentialling system focused on ensuring that basic professional and facility standards are upheld. This has been criticized for its focus on punishing those who fail to meet standards, while providing minimal incentives for others to improve practices (Seddon 2003). Although a recognized problem, there are fewer quality initiatives in the Hong Kong, Korean, Japanese, Singaporean or Taiwanese systems, where the tendency is towards developing methods of accreditation and routine reporting of medical errors. This reflects a variety of factors: policy makers, service providers and the public have yet to fully embrace the concept; the dominant private sector and medical profession are resistant to quality control regulations; a lack of service quality data; and an assumption that market competition promotes service quality.

Public health

Crude health indicators across the eight case-study territories were listed and discussed in Chapter 1, where it was noted that, in all eight bar China, health status by these measures is among the world's best. Chapter 1 also noted the fundamental difference between personal and public health, and the often minimal government commitment to public health.

Limited financial commitment by government to public health is certainly confirmed by the case studies in this book, but also confirmed is the state's key role. The case studies also show that different territories have different public health priorities, in keeping with international experience (Beaglehole 2003). For instance, emphasis in New Zealand is presently on reducing health inequalities. By contrast, a primary concern in China is improving disease control.

Singapore possibly represents the strongest and most coherent commitment to public health, which is evident beyond the health sector in the government's general philosophy of promoting healthy living. The armed forces appear to play a significant role in public health, while workplace-based exercise programmes are common. Added to this are public campaigns advocating healthy consumption patterns. Notably, Singapore's public health infrastructure is highly centralized and its response to the 2003 SARS outbreak included extensive use of quarantine and fines for non-compliance. New Zealand also has a relatively centralized public health infrastructure featuring a series of district offices funded and coordinated by the Ministry of Health. New Zealand is notable for the fact that its present health policy and system has strong public health underpinnings, with providers required to focus on several population-based goals and targets. A core aim of the new multidisciplinary primary health organizations is to practise preventive medicine and keep enrolled populations well.

Australia's federal system creates some complications in terms of public health responsibilities. Its response has been to develop national programmes in areas such as AIDS/HIV, cancer screening and tobacco control, which are incorporated in Public Health Outcome Funding Agreements between the Commonwealth and state governments. In Japan, a prominent public health feature is an elaborate screening programme, run through a national network of public health centres. Again, history has played a role here, with screening seen to be a source of prior disease eradication. In Korea, a range of basic public health services and programmes exists, but these are not a core component of health policy due to the view that health is an individual responsibility. Taiwan has a long history of public health administration and a comprehensive network of district offices coordinated by the central Department of Health. However, in a system where social insurance drives personal health, public health takes a back seat.

In Hong Kong, a separate Department of Health undertakes public health responsibilities. The importance of public health has grown in recent years following the Asian 'bird flu' outbreak of 1997. In 2003, the SARS outbreak exposed a series of problems with the public health system. In response, a new Centre for Health Protection was created with enhanced powers and a directive to work closely with all other players in the health sector and with health authorities in

China. Finally, China faces a list of public health challenges, such as dealing with a growing number of HIV/AIDS infections, reducing tobacco consumption and alleviating detrimental environmental conditions. Moreover, the SARS epidemic uncovered flaws in China's public health administration, with ramifications for wider government. These included collecting and disseminating data in a robust, transparent and consistent manner and cooperating with international authorities such as the World Health Organization, coordinating between the different levels of government and the 'parallel' health management structures, and extending the reach of disease prevention and health promotion services and health care facilities.

Rationing and demand management

With the exception of China, how to manage increasing service demand and limit service funding and availability is a key challenge across the case-study countries. Each health system provides a unique response, again confirming the considerable international divergence in cost-containment approaches (Coulter and Ham 2000; Hughes and Light 2002; Ham and Robert 2003).

New Zealand has been experimenting with explicit rationing policy since 1992. At the funding level, it has variously attempted to develop lists of services to be publicly funded, to define who should be eligible for state assistance, to contract service providers for set service volumes, and to experiment with capped, global budgets requiring providers to decide how to ration resources. At the service level, scoring systems for the clinical assessment and prioritization of non-urgent patients have been introduced. In the early 1990s, a separate agency was created to control public pharmaceutical expenditure. The results in New Zealand have been mixed and rationing policy continues to evolve. Australia's cost-containment techniques differ from those of New Zealand. It has experimented with case-mix and diagnosis-related group funding, introduced provider 'productivity improvement' programmes, established a Health Technology Advisory Committee to assess whether new and costly technologies should be funded, created a specific pharmaceutical expenditure management agency, and ventured into targeting eligibility for selected services and funding. It has also introduced scoring systems for prioritizing hospital patients.

There have been quite different approaches in the five 'Asian' territories. Singapore's general strategy in health policy is aimed at keeping costs down and reducing direct government responsibility for meeting health care demands. It has done so by placing limits on the services that can be paid for from individual savings accounts, and by controlling aspects of the health system. These include public hospital costs and reimbursement rates, hospital bed numbers, the size of the medical workforce, and the introduction of new technology. Singapore has also viewed co-payments as crucial to its philosophy that there should be incentives not to over-patronize health services, and that costs should be partly borne by service users. The implication is that, for the less wealthy, service access is restricted.

The citizens of Japan, Korea and Taiwan each enjoy unlimited access to a full complement of services. There are questions over how long these health systems can sustain present arrangements. Meanwhile, each contains incentives for cost containment and rationing. Japan's fee schedule, which reduces payments to services where provision is expanding and increases payments for services where demand appears to be diminishing, is a key cost-control mechanism. Japan has also experimented with a diagnosis and procedure combination system that standardizes reimbursement rates for hospital services. Korea's low health care expenditure is partly a function of a strong economy. With growth slowing and health care demand increasing, there are concerns about rising health care costs. High patient co-payments, accounting for around 41 per cent of total health expenditure, along with strict limits on the services insurance will pay for, are presently the main cost-control devices. It is likely that, in the future, the national insurance scheme will need to move from simply reimbursing provider claims to adopt the role of a purchaser that carefully assesses population needs and service costs. Korea has also focused on reducing pharmaceutical expenditure with the introduction, in 2000, of a separation between drug prescribing and dispensing. Taiwan's insurance system, combined with the subsequent implementation of global budgeting, has been attributed to stemming growing health care costs and funding deficits. Taiwan has also recently recognized the need to reduce fraudulent insurance claims and administrative inefficiency. Nonetheless, it faces challenges regarding how to reduce apparent over-consumption.

Following phenomenal health system growth and demand throughout the 1990s, Hong Kong has experienced economic deflation and health funding deficits. In response, the government has produced various policy statements. In practical terms, the Hospital Authority has initiated the use of New Zealand-style scoring tools on a restricted basis, introduced hospital emergency department charges to deter non-urgent patients, and begun the development of new technology assessment techniques. The Hospital Authority has also had an ongoing drive to improve efficiency across its hospitals and recently took over responsibility for the government's general practice outpatient clinics, one of the aims of which is to reduce pressure on hospital facilities.

IS THERE AN ASIA-PACIFIC HEALTH POLICY MODEL?

A question that arises from the discussions above and throughout this book is whether it is possible to construct an analytical model that assists understanding of the eight Asia-Pacific systems. The answer appears to be no. For coherent model development, it would be necessary for each of the eight territories to exhibit a series of similar traits. As noted in the first section of this chapter, some common themes are germane to them all. Similarly, as in the second section of this chapter, it is possible to consider each of the systems in terms of universal functions and issues. But these factors do not lend themselves to construction of a unique Asia-Pacific health policy model. This said, conceptual similarities noted in the previous section between elements of selected systems are conducive to model building.

For example, the commitment in Korea, Taiwan, Singapore and Hong Kong to high levels of private funding and provision, and in the first three of these jurisdictions to state-controlled insurance, is in keeping with the notion of 'productivist welfare capitalism'. A defining characteristic of this is that 'social policy aims chiefly to boost economic development. It does not have an independent status, but rather is subordinate to, and facilitative and supportive of, the core task of the developmental state, which is the promotion of economic development' (Holliday and Wilding 2003: 165). However, it has been argued that the 'productivist' approach is under threat (Ramesh 2003), an argument to which the discussions in this volume add weight. Each of these four societies is engaged in what appears to be an inevitable politically led march towards greater state involvement in health care funding and provision. This is being driven not only by the pressures outlined in Chapter 1, but also by a growing concern, independent of the economy, and fuelled by issues such as SARS, HIV/AIDS and international debates over health inequalities and the value of a healthy population, for robust and accessible health services and health promotion.

Further complicating the prospect of model building across these four territories, it has been asserted that, at a finer level, there is considerable divergence in their approaches to social and health policy. Hong Kong and Singapore might be described as 'liberal', emphasizing the market where possible, whereas Korea and Taiwan (and perhaps also Japan) might be viewed as 'conservative', with strong commitment to social insurance linked to employment and funded by personal contributions (Ramesh 2004). These departures are supported by material in this book. In terms of health policy, funding and organization, the four systems differ substantially.

Elsewhere, it is difficult to find similarities that might facilitate modelling. China is an obvious outlier that defies conceptual description. Australia, Japan and New Zealand are each advanced capitalist democracies. Both Australia and New Zealand are steadfast welfare states in the 'social democratic' tradition (Esping-Andersen 1990). However, beyond a general dedication to higher proportions of public funding in each of these three countries, the health systems, and surrounding policies, diverge.

CONCLUSIONS

This book has analysed the health policies and systems of eight Asia-Pacific territories. The eight studies provide considerable material for assisting understanding of health policy across a diverse set of health systems. However, there are clearly difficulties in comparing the health policies and systems of such a range of jurisdictions, or identifying elements of the different systems that might be compared. This is to be expected from eight systems with distinctive combinations of regulation, funding and service provision. A key question is whether there may have been greater utility in attempting to compare three or four locations, or whether deeper insights could have been gained from comparing specific policy areas, such as cost containment, funding or primary care organization. However, there remain strong reasons for the eight-study whole-system approach.

First, considering the various systems together offers a wide range of perspectives on why and how health policies are developed and implemented, and how health services are organized in different parts of the region. The eight cases, therefore, provide substantial baseline information. Second, looking at the systems comparatively facilitates analysis of the way in which different combinations of policies in individual health systems function. Third, as outlined in

Chapter 1, given the importance of health policy and systems today as a contributor to state capacity and the international political economy, the need for studies that consider multiple systems in their entirety is heightened. This is so insights can be gained into issues such as how primary and secondary care and the public and private sectors intersect with one another in different systems, how funding impacts on service organization, how governments approach cost containment, and how public health fits with personal health and contributes to health gain.

This volume is a starting point and leaves several questions unanswered. Many of the topics covered could be usefully extended. There is a need for more research into health policy in the region – for comparisons between Asian and Western countries, and between developed and developing Asia-Pacific countries – and into the extent to which different policy responses, funding and service arrangements, each of which exists within a specific context, might be transferable.

REFERENCES

Barker, C. (1996) *The Health Care Policy Process*. London: Sage Publications.

Beaglehole, R. (ed.) (2003) *Global Public Health: A New Era*. Oxford: Oxford University Press.

Blank, R.H. and Burau, V. (2004) *Comparative Health Policy*. Houndmills: Palgrave Macmillan.

Coulter, A. and Ham, C. (eds) (2000) *The Global Challenge of Health Care Rationing*. Buckingham: Open University Press.

Esping-Andersen, G. (1990) *The Three Worlds of Welfare Capitalism*. Cambridge: Polity Press.

Ham, C. and Robert, G. (eds) (2003) *Reasonable Rationing: International Experience of Priority Setting in Health Care*. Buckingham: Open University Press.

Hill, M. and Hupe, P. (2002) *Implementing Public Policy*. London: Sage Publications.

Holliday, I. (2003) Health care, in I. Holliday and P. Wilding (eds) *Welfare Capitalism in East Asia: Social Policy in the Tiger Economies*. Houndmills: Palgrave Macmillan.

Holliday, I. and Wilding, P. (2003) Conclusion, in I. Holliday and P. Wilding (eds) *Welfare Capitalism in East Asia: Social Policy in the Tiger Economies*. Houndmills: Palgrave Macmillan.

Hughes, D. and Light, D. (eds) (2002) *Rationing: Constructed Realities and Professional Practices*. Oxford: Blackwell.

Hussey, P. and Anderson, G.F. (2003) A comparison of single- and multi-payer health insurance systems and options for reform, *Health Policy*, 66(3): 215–28.
Kovner, A. and Jonas, S. (eds) (2002) *Health Care Delivery in the United States*, 7th edn. New York: Springer.
Mossialos, E., Dixon, A., Figueras, J. and Kutzin, J. (eds) (2002) *Funding Health Care: Options for Europe*. Buckingham: Open University Press.
OECD (2003) *OECD Health Data 2003*. Paris: Organization for Economic Cooperation and Development.
Putnam, R. (1993) *Making Democracy Work: Civic Traditions in Modern Italy*. Princeton, NJ: Princeton University Press.
Ramesh, M. (2003) Globalisation and social security expansion in East Asia, in L. Weiss (ed.) *States in the Global Economy: Bringing Domestic Institutions Back In*. Cambridge: Cambridge University Press.
Ramesh, M. (2004) *Social Policy in East and Southeast Asia: Education, Health, Housing and Income Maintenance*. London: Routledge Curzon.
Roberts, M., Hsiao, W., Berman, P. and Reich, R. (2004) *Getting Health Reform Right: A Guide to Improving Performance and Equity*. New York: Oxford University Press.
Rose, R. (1993) *Lesson Drawing in Public Policy*. Chatham, NJ: Chatham House.
Scott, C. (2001) *Public and Private Roles in Health Care Systems: Reform Experiences in Seven OECD Countries*. Buckingham: Open University Press.
Seddon, M. (2003) Aiming for a quality health service: quality improvement in the New Zealand health sector, in R. Gauld (ed.) *Continuity Amid Chaos: Health Care Management and Delivery in New Zealand*. Dunedin: University of Otago Press.
Walt, G. (1994) *Health Policy: An Introduction to Process and Power*. London: Zed Books.
Wilsford, D. (1994) Path dependency, or why history makes it difficult but not impossible to reform health systems in a big way, *Journal of Public Policy*, 14(3): 251–83.

NAME INDEX

6, P., 6
Abello, A., 92
Adam, B., 220
Ahmad, E., 31
Ajwani, S., 218
Altenstetter, C., 7, 11
Andersen, R.M., 78
Anderson, G., 4, 82, 83, 231
Arai, Y., 2
Aroni, R., 111
Ashton, T., 203

Barker, C., 226
Barr, M., 170
Barrett, M., 205
Beaglehole, R., 8, 176, 203, 236
Bei, N., 28
Bernstein, T., 34
Bessell, T., 111
Bjorkman, J.W., 7, 11
Blank, R., 3, 150, 226
Bloom, G., 28, 32, 34, 39, 40, 42
Bonita, R., 8, 176
Boston, J., 203
Britt, H., 108
Brook, R., 86
Brown, T., 217
Bullen, C., 217
Bureau, V., 3, 150, 226
Burrows. K., 102

Butler, J., 102
Butzback, O., 2

Cameron, A., 102
Campbell, J.C., 2, 123, 133, 139, 143
Carrin, G., 40
Catchlove, B., 106
Chan, A., 11
Chang, R.E., 85
Cheng, C.M., 82, 84, 85
Cheng, S.H., 80, 83
Chew, S.B., 161, 162
Chi, C., 74
Chiang, T.L., 74, 75, 77, 79, 80, 81, 83, 84, 85, 86, 87
Choa, G.H., 176
Chu, C.L., 80
Collins, C., 176
Cook, S., 26, 40
Coppell, K., 217
Coulter, A., 4, 11, 238
Creech, W., 206
Cumming, J., 3

Dalziel, P., 203
Davis, P.B., 6, 202, 203, 219
de Boer, M., 215
Deeble, J., 117
Denniss, R., 112
Dixon, A., 8, 9

Docteur, E., 16
Donelan, K., 206
Dong, H., 31
Dong, W., 32, 38
Dow, D., 202
Du, Y., 41
Duckett, S., 92, 98, 100, 117

Eddy, D., 86
Eitel, E.J., 176
Ellwood, P., 86
Endacott, G.B., 176, 178

Fang, J., 41
Feng, X., 40
Fitzgerald, P., 107
Fitzjohn, J., 220

Gao, J., 32, 33
Gauld, R., 2, 3, 176, 202, 205, 209, 219, 221
Gray, G., 100
Goddard, M., 111
Goodman, J., 167
Goh, C.T., 149, 158
Gong, H., 34, 36
Gong, Y., 33
Gosden, T., 106
Gould, D., 176
Gu, E., 3
Gu, X., 32

Hailey, D., 111
Hall, J., 3, 100
Ham, C., 4, 6, 7, 11, 238
Harris, A., 111
Harvey, K., 108
Hay, I., 202, 203
Hayes, L., 92
Healy, J., 11
Hefford, M., 215
Henry, D., 111
Higuchi, T., 131
Hill, M., 226
Hill, S., 111
Hinton, A., 176

Ho, S., 178
Holliday, I., 1, 2, 3, 11, 13, 156, 235, 240
Hong, W.H., 80
Hopkins, S., 102
Horn, J., 25
Hornblow, A., 220
House, J., 92
Hsiao, W.C., 81, 150, 159, 163
Hu, T.W., 86
Huang, P., 84
Huang, W.Y., 79
Huang, Y., 31
Hughes, D., 238
Hunter, D., 6
Hupe, P., 226
Hussain, A., 32
Hussey, P., 4, 82, 83, 231

Ikegami, N., 2, 3, 123, 133, 139, 143

Jackson, T., 100
Jonas, S., 232

Kelliher, D., 28
Khan, A., 34
Kidd, M., 102
Kindig, D., 87
King, A., 209
Korda, R., 92
Kovner, A., 232
Kuo, S.W.Y., 70
Kwon, S., 51, 52, 58, 62, 64, 67

LaFortune, G., 17
Lee, K.Y., 150
Lee, L., 35
Lee, M.L., 85, 87
Lee, R.P., 74
Lee, W.K.M., 166
Leong, C.H., 193
Li, C., 31
Li, L., 43
Li, P., 34
Liaw, S.T., 109

Lieberthal, K., 28
Light, D., 238
Lim, L.Y.C., 148
Lim, M.-K., 2, 37
Lindblom, C., 115
Liu, C., 43
Liu, E., 191
Liu, J.H., 84
Liu, Y., 28, 33, 39
Liu, C.-T., 2
Lofgren, H., 111
Lokuge, K., 112
Low, L., 150, 151, 159, 160, 161, 162, 164, 166
Lu, J.F., 81
Lu, X., 34

MacKenzie, D.J.M., 179
McGoohan, E., 217
McKee, M., 11
McCallum, J., 102
McClelland, A., 92
McManus, P., 110
Malcolm, L., 205
Marshall, K., 2
Massaro, T., 160, 161, 163
Mathers, C., 93
Mathews, J., 93
Mays, N., 3
Meng, Q., 31, 32, 38
Mills, L.A., 178
Miners, N., 178
Mitchell, A., 111
Moran, M.,., 11
Morrell, S., 93
Mossialos, E., 7, 8, 9, 231
Murray, M., 108

Nichols, L.M., 3

O'Brien, K., 43
O'Grady, G., 220
Oi, J., 28
Oksenberg, M., 28
Ovretveit, J., 9
Oxley, H., 16

Pauly, M., 167
Peacock, S., 115
Peabody, J.W., 84
Peterson, M.A., 11
Phillips, D., 11
Prescott, N., 164, 166, 170
Putnam, R., 228

Rahim, L.Z., 166
Ramesh, M., 2, 3, 156, 161, 240, 241
Ranade, W., 7, 11
Rawski, T., 28
Richardson, J., 111
Riskin, C., 34
Robert, G., 238
Roberts, M., 3, 226
Roberts, P., 219
Rose, R., 227
Runciman, W., 104
Russell, M., 218

Salkeld, G., 111
Saltman, R., 8, 11
Satinsky, M., 10
Saw, S.H., 148, 149
Sayer, G.R., 176
Schofield, D., 93, 100, 102
Scott, C., 11, 232
Scotton, R., 92, 100
Seddon, M., 219, 236
Segal, L., 115
Sen, K., 3
Shin, Y., 2
Shue, V., 28
Simmons, G., 217
Sinn, E., 176
Sloan, C., 108
Smith, J., 102
Solinger, D., 26
Somjee, G., 165
Stent, R., 205
Stiglitz, J., 28

Tan, N., 147
Tan, T.M., 161, 162
Tang, K.-L., 2, 11

Tang, S, 25, 31, 32, 33, 38, 40
Thomas, E., 104
Toh, M.H., 150, 151, 159, 162, 164
Tomba, L., 31
Trevedi, P., 102
Tuohy, C., 11

Upton, S., 203

Vaithianathan, R., 100
van de Ven, W., 86

Walker, A., 92, 110
Walt, G., 226
Wang, H., 34, 40
Wang, X., 28
Wedeman, A., 34

Wellington, A.R., 178
White, K., 107
Whitehead, M., 78
Wilcox, S., 102
Wilding, P., 2, 11, 13, 240
Wilsford, D., 228
Wilson, R.M., 6, 104
Wong, Y.N., 160, 161, 163
Woo, W., 28

Xiong, Y., 35
Xu, S., 25

Yue, S.Y., 191
Yuen, P., 175, 193

Zhan, S., 31

SUBJECT INDEX

APEC, 2
ASEAN, 2
Australia, 1, 7, 8, 9, 12–19, 91–121, 158
  health financing, 93–6
    Commonwealth government dominance, 95
    expenditure trends, 96
    insurance, 99–102; decline, 100; politics, 100; premiums, 102; inequitable distribution, 102; 'adverse selection', 102
    private hospitals, 96
    Medicare, 94, 97–9, 100; 'bulk billing', 98, 99; fee schedules, 98; funding formula, 97–8; Medicare 'levy', 98–9
  health status, 92–3
    Aboriginal, 93
    inequalities, 92–3
  health workforce, 106–7
    general practice, 106–7
  hospitals, 102–6
    access barriers, 104
    DRG payments, 104
    hospital beds, 103; distribution, 103
    inpatient trends, 105–6
    private hospitals, 104; growth, 105–6
    quality, 104–5; adverse events, 104; improvement, 104–5
    same-day procedures, 104, 105
    utilization, 103–4
    waiting lists, 104
  integrated care, 115
  medical service utilization, 106–7
  pharmaceuticals, 108–112
    co-payments, 109; concessions, 109
    expenditure growth, 110
    generics, 109–110
    National Medicines Policy, 108
    Pharmaceutical Benefits Advisory Committee, 111–12; politics and implications, 111–12
    Pharmaceutical Benefits Scheme, 108–9, 110; listing guidelines, 110–11
  policy challenges, 112–16
    Commonwealth and state government responsibilities, 114–16
    public versus private provision, 113–14; market-based organization, 114
    universalism versus selectivism, 113
  public health, 93

Asia
  financial crisis, 2
  images of, 2
  mega-cities, 1
  urbanization, 1
  welfare models, 2, 240–1
Asia-Pacific
  health care arrangements, 2
  health care model, 240–1
  interconnectedness of, 2
  social development, 2

Britain, 4, 181, 206

China, 1, 2, 7, 12–19, 23–47, 181, 184
  health system
    access, 27
    accountability, 31
    background, 24
    'barefoot' doctors, 27
    challenges, 35–6
    competition, 30
    early history, 25–7; and organization, 25; and policy, 25; and service expenditure, 30–1, 32–3
    financing, 37–42
    founding, 25
    health care providers, 30
    improving life expectancy, 25
    present organization, 29–31; rural areas, 32–3; urban areas, 32
    public health, 25
    quality, 36
    rural—urban development, organization and differences, 26–7
    technology, 37
    traditional medicine, 27
  health workforce remuneration, 31
    and patient charges, 31
    and underfunding, 31
  health workforce training, 36–7
  HIV/AIDS, 35–6
  next phase of transition, 34–43
    creating appropriate institutional arrangements, 42–3; trust problems, 42
    health financing, 37–42; rural, 39–41; urban, 38–9
    health system fragmentation, 41–2
    new policy environment, 34–5
    service ownership patterns, 37
    workforce, 36–7
  SARS, 34, 35, 43
  transition to market economy, 27–9
    financial support and benefits, 32, 38, 41
    impact on health system, 29–31
    impact on rural health care, 32–3
    impact on urban health care, 32
    insurance, 32, 38–9, 40–1
    management of transition, 28
    uninsured, 32 ,
    weak institutional arrangements, 28–9
clinical guidelines, 59
comparative policy, 10–12, 225–43
  aims of, 11
  design, 11
  difficulties of, 11
  funding, 230–34
  hospital care, 235
  insurance, 231–2
  integration, 235–6
  'path dependency', 228–9
  policy transfer, 227–8
  primary care, 234
  provision, 234–6
  public health, 236–8
  quality, 236
  rationing and demand management, 238–40
  regulation, 229–30
  traditional medicine, 234–5
  types of study, 11–12

Subject index 251

determinants of health, 6
DRG-based payments, 58, 66, 104

fertility rates, 14
  see also individual chapter entries
financing, 9
  GDP expenditure on health, 16, 231
  insurance, 7, 9, 13, 231–2
  public expenditure, 16
  see also individual chapter entries
France, 4

Germany, 67n

health care
  access, 4, 231
  differences between and other goods and services, 7
  government commitment to, 3–4
  organisational forms, 10
  providing, 10
  'safety net', 227
  see also individual chapter entries
health policy
  changing ideas about, 7
  citizen participation in, 5
  collaborative model, 7
  comparative, 10–12, 225–43
  complexity, 7
  'cross sector' policy, 6
  defined, 3
  economic liberalism, 3
  government commitment to, 3–4, 225–6
  importance of, 3
  interest groups, 7, 227
  market model, 3, 7
  medical profession, 227
  policy transfer, 227–8
  pressures on, 4, 231
    ageing populations, 4, 35
    demographic change, 4
    emerging diseases and health risks, 6
    expanding scope, 5, 10
    increasing demand, 4, 10, 233
    limited funding, 4, 233
    patient satisfaction, 5
    responses to, 226
    service quality, 5
  rationing and prioritization, 4
  reforms, 14
  role of politics, 226
  see also individual chapter entries
health status,
  environmental and lifestyle factors, 17
  infant mortality rates, 14, 16
  life expectancy, 16
  obesity, 17
  tobacco consumption, 17, 35
  see also individual chapter entries
health system
  collaboration, 5
  financing, 9
  government dominated, 7
  integration, 10
  new ways of organizing, 5
  'path dependency', 228–9
  policy transfer, 227–8
  pressures on, 4–6
  private sector involvement, 5
  provision, 234–6
  public health, 236–8
  public—private mix, 8
  purchasing, 9
  rationing, 238–40
  regulation, 8–9, 229–30
  social insurance, 7
  structure, 7–10
  see also individual chapter entries
HIV/AIDS, 6, 35–6, 93, 123, 169, 237, 238, 240
Hong Kong, 12–19, 158, 174–99
  Avian Flu, 195
  Centre For Health Protection, 196, 197
  'contract medicine', 186–7
  Department of Health, 180, 185
  'Harvard Report', 191–4
    findings, 192

health integrated systems, 192
Health Security Plan, 192
  recommendations, 192
  responses, 193; government response, 193–4
  terms of reference, 191–2
health insurance, 191
health policy,
  challenges, 189–96
  defined, 179, 180; ill-defined, 189–90
  history, 176–81
  hospital bed ratios, 179
  incrementalism, 182–3
  laissez-faire, 176
  medical profession, 182, 183
  'piecemeal' nature of, 181
  preparatory committees, 183
  process, 181–3
  White Papers, 179
  working parties, 182–3
health system
  fee structures, 189
  hospitals, 176–7, 178, 179, 180; camp beds, 179; early development, 176–7; semi-private beds, 191; tripartite system, 177; waiting lists, 178, 189
  integration, 187
  key structures, 181–2
  post-war, 178
  primary care, 178; charges, 186; 'contract medicine', 186–7; government outpatient clinics, 179, 185, 189; reviews, 180–1
  private hospitals, 185–6; private sector dominance, 186
  public health administration, 177; Department of Health, 180
  reviews, 180–1
  shortcomings, 175, 189–90
  uncoordinated, 184, 189

health workforce,
  medical profession, 177, 191; policy influence, 182, 183; self-regulation, 187; specialist register, 184
  medical personnel, 184; public-private imbalance, 184
  nursing shortages, 178
Hospital Authority, 180, 185, 226
  charges, 185, 189
  improving service standards, 190
  market share, 185
  Provisional Hospital Authority, 180
Hospital Services Department, 180
infectious diseases, 177, 178
Medical and Health Department, 179
  management style, 179
  patient complaints, 187
  policy challenges, 189–96
    compartmentalization, 189
    ill-defined policy, 189–90
    increasing costs, 190
    increasing demand, 190
    poor communication, 189
    service waiting times, 190
  population growth, 177
  preventive medicine, 188
  'Scott Report', 180, 191
  SARS, 176, 189, 195–6
  traditional medicine, 176, 181, 184–5, 186, 187–8
    Chinese medicine council, 188

India, 1
Indonesia, 1
infant mortality rates, 14, 16
  see also individual chapter entries
integration, 10, 115, 187, 201, 203, 204, 212, 218, 235–6

Japan, 7, 8, 9, 12–19, 58, 67n, 71, 122–45, 192
  health financing, 130–43
    adverse selection, 134
    cream skimming, 134
    Citizens' Health Insurance, 131–2
    co-payments, 132
    cross-subsidization, 133, 136
    Diagnosis and Procedure Combination, 142–3
    elderly insurance, 133, 136
    expenditure differences, 137
    fee schedule, 138–43; fee setting process, 140–41; maintaining 'balance', 141; regulatory device, 138–40
    present system, 134–43
    reform proposals, 135–6; elderly insurance, 136
    risk adjustment, 134
    social insurance, 130–43; development, 130–32; premium increases, 134–5; pressures for mergers, 135; reform proposals, 135–6
  health status, 123
  health system, 124–30
    accountability, 130
    indigenous system, 124–5; role of family, 125
    Meiji era, 125–8; hospitals, 126
    post-war development, 128–9; American influence, 128
    present system, 129–30, 134–43; no gatekeeping, 129; physician organization, 129; waiting lists, 129
    quality, 129–30; medical error, 129–30
  HIV/AIDS, 123, 157
  hospitals,
    geriatric inpatients, 129, 133
    Meiji era foundations, 126; link with physicians, 126

  Japan Medical Association, 128, 130, 140–1
  Japan Medical Corporation, 127–8
  market competition, 140
  medical training and practice, Meiji era, 125; hierarchical system, 127; Western medicine ascendance, 125
    post-war developments, 128
    remuneration, 138
    traditional medicine, 125
  pharmaceuticals, 138, 140
  public health, 137; screening, 137, 144n
  rationing, 123
  traditional medicine, 124–125, 127

life expectancy, 16

medical profession, 7, 18, 19, 227
  see also individual chapter entries

New Zealand, 1, 4, 7, 8, 9, 12–19, 192, 200–24
  Accident Compensation Commission, 212, 221n
  area health boards, 203
    performance, 203
    positives and negatives, 203
  'booking system', 215–6
  clinical guidelines, 204, 215
  demographics, 213
  district health boards, 206–12, 215
    complexity, 210–11
    Maori involvement, 209, 210
    ministerial control, 209
    Ministry of Health, 207
    policy requirements, 207; enhancing primary care, 207; needs assessments, 207; prioritizing, 207; reducing inequalities, 207, 218

political aims, 207
population-based funding, 213
prioritization, 215
scope, 207
'shared services' agencies, 210
strategic plans, 210
structure, 209–10; governance arrangements, 209; sub-committees, 209
funding, 214
health care demand, 213
reduction strategies, 214
service efficiency, 213
health financing, 212
allocation, 212
growth, 212–13
hospital funding, 213–14
Health Funding Authority, 205–6, 215
focus, 205
negatives, 205–6
positives, 206
service integration, 218
health policy
challenges, 201–2
competition, 201
population health focus, 201
shifting goals, 201
'health reforms', 203–5
Core Services Committee, 204, 215
Crown health enterprises, 204
independent practitioner associations, 205, 211
negatives, 204–5
positives, 205
Public Health Commission, 204
regional health authorities, 203–4, 205
health system
challenges, 201–2
successive change, 201; impact on institutions, 201
health workforce, 219
Health Workforce Advisory Committee, 220

historical developments, 202–6
pre-1938, 202
Social Security Act, 1938, 202; policy compromises, 202
source of contemporary problems, 202–3
independent practitioner associations, 205
information systems and technology, 218–9
integration, 201, 203, 212, 218
Maori health, 205
National Health Committee, 215
New Zealand Health Strategy, 209
Pharmac, 205, 207
cost containment strategies, 214
pharmaceuticals, 205,
Primary Health Organizations, 205, 210–11, 217
concerns about, 211;
policy challenges, 221
prioritization, 204, 206, 214–5; 'booking system', 215–6
Core Services Committee, 215
district health boards, 215
Health Funding Authority, 215
National Health Committee, 215
public health, 216–8
'lifestyle' diseases, 217
health inequalities, 218
organization, 216–17
screening, 217
quality, 219
approaches, 219
medical errors, 219
SARS, 217
waiting lists, 204–5, 211, 215–6, 220, 221n

obesity, 17, 188
OECD, 16, 17, 49, 59, 61, 65, 82, 83, 92, 157, 203, 212, 213, 226, 231

Subject index

Papua New Guinea, 1
pharmaceutical industry, 7
  see also individual chapter entries
population ageing, 35
practising physicians, 16–17
  see also individual chapter entries
primary care, 7, 234
  see also individual chapter entries
'productivist welfare capitalism', 1, 240
providing, 10
public health, 1, 6, 7, 236–8
  limited funding allocation, 8
  see also individual chapter entries
purchasing, 9

quality, 36, 236
  see also individual chapter entries

rationing and prioritisation, 4, 238–40
  see also individual chapter entries
regulation, 8–9

SARS, 2, 6, 34, 35, 43, 85, 157, 168–9, 176, 189, 195–6, 217, 227, 237, 238, 240
Singapore, 1, 7, 9, 12–19, 146–73, 192
  birth control, 148–9
  health care development, 148–9
  health financing,
    expenditure, 157–8; growth, 149, 159; pressures on, 164
  health policy,
    ageing population, 164
    government control, 160–3
    'healthy living' campaigns, 165
    lessons, 163–5
    'moral hazard', 159
    personal responsibility, 158–9
    philosophy, 149–50
    rationing, 162–4, 167;
      Australian comparisons, 163
  health system,
    access inequalities, 166–7

accountability, 151
government control, 160–3
government outpatient clinics, 155
health care 'clusters', 152
hospitals, 150–52, 169;
  'privatization', 151;
  performance, 151–2; fees,
  161 organization, 152
primary care, 156
private practitioners, 155
public health, 156–7; HIV/AIDS, 157, 169; SARS, 157, 168–9; National Service, 165
reforms, 147; hospitals, 149;
  medical savings accounts, 149; pre-reforms, 150
strengths, 169
voluntary organizations, 156
health workforce, 148, 160–1, 167
history and politics, 147–8
hospital beds, 148
medical savings accounts, 149, 152–6, 157–9, 161
  ElderShield, 156, 226
  government control, 161
  Medifund, 155, 227
  Medisave, 153–5, 159;
    contributions, 153; coverage, 153–5
  MediShield, 153, 155; coverage, 155
  philosophy, 149–50, 158–9
  pressures on expenditure, 164
  rationing, 162–4, 167
  shortcomings, 157, 166–7
National Service, 165
  fitness regime, 165
  wider implications, 165
population ageing, 164
  health care utilization, 164
  health policies, 164
traditional medicine, 165
Solomon Islands, 1
South Korea, 7, 8, 9, 12–19, 48–68
  clinical guidelines, 59

health expenditure, 59–60
  physician fee rises, 60
  pressures on, 60
  public-private divide, 60
health system, 49
  financing, 52–4
  history, 49–52
  reforms, 49; financing, 49;
    pharmaceutical, 49, 63–5;
    health insurance, 62–3
health services
  delivery, 54–9
  duplication, 56
  hospitals, 56; physician-owned, 56; licensing, 57; quality, 57
  gatekeeping, lack of, 56
  private sector dominance, 49
supply, 56
national health insurance, 49–50
  benefits of single insurer, 63
  establishment, 50–52; influence of farmers on, 51–2
  prior insurance arrangements; contributions to, 53–4;
    limited benefit coverage, 51, 52–3; low government subsidy, 53
  contributions to, 54
  payment system, 57–9; DRG-based payment, 58–9, 66;
    effects of, 58; fee regulation, 58; impact of, 59
  reforms, 62–3; pressures for, 62–3
  policy challenges, 63, 66
medical technology, 58
patient co-payments, 54
pharmaceutical consumption, 65
pharmaceutical reforms,
  aims of, 64
  opposition to, 65
  reasons for, 63–4
population health, 60–62
  life expectancy, 61
  limited population health policy, 62
  major causes of illness and death, 61; impact on economy, 61
  traditional medicine, 54, 64, 67n
Sweden, 4, 192

Taiwan, 1, 7, 8, 9, 12–19, 69–90, 158, 184
  health policy objectives, 78
  health system,
    dual systems, 74–5;
      dominance of Western medicine, 75
    equity of access, 78–81
    health care expenditure, 81, 82, 83; increasing, 81, 83
    history, 71–4
    health care providers, 77
    hospital accreditation, 83–4;
      and acute bed numbers, 83–4
    hospital beds, 76, 83–4
    hospital ownership, 76; private dominance, 76
    hospital distribution, 79
    macro-economic efficiency, 81–2
    micro-economic efficiency, 82–5
    pharmacy, 77
    quality, 84–5
  health service utilization, 83
  health workforce,
    description, 75
    training, 75
    growth and size, 75 6
    physician supply, 79, 83
  national health insurance, 77–8
    benefits, 80
    co-payments, 83
    global budgeting, 82
    inequalities, 80–1
    need for improved incentives, 85
    objectives, 78
    premium increases, 82

Subject index 257

prior insurance arrangements, 77
pressures for national insurance, 78, 81
public satisfaction, 82
reform proposals, 85–7;
  equalization fund, 85–6;
  population health purchasing, 87; politics of, 87
political and economic history, 70
population health,
  life expectancy, 70
  major causes of illness and death, 70–1;
public health administration, 71–4
  evolution, 71–2
  expenditure, 74
  funding sources, 74
  present structure, 72–4
  under Japanese control, 71
SARS, 85
traditional medicine, 74–5, 80
traditional medicine, 54, 64, 67n, 74–5, 124–125, 127, 165, 176, 181, 184–5, 186, 187–8, 234–5

Timor Leste, 1
tobacco consumption, 17, 93
  gender differences, 17
traditional medicine, 14, 17, 19, 54, 64, 67n, 74–5, 80, 124–125, 127
types of health care
  personal health, 8
  primary care, 8
  public health, 8
  secondary care, 8
  tertiary care, 8

United Nations, 3
  Millennium Development Goals, 3
United States, 1, 58, 112, 138, 142, 149, 152, 158
urbanization, 1
  challenges, 1
  inequalities, 1–2

World Bank, 3, 31
World Health Organization, 3, 61, 238

Open up your options

- Education
- Health & Social Welfare
- Management
- Media, Film & Culture
- Psychology & Counselling
- Sociology
- Study Skills

for more information on our publications visit **www.openup.co.uk**

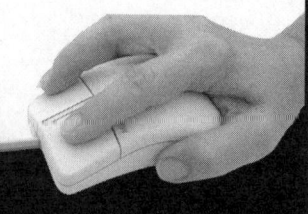

OPEN UNIVERSITY PRESS
McGraw - Hill Education